201 IcebREAKERS

201 ICEBREAKERS

Group Mixers, Warm-ups, Energizers, and Playful Activities

Edie West

McGraw Hill

New York   San Francisco   Washington, D.C.   Auckland   Bogotá
Caracas   Lisbon   London   Madrid   Mexico City   Milan
Monteal   New Delhi   San Juan   Singapore
Sydney   Tokyo   Toronto

Libary of Congress Cataloging-Card: 96-077804

The sponsoring editor for this book was Richard Narramore, the editing supervisor was Fred Dahl, and the production supervisor was Donald Schmidt. It was set in New Century Schoolbook by Inkwell Publishing Services.

Printed and bound by Edwards Brothers.

 This book was printed on recycled, acid-free paper containing a minimum of 50% recycled de-inked fiber.

CONTENTS

Getting to Know You Better   **175**

Grouping People   **221**

Introducing a Topic 245

Meeting Starters 291

Mental Aerobics 307

Find the Perfect Icebreaker for Your Group!

	Energizing a Long, Dry Presentation	Especially for Big Groups	For Non-icebreaker Types	Getting Closure	Getting to Know You	Getting to Know You Better	Grouping People	Introducing a Topic	Meeting Starters	Mental Aerobics	Outdoor Activities	Physical Energizers	Pure Fun	Self-Disclosure	Team Building	Winding Down/Relaxation
Energizing a Long, Dry Presentation																
ABCs	•			•								•				
Almanac	•					•							•		•	
Doodle Do	•			•		•										
Fidgets	•		•						•			•	•			
Full as a Tick	•		•	•				•	•	•						
In Sync	•										•	•	•		•	
Opinion Poll	•				•	•						•				
Out of the Box	•											•				
Party Mix	•					•								•	•	
Payola	•							•							•	
Peculiarities	•					•							•			
Pink Slips	•											•				
Teensy Triathlon	•											•				
The Scrambler	•		•						•		•		•		•	
Theme Work	•									•					•	
You Said It!	•								•	•		•				
Especially for Big Groups																
At the Fair		•										•			•	
Balloon Stampede		•				•					•	•	•		•	
Bumper Collision		•				•						•	•			
Creative Congratulations		•				•						•	•			

	Energizing a Long, Dry Presentation	Especially for Big Groups	For Non-icebreaker Types	Getting Closure	Getting to Know You	Getting to Know You Better	Grouping People	Introducing a Topic	Meeting Starters	Mental Aerobics	Outdoor Activities	Physical Energizers	Pure Fun	Self-Disclosure	Team Building	Winding Down/Relaxation
Double Take		•			•							•				
Getting the Goods		•			•	•						•				
Good Sports		•					•				•	•	•			
Happy Birthday!		•			•		•						•			
How Quickly They Forget		•			•							•				
Marching Orders		•										•	•		•	
Motor Mania		•		•						•		•	•		•	
Octopuses		•			•							•	•		•	
On All Sides		•			•							•				
Shake It Up		•			•		•					•				
Significant Events		•			•	•						•		•		
Stringing Us Along		•		•	•							•				
Swing Your Partner		•			•							•				
The Domino Effect		•						•			•	•	•		•	
The Hummer's Parade		•		•			•								•	
The Line Up	•	•				•						•	•		•	
The Wink		•			•							•	•			
For Non-icebreaker Types																
A Contradiction in Terms			•					•		•						
Best and Worst			•			•			•						•	
Good News, Bad News			•	•				•	•						•	
In or Out			•	•				•						•		
Missing Links		•	•		•							•				
Musical Instrument		•	•		•	•		•							•	
Road Signs	•		•					•	•	•						
Trivia X-O	•		•	•				•		•					•	

	Energizing a Long, Dry Presentation	Especially for Big Groups	For Non-icebreaker Types	Getting Closure	Getting to Know You	Getting to Know You Better	Grouping People	Introducing a Topic	Meeting Starters	Mental Aerobics	Outdoor Activities	Physical Energizers	Pure Fun	Self-Disclosure	Team Building	Winding Down/Relaxation
You Are What You Drive			•		•	•										
You're a Poet and Don't Know It			•	•		•		•		•				•	•	
Getting Closure																
Alice's Anthology			•	•				•		•				•	•	
Arrivals and Departures			•	•				•	•							
Bloom Where You're Planted				•												
Hit the Deck				•				•				•	•		•	
If I Had a Hammer			•	•				•								
Leaf It to Me				•											•	
Leaving Tips			•	•												
New! Improved!				•				•					•			
Pie a la Mode				•				•							•	
Q & A	•		•	•				•		•						
Sculpt-a-Team		•	•	•										•	•	
Star Light, Star Bright				•					•						•	
Swan Song				•								•	•		•	
This Is My Country		•		•	•	•		•							•	
YMCA		•		•				•			•	•	•		•	
Getting to Know You																
Alliteration Affiliation					•					•						
Balloon Bonding					•	•						•	•		•	
Days of Our Lives					•	•								•		
Favorite Things					•	•										
Four of a Kind	•				•	•										
Goin' Fishin'					•											
Jack-in-the Box					•	•						•				

	Energizing a Long, Dry Presentation	Especially for Big Groups	For Non-icebreaker Types	Getting Closure	Getting to Know You	Getting to Know You Better	Grouping People	Introducing a Topic	Meeting Starters	Mental Aerobics	Outdoor Activities	Physical Energizers	Pure Fun	Self-Disclosure	Team Building	Winding Down/Relaxation
Know-It-All					•											
Make Your Points					•			•				•	•			
Name That Team					•	•			•						•	
Personal Ads					•			•							•	
Pick Pocket					•	•							•		•	
Pick Up Ticks	•				•							•				
ShareWear		•			•	•								•	•	
The Name Game					•					•						
Time Capsule					•	•								•	•	
Two to Tango					•		•									
Vanity Plates			•		•	•							•			
Whodunit	•				•	•						•				
Getting to Know You Better																
A Star Is Born						•									•	
Associations					•	•								•	•	
Baggage Claim					•	•										
Birth Right						•	•					•				
Flake to Flake		•			•	•		•				•			•	
Generation Gap						•	•	•								
Hi. How Are Ya'?		•			•	•						•				
If You Could Be …	•					•		•				•		•	•	
Let the Good Times Roll					•	•						•			•	
Life's Little Suitcase			•		•	•								•		
Me, Myself, And I					•	•								•	•	
Most Like Me					•	•								•	•	
My Hero!					•	•									•	

	Energizing a Long, Dry Presentation	Especially for Big Groups	For Non-icebreaker Types	Getting Closure	Getting to Know You	Getting to Know You Better	Grouping People	Introducing a Topic	Meeting Starters	Mental Aerobics	Outdoor Activities	Physical Energizers	Pure Fun	Self-Disclosure	Team Building	Winding Down/Relaxation
Notebook of Lists	•					•										
Pickle Barrel				•		•									•	
Quick Quotes				•		•		•						•		
Refrigerator Magnetism					•	•										
Role Call						•		•							•	
Shaping Up!					•	•								•	•	
Spanning the Globe					•	•		•				•				
Superlatives					•	•								•	•	
Used Car Lot					•	•								•	•	
Wordy Connections						•		•					•	•	•	
Grouping People																
Canine Kibitzing							•					•				
Easy Money					•		•									
Going Nuts		•			•	•	•									
Let's Face It					•		•						•			
P.A.N.I.C. Club					•	•	•	•					•		•	
Street Gangs							•	•	•						•	
The Big Dipper							•					•			•	
Traffic Noise							•					•				
Upset the Fruit Basket					•		•					•	•			
Introducing a Topic																
Blockbuster				•				•	•							
Bouncing Back								•					•			
Constructive Feedback								•							•	
Create-a-Character						•		•							•	
Doggone It								•								

	Energizing a Long, Dry Presentation	Especially for Big Groups	For Non-icebreaker Types	Getting Closure	Getting to Know You	Getting to Know You Better	Grouping People	Introducing a Topic	Meeting Starters	Mental Aerobics	Outdoor Activities	Physical Energizers	Pure Fun	Self-Disclosure	Team Building	Winding Down/Relaxation
Doom & Gloom								•	•							
Fifty Ways				•				•					•			
First Things First				•				•						•		
Full Plate				•				•								
Letters to the Editor						•		•								
Look on the Bright Side								•		•						
Orange You Smart			•	•				•		•		•			•	
Pictures Don't Lie								•							•	
Piece by Piece				•			•	•					•		•	
Questionable Conversation					•	•		•								
Recipe for Teamwork				•				•							•	
Sensory Expression				•				•					•			
Show and Hide	•			•				•				•				
Spinning an Ideal Yarn				•				•							•	
The Domino Challenge								•					•		•	
The Tortoise and the Hare			•					•								
Up, Down, All Around the Town							•	•							•	
Your Heart on Your Sleeve				•				•					•	•		
Meeting Starters																
Auto Biography						•		•	•							
Building an Agenda								•	•			•				
Can It!				•				•	•							
Here We Are			•			•		•	•						•	
I Spied	•							•	•						•	
It's a Toss Up								•	•						•	
Story Time	•							•	•						•	

	Energizing a Long, Dry Presentation	Especially for Big Groups	For Non-icebreaker Types	Getting Closure	Getting to Know You	Getting to Know You Better	Grouping People	Introducing a Topic	Meeting Starters	Mental Aerobics	Outdoor Activities	Physical Energizers	Pure Fun	Self-Disclosure	Team Building	Winding Down/Relaxation
Tuning Up									•			•			•	
What in the World?	•								•				•		•	
Mental Aerobics																
Air Waves								•		•			•		•	
Evolutionary Idea	•		•			•		•		•					•	
Funny Fables							•	•		•			•			
News Edit										•			•			
Oxymorons								•		•			•			
Pavlov				•				•		•		•	•		•	
Phobia Mania								•		•			•			
Radio City								•		•			•		•	
Say It with Flowers										•			•		•	
Street Smarts						•		•		•			•		•	
The Lettermen								•		•	•				•	
Wordplexing			•							•			•			
Outdoor Activities																
Ball Bobble								•			•	•	•		•	
Beach Party											•	•	•		•	
Cheers!				•							•	•	•		•	
Fast Forwarding											•	•	•			
In Shape											•	•	•		•	
The Waves	•	•									•	•	•		•	
Yard Sticks		•									•	•	•		•	
Physical Energizers																
Advanced Placement											•	•	•		•	
Bicycle Built for Two												•	•		•	

	Energizing a Long, Dry Presentation	Especially for Big Groups	For Non-icebreaker Types	Getting Closure	Getting to Know You	Getting to Know You Better	Grouping People	Introducing a Topic	Meeting Starters	Mental Aerobics	Outdoor Activities	Physical Energizers	Pure Fun	Self-Disclosure	Team Building	Winding Down/Relaxation
Dynamic Duos							•					•	•		•	
Health Club												•	•			
Line Language	•											•	•		•	
Off the Wall								•				•			•	
Snap Shot											•	•			•	
Swimming Lessons		•									•	•	•			
The Shape You're In					•	•		•	•		•	•	•		•	
Weak Days	•					•						•	•			
Pure Fun																
Clean Machine													•		•	
Crazy Captions			•							•			•		•	
Hot Air Express												•	•		•	
Oink, Oink, Oink!												•	•			
Rubbery Band												•	•		•	
Story Telling				•									•		•	
Who's the Dummy?						•							•		•	
Self-Disclosure																
Bear It and Grin!						•		•						•		
Boy, Was My Face Red!						•		•						•		
Memory Lane						•								•	•	
Pillow Talk						•								•		
Pin 'em Down						•								•	•	
Projection					•	•								•		
Things That Are …						•								•	•	
Team Building																
Happily Ever After						•		•				•	•		•	

	Energizing a Long, Dry Presentation	Especially for Big Groups	For Non-icebreaker Types	Getting Closure	Getting to Know You	Getting to Know You Better	Grouping People	Introducing a Topic	Meeting Starters	Mental Aerobics	Outdoor Activities	Physical Energizers	Pure Fun	Self-Disclosure	Team Building	Winding Down/Relaxation
Paper Dolls												•	•		•	
Personification				•				•	•				•		•	
Rhymes Revisited						•		•					•		•	
Star Quality								•							•	
Thanks Giving									•						•	
Warning Signs				•		•		•						•	•	
We're All in the Same Boat	•											•	•		•	
Winding Down/Relaxation																
Energy Sources								•								•
On Your Toes												•				•
Stress Re-leaf				•				•	•							•
The Eye of the Beholder						•		•			•					•
Tune-Up			•	•								•				•

Preface

Someday I will write a book called *The Uses for and Benefits of a Smile*. I suspect it may take a lifetime of compiling data, and not enough pages in one book to contain it all.

A few years ago, when I was in the midst of a "Who do I want to be and what do I want to do next?" dilemma, a listening friend asked me a question of significance: "What do you enjoy doing most, and what gives you the greatest sense of satisfaction?" Without a moment's hesitation, I responded, "I like to make people smile."

I'm not a comedian. My sons will ungraciously attest to that: "Mom, give it up. You messed up the punch line *again*." So, then. How to bring smiles? Not too difficult a question to answer. I was already doing it. Creating and using icebreakers and games—activities that raise comfort levels; that encourage openness to self-understanding and foster an appreciation of and compassion for others; that draw people out of the past and into the moment; that put a novel spin on an idea; that stimulate creative thinking; that ease the defensive barriers to our human vulnerability—that make people smile inside and outside. Let me give you an example. A few years ago six other travelers and I were scheduled on a flight to Albany that was postponed and ultimately canceled four hours later due to inclement weather. An option presented to us was to travel by van through sleet and snow about two hundred miles to our destination. We took the opportunity and boarded the van at 11:00 p.m.

After about thirty minutes of listening to my fellow travelers complain and grumble, I took a major risk. I boldly told the other passengers that there was no reason that we shouldn't have an enjoyable trip from now on even though the past several hours had been so miserable. I then announced that I would lead them through some activities (icebreakers) so we could get to know one another and have a good time until we got to our destination.

Only strangers would demonstrate the patience and politeness my companions did that evening. Following my description of games that I was ready to begin, I looked for supportive nods and utterances that would give me the courage I needed to introduce a simple activity for remembering names. The persons sitting on either side of me responded enthusiastically first, which I attributed to their youth; the three men in the middle seat reluctantly affirmed that they would try the first game. We (I had support by then) asked the man in the passenger seat next to the driver for the go-ahead. He ignored me and two other travelers.

Nevertheless, I moved right along. "In this first icebreaker," I announced, "which I'm sure is familiar to you, one person will begin by introducing himself and then each successive person will repeat the names of the people before him and then add his own name to the list. We will learn names easily this way."

The first person, who was in the back to my left, gave his name and passed to me. I repeated his name, then added my name. The person to my right repeated the first man's name, my name, and then added his name. Play then passed to the middle seat where each person in turn, followed the pattern. Sometimes people missed and had to begin again.

By now, the people in the middle seat were turned around and enjoying the company of the three of us in the back seat and we were all smiling. But the frosting on the cake—that existential moment of spontaneous exuberance, laughter and hand clapping—came for all of us when the second row had completed the task, and from the passenger seat next to the driver, came all of our names loudly repeated, in order, correctly, and with fervor (although without the speaker turning his head or batting an eye). We all cheered and I quickly moved on to the next icebreaker.

When we finally reached Albany five hours later, all of us agreed that the ride seemed much shorter than we had expected. We exchanged business cards, and some of us have actually kept in touch.

I haven't shared the Newark to Albany story so that you will descend upon unsuspecting souls in airports, but as a challenge to add to the list that follows more unlikely places and times to use the icebreakers contained in this book:

> parties
> weddings
> long lines
> athletic events
> marketing events
> lunchrooms
> sales meetings
> presentations
> training sessions
> book clubs
> Internet conversations
> church/synagogue services
> youth group events
> hikes and bicycling trips
> lunches and dinners
> bedtime
> bridal and baby showers

Acknowledgments

Many thanks to Richard Narramore, editor at McGraw-Hill, who invited me to gather my icebreaker ideas into a book for others to enjoy, and who worked patiently with me until the project was completed.

Thanks to Carole Anne Turner, my in-house editor and designer of activity sheets, who contributed ideas, enthusiasm, and her own wonderful smiles.

Thanks to Ron Greene, my son, my right-hand computer expert, who came through at the final moment, taking time away from studying for law school finals to help pull the pieces together.

Thanks to my husband Glenn, who encouraged me to write, enthusiastically listened to progress reports, and brainstormed ideas with me on many occasions. (And who already has at least six ideas about what my next venture could be.)

And thanks to the many friends and family members who gave me ideas and encouragement.

But, most of all, thanks to my parents who lovingly taught me to play.

Edic West

INTRODUCTION

When I deliver Games sessions for people who are likely to use the activities, I begin the program with the following explanation, "You will be playing games, some of which will be useful to you as is, some of which you will need to adapt to fit your particular needs, and some of which you will never admit to having played."

The same is true for this book. Feel free to use, adapt, or discard as you see fit. And if you have a variation, tip, or new icebreaker to share, please send it to me at:

Edie West
8327 Southern Oaks Court
Lorton, Virginia 22079
fax: 703-690-9378
email: ediewest@aol.com

We divided *201 Icebreakers* into categories that we thought would help you with selecting an icebreaker for a particular use or purpose. You will find the categories listed in the Table of Contents. But, since each icebreaker fits into many categories, we have included a matrix with suggestions for multiple uses. Beyond that, we are sure that you will find your own categories to put them in.

Each icebreaker is formatted the same way:

- ✓ Title
- ✓ Purpose: suggested uses
- ✓ Group size: the number of participants we know works
- ✓ Level of physical activity: actual physical engagement
- ✓ Estimated time: educated guess
- ✓ Props: materials, equipment, and supplies needed
- ✓ Summary paragraph: additional thoughts that may be helpful to you
- ✓ Instructions: step-by-step for you, the leader
- ✓ Variations: for you to adapt the icebreakers
- ✓ Tips: for you, the leader
- ✓ Notes: for your thoughts and observations

In italics on each page is an introduction *just for you*. Feel free to use any or all of this section when you introduce icebreakers with your own audiences.

Many of the icebreakers require additional information for you or sheets or cards for participants. In most cases, you will find what you need for each icebreaker on the page following it. Feel free to copy, cut, or use them any way you would like.

Now that you have the contents of icebreakers, the only ingredient missing is you—your leadership, your enthusiasm, your wonderful sense of play. Remember, if you smile, others will, too!

Edie's Top Ten Favorite Icebreakers

(In aphabetical order)

1. Birth Right allows participants to commiserate and celebrate—two important bonding experiences. I remember one group who gave themselves license to challenge all rules for the remainder of the session because they were middle children. What else did I expect? (Page 184)

2. Purely for the humor of it, Canine Kibitzing is always a favorite with me. (Page 223)

3. Missing Links is an appropriate activity for people in any situation, from those who sit next to each other in a crowd of a thousand to members of a small team brought together to resolve issues. (Page 85)

4. Everyone's favorite is Happy Birthday. Often people find others who have the same birthday, or will make comments like, "Yours is January 19th? That's my mother's birthday!" Any excuse for a celebration. (Page 55)

5. I like Marching Orders because I love a parade! (Page 58)

6. The last time I used Motor Mania, one group became a Jacuzzi. I've been leading this activity for years—first time for a Jacuzzi. (Page 60)

7. I like Orange You Smart because participants enjoy the light competition, strategy, and fresh rolling fruit, *and* important words and concepts get reinforced. (Plus, the room smells great for the remainder of the time!) (Page 267)

8. A balloon sculpture becomes a metaphor for team cohesion in Sculpt-a-Team, and everyone participates equally in the shaping of it. I like the simplicity and peacefulness. (Page 120)

9. The Line Up is light competition that always works; participants get physically energized, and I enjoy the challenge of thinking of new ways to have people "line up." (Page 73)

10. Participants become very creative with Yard Sticks: bodies lying end to end, feet end-to-end, or arms stretched finger-to-finger. It is pure pleasure to watch the unleashing of group ingenuity. (Page 347)

ENERGIZING A LONG, DRY PRESENTATION

ABCs

Purpose

Physical energizer; Energizing a long, dry presentation; Getting closure

Group Size

12-26

Level of Physical Activity

Medium

Estimated Time

2-5 minutes

Props

None

This activity uses light competition as participants name words that reinforce content. Use it midway through a session as an energizer and reinforcer, or at the conclusion of a session to get closure. It also may be used periodically in longer sessions. Caution: Some participants may consider this activity to be too simple.

My niece, Wendy Fay, taught my children to play the Alphabet Game when they were young. The purposes were to pass time pleasurably while traveling in a car and to reinforce reading skills. We are now a family of adults who still play the Alphabet Game when riding long distances.

Instructions

1. Ask participants to stand and line up (or stand in place at their seats).
2. Tell participants that this is a very simple exercise.
3. Explain the rules:
   - I will say the letters of the alphabet in order to participants standing in line, beginning with the letter "A" for the person at the head of the line.
   - When a letter of the alphabet is said, the participant whose turn it is should name a word related to the content of the gathering that begins with that letter of the alphabet.
   - If the participant says a word in three seconds, he or she remains standing.
   - If a participant cannot think of a word in time, or says one that does not qualify, he or she sits down and the next participant must name a word that begins with that same letter.
   - Play continues with that letter until a participant correctly states a word within the three-second time limit.
   - Play continues until the alphabet is finished or until all players are seated.
   - The last person or persons standing are the winners.
4. Begin the activity.

Variations

1. Create teams and have them list words on a paper that begin with every letter of the alphabet. The first group to finish wins.
2. Create teams and follow the same instructions that are listed for the activity.
3. Have all players seated in groups, for example by table. The leader then calls letters of the alphabet randomly and one person from a group stands if they have a word. The first person standing with a correct word scores a point for their team. The team with the most points wins.

Tips

1. You decide how seriously you want the words to be linked to the content, and enforce exactness of words accordingly.
2. On really tough letters, after three tries, ask for help from people sitting. If one of them can give a word, that person gets to play again.

Notes

_____

_____

_____

_____

_____

_____

_____

_____

_____

_____

Almanac

Purpose

Getting to know you better; Team building; Energizing a long, dry presentation; Pure fun

Group Size

6-24

Level of Physical Activity

Medium

Estimated Time

2-3 minutes each time

Props

Almanac Activity Sheet, cut into cards

In this activity, participants will pool their knowledge of a given topic to create the best almanac entry they can. Almanac is a good activity for participants at any level of an organization. Use it any time during a session for getting participants to connect, and to learn something in the process.

Almanacs are interesting books to leaf through. I am amazed at the wealth of information jammed into 1,000 or so pages. You may find sections on Expectation of Life Statistics and World Exploration / News of Today marked with the history of yesteryear. It's fascinating. I wonder what process editors use to decide what to include?

Instructions

1. Organize participants into groups of four to six people.
2. Explain that the groups are going to work together to create a verbal almanac.
3. Give each group one card with one category on it.
4. Instruct groups to have a three-minute discussion around the topic on the card. For instance, if the card says weather, they should have a discussion about anything they know about weather. One person may know what the prediction is for weather conditions for the next two days; another may know about the clean-up process from the last volcanic activity; another may know about ideal weather conditions for a person suffering with osteoporosis.
5. After three minutes, tell them that time is up, and the next time they will get a different card.

Variations

1. Ask participants to capture comments on flip chart paper or note paper and post when time is up.
2. Give each group the same topic and hear comments from each group afterwards.

Tips

Give each group a different topic. Each time, switch the topics between groups.

ALMANAC ACTIVITY SHEET

Health

Nutrition

National News

World News

Environment

Astronomy & Space

World History

Geography

Entertainment

Business and the Economy

Sports—Olympic Athletes

Doodle Do

Purpose

Getting closure; Getting to know you better; Energizing a long, dry presentation

Group Size

10-40

Level of Physical Activity

Low

Estimated Time

Ongoing

Props

Paper tablecloths; colored pencils

This activity encourages creativity and keeps your group alert by providing paper tablecloths and colored pencils for them to draw or take notes during your presentation. Either introduce this in the beginning of the session for people to get to know others better; bring it out after lunch as an energizer; or end the session with people sharing their graffiti.

Doodling is therapeutic. Some people doodle because they have an artistic bent that cries to be unleashed; others doodle out of boredom or in a desperate attempt to remember thoughts, facts, or ideas.

Instructions

1. Cover the tables with paper tablecloths and put colored pencils on each table within everyone's reach.
2. Explain to participants that people doodle for various reasons, and that doodling is not restricted by age or artistic talent. Explain that the paper and pencils on the table are provided for their doodling pleasure.
3. Invite participants to record their emotions, thoughts, ideas, artistic expressions, information, stories, and questions on their tablecloths throughout the session.
4. After a period of time, encourage participants to take five minutes to share their doodles with their tablemates and discuss any pertinent questions they've recorded.

Variations

1. Recommend topics for participants to draw or write about.
2. Limit the doodling to pictures.

Tips

1. It's fun with crayons, too.
2. Encourage lavish design and use of color.

Fidgets

Purpose

Physical energizer; For non-icebreaker types; Pure fun; Meeting starter; Energizing a long, dry presentation

Group Size

6-45

Level of Physical Activity

Medium

Estimated Time

Ongoing

Props

Legos, Googolplex, Tinker Toys or some such creative building sets

This activity is in the category of "Do Little—Gain Much." People will enjoy having creative building sets to "fidget" with during long sessions or breaks. All types of groups enjoy this.

One time when I was delivering facilitator training, I took along my sets of Googolplex for people to fiddle with during the workshop. Near the end of the workshop, I asked the group to list the ideas that were most helpful to them from the entire day. I have been facilitating for most of my adult life in one fashion or another; and this particular workshop gives participants very useful processes and tools. Despite that, number one on the list of helpful ideas was Googolplex. When I asked them about it, participants responded that the Googolplex helped keep them focused and attuned to everything that was talked about. Needless to say, Googolplex has become an essential tool in my facilitation bag.

Instructions

1. Purchase toy creative building sets such as Googolplex, Legos, Tinker Toys.
2. Put them in open containers on tables within reach of participants.
3. When the session starts, explain that the building sets are provided for them to fidget with as they listen to and participate in the session.
4. Stand or sit and watch what happens.

Variation

Put colored pencils, markers, or crayons with paper on the table instead.

Tips

1. You will be amazed at the results: creativity, team building, open conversations, cooperation, collaboration, achievement, and a more focused interest in the topic.
2. I have seen so much benefit come from this simple activity that I don't travel anywhere without my Fidgets. They're great for meetings, training sessions, and lengthy speeches.

Full as a Tick

Purpose

Mental aerobics; Meeting starter; Energizing a long, dry presentation; For non-icebreaker types; Pure fun; Introducing a topic; Getting closure

Group Size

5-25

Level of Physical Activity

Medium

Estimated Time

3 minutes each time

Props

Objects

This activity is "as easy as pie" once participants get the hang of comparing objects to different things. Use it as an energizer after breaks or, since it relates to the topic, use it to provide focus and attention. Good for any group in a training session or meeting.

A simile is defined in The American Heritage Dictionary, Second College Edition *as "a figure of speech in which two essentially unlike things are compared, often in a phrase introduced by like or as, as in 'He was as strong as a bull.'"*

Instructions

1. After a break, bring out an object and pass it around for people to touch and think about.
2. Explain that this activity is called Full as a Tick. The purpose of the activity is to create similes about the object that relate back to the topic (or organization or group).
3. Remind participants that simile phrases often begin with *like* or *as*. Give an example such as "Delivering a speech is like opening a bottle of Coke; if you don't taste and hear the carbonation in the beginning, you assume the rest will be flat."
4. Instruct participants to think of one or more similes that relate to their topic using the object they have in their hands.
5. After two minutes, ask participants to share their similes with the group.

Variations

1. Have small groups work on similes to share with other groups.
2. Ask participants to list similes on a flip chart.
3. As you pass an object around, ask participants to spontaneously name a simile.
4. Use the activity several times during a lengthy session, bringing different objects each time.

Tips

1. Almost any objects will work, but the activity is better received if you use objects that are fun. Examples include: curling iron, top hat, football helmet, music box, teddy bear.
2. Keep it light.
3. This is not a good activity for serious sessions where people may be hostile or antagonistic about the content of the session.

IN SYNC

Purpose

Physical energizer; Team building; Outdoor activity; Energizing a long, dry presentation; Pure fun

Group Size

18-200

Level of Physical Activity

High

Estimated Time

3-4 minutes in the beginning, 30 seconds at various times during the session

Props

None

In this activity, participants will engage in synchronized movements like the wave, but better. Use this activity with groups who respond to a challenge and to movement.

Synchronous: a buzz word for the nineties, meaning "happening, existing, or arising at precisely the same time" (Merriam Webster's Collegiate Dictionary, Tenth Edition).

Instructions

1. Organize participants into groups of eight to twenty. Ask them to choose a group name.
2. Give them one minute in their groups to decide upon a synchronous movement they could all do that would be relaxing and energizing. Give examples such as the wave, a dance step, and an exercise routine.
3. After one minute, ask the groups to demonstrate their movements for the other groups.
4. Explain that during the session you will give the name of a group and say, "In sync." At that time they should stand up and repeat their group movement. When you say "Out of sync," they should return to their seats.
5. Tell them they may change their movement anytime they like as long as the whole group changes, maintaining synchronicity.
6. Choose one group and say, "(Group name), in sync."
7. Do the activity whenever you feel they're ready for a break/energizer.

Variations

1. Give each group a card with a movement on it for them to perform.
2. Forget movement; use the time for groups to get together and talk.

Tips

1. The seating arrangement makes little difference with this activity. It works even if seating is theater style. Rows of seats become groups. Groups will just stand in place and perform their movement.
2. Groups do not have to be seated together for this one. Wherever they are, they stand and perform with the original group.

Opinion Poll

Purpose

Getting to know you; Getting to know you better; Physical energizer; Energizer for a long, dry presentation

Group Size

10-30

Level of Physical Activity

High

Estimated Time

2-5 minutes

Props

Opinion Poll Activity Sheet for leader; flip chart and marker or overhead projector and screen

The group will enjoy giving and hearing opinions about a variety of topics, from the weather to a favorite color. This is a quick, fun way to get a group on their feet. Use it with any group, any time during a session for a quick stretch.

> *"What is your opinion?" can either be an innocent inquiry or a question laden with expectations—a truly leading question often asked of one party by a second party after discovering a disagreement with a third party. In that situation, the underlying, albeit presumed, message behind the question is, "I'm directing this question to you because I think that you will support my opinion. I'm right, aren't I???"*

Instructions

1. Tell participants that you will be taking a quick poll of their honest opinions.
2. Explain the rules:
   - I will read a statement that contains two or three choices for completion.
   - When I read the choices a second time, you should respond with your opinion by standing when your choice is stated.
   - We will count the numbers of people who hold each opinion.
3. Give an example, such as "The season of the year that I prefer is summer, autumn, winter, or spring." Then call out each of the four choices in turn and count how many people stand for each choice.
4. Put responses to the poll on a flip chart or transparency for all to see.

Variations

1. Tell participants at the beginning of the session that you will be conducting a poll later on and ask them to write a topic on a 3″ × 5″ card for you to use. Use these topics for your poll.
2. Use this as a quick, easy way to take a poll on organizational issues or ideas.

Tips

1. Explain that this is a forced choice activity; they should give an opinion even when they don't particularly prefer any of the choices.
2. Keep this light, fun, and quick with minimal discussion.
3. If people say "I change my mind," tell them it's too late.

Notes

_____

_____

_____

_____

_____

_____

_____

_____

_____

OPINION POLL
ACTIVITY SHEET

1. Which season of the year do you prefer: winter, spring, summer, or fall?

2. Which type of music do you prefer: classical, country, jazz, or heavy metal rock?

3. Which type of food do you prefer: Italian, Mexican, Chinese, or French?

4. Which type of exercise do you prefer: swimming, aerobics, running, or bicycling?

5. Which type of ice cream do you prefer: vanilla, bubble gum, coffee, or mint chocolate chip?

6. Which type of vacation do you prefer: camping by a lake, biking across Canada, a chalet at a ski resort, or backpacking in the wilderness?

7. Which color do you prefer: green, brown, orange, or purple?

8. Which activity would you prefer to do on a Friday night: rent a video, go to the opera, attend a Monster Truck show, or participate in country line dancing?

9. Which is your favorite holiday: Fourth of July, St. Patrick's Day, Thanksgiving, or Labor Day?

10. What is your best time of day: morning, afternoon, evening, or night?

Out of the Box

Purpose
Energizing a long, dry presentation; Physical energizer

Group Size
6-40

Level of Physical Activity
High

Estimated Time
2-4 minutes

Props
One box; one bowl or basket; Out of the Box Activity Sheets I and II
This activity will energize everyone as they anticipate their number being chosen. Use it in a session that is long or dry or has stretches of sitting. It is great for groups that are not used to engaging activities. Since participants are leading, the activities are more acceptable.

I think the world would be a better place if everyone decided to do one out-of-the-box thing each day. Think how that would open us up to new ideas.

Instructions
1. Cut out Energizer Slips from Activity Sheet I and put them in a box.
2. Pass out double numbers to participants from Activity Sheet II. Ask them to tear off one of the numbers to put in the basket or bowl.
3. Explain to participants that periodically throughout the session, you, the leader, will choose a number from the bowl and announce it. The person who has that number will come forward and choose a slip from the box. The slip will give the person directions for leading the group in an energizing experience.
4. Choose a number each time you want the group to get up and get energized.

Variations
1. Use the same group of numbers for energizers and door prizes so the group is in suspense about what the slip will reveal.
2. Give each participant a number and explain that they each must be prepared with an energizing activity to lead the group in when their number is called.

Tip
Give examples of types of activities. Or call your own number and lead the first one.

OUT OF THE BOX
ACTIVITY SHEET 1

Jumping Jacks

Toe Touches

Arm Circles

Jogging in Place

Kick Line

High Knee Lifts

Spell Out YMCA with Body Language

The Wave

Lead a Cheer

The Hokey Pokey

Deep Breathing and Stretching

Bumper Cars

Creative Handshaking

Bunny Hop Around the Room

Hand Jive

The Itsy Bitsy Spider

Sing a Round of Row, Row, Row Your Boat

Shoulder Rubs

The Bump

Make a Toast

OUT OF THE BOX
ACTIVITY SHEET 2

1	1
2	2
3	3
4	4
5	5
6	6
7	7
8	8
9	9
10	10
11	11
12	12
13	13
14	14
15	15
16	16
17	17
18	18
19	19
20	20
21	21
22	22

23	23
24	24
25	25
26	26
27	27
28	28
29	29
30	30
31	31
32	32
33	33
34	34
35	35
36	36
37	37
38	38
39	39
40	40

Party Mix

Purpose	Getting to know you better; Team building; Self-disclosure; Energizing a long, dry presentation
Group Size	6-40
Level of Physical Activity	Low
Estimated Time	6-10 minutes, per time, per group
Props	Party Mix Activity Sheets, cut into cards, one set of cards per group

Participants will take turns answering nutty, twisted, and wholesome questions in this activity. Use this with multiple groups as a team building exercise. If you only have one group, tailor the questions to match that group.

> *Everything is questionable. This doesn't mean that some things are not answerable; it just means everything is questionable. Absolutes become absolutes because we've answered the questions. If you ask someone why they believe a certain way, they'll often answer "Because it's so" or "It has been proven to be true." These answers can be interpreted as, "I've had my questions answered." Or so one would think. But sometimes people haven't asked any questions. Faith is not the acceptance of anything given; faith is a study of the answers to the questions and an acceptance of those answers.*

Instructions

1. Organize participants seated at tables in groups of five to eight.
2. Put Party Mix card piles face down in the middle of each table.
3. Explain the rules:
   - Participants will take turns choosing a Party Mix card from the center of the table.
   - Each participant will then choose a corresponding Question card. For example, a person who chooses a Nut Party Mix card will then choose a Nut Question card.
   - Participants will then answer the questions aloud for group members to hear.

Variation

Participants could read the questions aloud and ask someone in the group to respond.

Tips

1. If possible, put Chex Party Mix™ on the tables for participants to enjoy while playing, and provide the recipe.
2. The questions follow the cards: pretzel questions are a bit twisted; nut questions are a bit crazy; and Chex™ questions are full-bodied.

PARTY MIX
ACTIVITY SHEET I

Pretzels	*Pretzels*
Peanuts	Peanuts
Chex	**Chex**

PARTY MIX ACTIVITY SHEET II

Pretzel Would you rather ride an elephant or a camel and why?	**Peanuts** What was your childhood nickname and why?	**Chex** Who has most inspired you in life and why?
Pretzel Would you rather shave your head or pierce your nose? Why?	**Peanuts** What was your best Halloween costume and why?	**Chex** What is the reason for man's existence on earth?
Pretzel Would you rather spend a week stranded in the jungle or at sea on a boat and why?	**Peanuts** What was your most embarassing moment and why?	**Chex** What historical person could teach you the most and why?
Pretzel Would you rather eat a monkey's brains or a pig's eye and why?	**Peanuts** Describe your worst haircut.	**Chex** Is there other intelligent life in the universe? Why?
Pretzel Would you rather bungee jump off a bridge or go over a waterfall in a kayak and why?	**Peanuts** What was the ugliest thing your parent made you wear as a kid and why?	**Chex** Who would you most like to be stranded on an island with and why?
Pretzel Would you rather live forever or never grow up and why?	**Peanuts** What was the best April Fool's joke you have heard of?	**Chex** What is the true definition of success and why?

Payola

Purpose   Introducing a topic; Team building; Energizing a long, dry presentation

Group Size   6-20

Level of Physical Activity   Medium

Estimated Time   1-5 minutes

Props   Play money ($100,000 per participant in different denominations); prizes with sale prices that match earning power; two envelopes per participant

Participants enjoy recognizing one another's contributions—without any cost to themselves. Use this activity to stimulate interest and keep the group energized.

> *Many parents wonder about the best way to get their kids to do work and to consider it a normal process (notice that I didn't say enjoyable) to assume responsibility. What I'm talking about is payment for services. Some call it allowance; others call it bribery. I, of course, preferred the inconsistent route —switching philosophies each time one appeared not to work. My parents were very consistent; work was not an option, but their paying me was. So I could do the work well and get my allowance, or I could do it less than well and not get an allowance. The emphasis was on quality. Aha!*

Instructions

1. Before participants arrive, put $100,000 each in various denominations in half of the envelopes and write "To Give" on them; then write "Recognition" on the remaining empty envelopes.

2. As participants arrive, give each one a full "To Give" envelope and an empty "Recognition" envelope.

3. Instruct them to use all of the money to reward one another for contributing insights, perspectives, or ideas at any time. Explain that the different denominations are to help them place value on the contributions.

4. Tell them that at the end of the session, they will get to spend their recognition dollars.

5. At the end of the session, allow participants to buy prizes using the dollars they've accumulated.

Variations

1. Have a pile of money on the table and ask participants to take from the pile to reward others.

2. Use chips rather than dollars.

Tips

1. You give out money, too, particularly in the beginning to get the ball rolling.
2. Don't be surprised if participants pool money at the end to buy joint prizes.
3. Encourage participants to include everyone in recognition. The purpose is not to exclude anyone; the purpose of the activity is to include everyone.

Notes

_____

_____

_____

_____

_____

_____

_____

_____

_____

_____

PECULIARITIES

Purpose   Getting to know you; Physical energizer; Pure fun; Energizing a long, dry presentation

Group Size   12-60

Level of Physical Activity   Low

Estimated Time   2-5 minutes

Props   Peculiarities Activity Sheet; simple prizes such as candy, stickers, or pens

Peculiarities is a quick, light, and easy way for individuals to find out about one another. It may be used at any time during a short or long session with participants who know one another well or are complete strangers, or to introduce the topic of diversity. For long sessions, I recommend using a few examples every hour or so to add interest and humor.

A peculiarity (according to Merriam Webster's Collegiate Dictionary, Tenth Edition) is "a distinguishing characteristic; oddity, quirk." While commonalities bring us together, peculiarities add interest—sometimes.

Instructions
1. Ask participants to stand.
2. Explain that the object of the activity is to discover peculiarities in the group.
3. Tell participants that you will read items on a list—one at a time. Ask them to come forward if they respond affirmatively to the category to receive a prize.

Variation   Pass out the list to participants and ask them to fill it out individually and then find others in the room who have marked the same categories. Include some that you know are owned by more than one person.

Tips
1. Keep this quick, light, and fun.
2. Add peculiarities to the list, perhaps relating to organizational quirks or norms or to specific peculiarities that you know about people in the group.

Notes   _____

_____

_____

PECULIARITIES ACTIVITY SHEET (FOR LEADER)

1. Was born on February 29
2. Has/had a dog named Spot, Midnight, Lucky, or Shadow
3. Is wearing an article of clothing that was chosen and purchased by someone else
4. Is wearing a family heirloom
5. Drives a Harley
6. Competes in sporting events such as running, skiing, etc.
7. Likes pizza with anchovies
8. Volunteers for charity fund drives
9. Was born in another state
10. Was born in another country
11. Has won a prize
12. Has never been to Florida
13. Writes songs or poetry
14. Has an organized, clean desk
15. Has a twin brother/sister
16. Has a shoe size of 13 or greater
17. Has milked a cow
18. Has been to the top of the Washington Monument
19. Collects stamps or other collectible
20. Remembers sodas for five cents
21. Has been to a Billy Joel concert
22. Has eight or more siblings
23. Prefers winter to summer
24. Has been on a radio or TV show
25. Restores old cars or trucks
26. Has won a prize or money from a mail-in form

Pink Slips

Purpose

Energizing a long, dry presentation; Physical energizer

Group Size

6-20

Level of Physical Activity

High

Estimated Time

2-4 minutes

Props

Pink Slips Activity Sheet
Use this activity with groups that are highly interactive to keep their interest, or with groups that are not very interactive to get them involved.

> *To my amazement, people who would not plan for interactive activities for themselves are often the ones who enjoy them the most. It's often the job of a leader to grant license to behave like an extrovert.*

Instructions

1. Copy and then cut out the Pink Slips Activity Sheet so that you have one Pink Slip per person.
2. Explain that we equate getting a pink slip with losing a job. The beauty of the "pink slips" in this activity is that they give people jobs.
3. Instruct participants to complete the activity on their pink slips sometime before the end of the session. After they do it, they should put their pink slips in a pile.
4. Periodically during the session, remind participants to complete their pink slip activities before the end of the session.
5. At the end of the session, review all pink slips.

Variation

Give out pink slips of paper and have participants choose and write down their own activities. Then redistribute the slips so that each person gets someone else's slip.

Tip

Make your own pink slips with the kinds of activities you think would be of the most benefit to your audience.

PINK SLIPS ACTIVITY SHEET

Shake hands with at least five people.

Ask two people about their hobbies.

Ask three questions during the session.

Offer someone a cup of coffee or other beverage.

Change seats twice during the session.

Find out the favorite football team of four other participants.

Push in ten chairs as people leave for the lunch break.

Pour water for three people.

Write down the pink slip activities of three other people.

Pull a chair out for one other person as they come back from lunch or a break.

Give three people genuine compliments.

Ask two people about their job roles.

Tell one joke or humorous story.

Straighten materials on the table during a break.

Give your opinion at least twice during the session.

Get up and stretch at a time when everyone else is sitting.

TEENSY TRIATHLON

Purpose Physical energizer; Energizing a long, dry presentation; Pure fun

Group Size 10-40

Level of Physical Activity High

Estimated Time 5 minutes each time

Props Teensy Triathlon Activity Sheet

Here's one way to offer different types of movement and have fun doing it. Use it any time people are in a long session, with any type of group.

Training needs a new term: "chair potatoes." We often ask people to sit for three or four hours, or many days in a row with only a walk to the rest rooms as exercise. Shame on us! There are many ways to offer movement that generate health and well-being—physically, emotionally, and mentally.

Instructions

1. Ask participants to stand and move to an open space in the room.
2. Explain that since it is healthy mentally and physically to engage in physical activity at intervals during a time of sitting and listening, you will introduce the Teensy Triathlon which they may all participate in.
3. Explain the rules to participants:
   - You will be working to perfect your own rhythm in three rounds of competition.
   - The three events are: one minute of running in place, one minute of swimming, and one minute of stationary biking.
   - We will run the Teensy Triathlon three times during the day: after the morning break, after lunch, and after the afternoon break.
   - If you are unable to do these activities, you are to choose three of your own that will give physical stimulation.
4. Demonstrate each activity (biking can be done while seated on a chair) and give participants two minutes to practice the moves.
5. Ask participants to step into position to begin. Explain that you will blow the whistle for them to begin running; after one minute, you will again blow the whistle to begin swimming; and after another minute, you will blow the whistle to begin biking.
6. Say "Ready, set" and then blow the whistle.

7. Following the activity, remind participants that they will have an opportunity to improve their form in the next round of competition.

8. Following the third round, distribute Teensy Triathlon medals.

Variations

1. Make it a partnering or group activity and have participants synchronize running, swimming, and biking.

2. Ask participants to suggest events, or have them design their own triathlon.

3. Use more humorous activities such as running up the side of one hill and down the other or paddling a canoe through thick mud.

Tips

1. Use fun props such as a sign that says Starting Line, water bottles, or sweatbands.

2. Use music during the exercise that matches the activity; for example, "Chariots of Fire" for running music or an Italian opera for biking music.

Notes

_____

_____

_____

_____

_____

_____

_____

_____

TEENSY TRIATHLON
ACTIVITY SHEET

The Scrambler

Purpose

Mental aerobics; Team building; Introducing a topic; Pure fun; Energizing a long, dry presentation; For non-icebreaker types

Group Size

5-50

Level of Physical Activity

Low

Estimated Time

5 minutes, periodically throughout the day

Props

Scrambler Activity Sheet

Many people come to seminars with an immediate need to do or accomplish a task. The Scrambler takes care of that need for some, is just plain fun for others, and may provide a way for you to introduce content. Use it after breaks as a mental energizer or group competition.

Many people like to have a point of focus—even if it's not the right one. I've observed in a crisis situation that some people will focus on a task that is relatively insignificant, just to focus and feel as if they are doing something.

Instructions

1. As participants enter the room, hand them Scrambler List #1 and invite them to try their luck while waiting for the class to begin.
2. When beginning the class, explain that the Scrambler is a list of words with meaning (names of vehicles, countries, desserts, flowers, and others you've added).
3. Organize participants into groups of three.
4. Tell them that after every break, you will hand out a new Scrambler List and they may spend time working with their groups to unscramble the words on their lists.
5. Explain that there will be prizes at the end of the day for the groups who unscramble the most words accurately.

Variations

1. Use it as an activity for already established groups.
2. Make it an individual challenge.
3. Scramble words that are from the content you're delivering or they're learning, or words around a theme (e.g., politics or channels of communication).

Tip

This is totally for fun. Set the stage for lightness.

Notes

_____

_____

THE SCRAMBLER
ACTIVITY SHEET

The Scrambler List #1—VEHICLES

gkuveaolbsnwg _ _ _ _ _ _ _ _ _ _ _ _ _

nmvniai _ _ _ _ _ _ _

gverroeanr _ _ _ _ _ _ _ _ _

uimioelsn _ _ _ _ _ _ _ _

vbusacotnertilemng _ _ _ _ _ _ _ _ _ _ _ _ _ _ _ _ _

kkctppruuic _ _ _ _ _ _ _ _ _ _

ewerethenigeleh _ _ _ _ _ _ _ _ _ _ _ _ _ _ _

mycecaharov _ _ _ _ _ _ _ _ _ _ _

iesxflnitiuin _ _ _ _ _ _ _ _ _ _ _ _ _

taunrs _ _ _ _ _ _

The Scrambler List #2—COUNTRIES

glaoan _ _ _ _ _ _

benitatedaarumires _ _ _ _ _ _ _ _ _ _ _ _ _ _ _ _ _ _

dneeazlawn _ _ _ _ _ _ _ _ _

lataindh _ _ _ _ _ _ _

lbgumxeuor _ _ _ _ _ _ _ _ _ _

aacciorst _ _ _ _ _ _ _ _

aaeginnrt _ _ _ _ _ _ _ _

bliiera _ _ _ _ _ _ _

madrenk _ _ _ _ _ _ _

trusaia _ _ _ _ _ _ _

The Scrambler List #3—DESSERTS

kepwpealinepsupieddonca _

risitamu _ _ _ _ _ _ _ _

aaabdignnndpu _ _ _ _ _ _ _ _ _ _ _ _ _

paocookhclteuandce _ _ _ _ _ _ _ _ _ _ _ _ _ _ _ _ _ _

nicalno _ _ _ _ _ _ _

uberberolycbrble _ _ _ _ _ _ _ _ _ _ _ _ _ _ _ _

fitukeconoroes _ _ _ _ _ _ _ _ _ _ _ _ _

pemerimineleguon _ _ _ _ _ _ _ _ _ _ _ _ _ _ _ _

vlabkaa _ _ _ _ _ _ _

hndadesugeotfu _ _ _ _ _ _ _ _ _ _ _ _ _

The Scrambler List #4—FLOWERS

achntyih _ _ _ _ _ _ _ _

eaazal _ _ _ _ _ _

enrdaiag _ _ _ _ _ _ _ _

goldaial _ _ _ _ _ _ _ _

dygeeraisrba _ _ _ _ _ _ _ _ _ _ _

foddilaf _ _ _ _ _ _ _

rymorgglonin _ _ _ _ _ _ _ _ _ _ _

nvboaiiluglea _ _ _ _ _ _ _ _ _ _ _ _

salacyedsubnke _ _ _ _ _ _ _ _ _ _ _ _ _

frosuwenl _ _ _ _ _ _ _ _ _

Answer Key

The Scrambler List #1—VEHICLES

Volkswagen bug
minivan
Range Rover
Limousine
Mustang convertible
pickup truck
eighteen wheeler
Chevy Camaro
Lexus Infiniti
Saturn

The Scrambler List #2—COUNTRIES

Angola
United Arab Emirates
New Zealand
Thailand
Luxembourg
Costa Rica
Argentina
Liberia
Denmark
Austria

The Scrambler List #3—DESSERTS

Pineapple upsidedown cake
Tiramisu
Banana pudding
Chocolate pound cake
Cannoli
Blueberry cobbler
Fortune cookies
Lemon meringue pie
Baklava
Hot fudge sundae

The Scrambler List #4—FLOWERS

Hyacinth
Azalea
Gardenia
Gladiola
Gerbera daisy
Daffodil
Morning Glory
Bougainvillea
Black-eyed Susan
Sunflower

THEME WORK

Purpose
Mental aerobics; Energizing a long, dry presentation; Team building

Group Size
12-20

Level of Physical Activity
Medium

Estimated Time
2-5 minutes

Props
CD or tape with bars of TV theme songs on it; CD or tape playback machine; paper and pens for each participant

    Once is not enough with this activity. Use this icebreaker after breaks and anytime you feel the need for an energizer.

> *My mother recently found in her chest of treasures a Rootie Kazootie bandanna that I had sent for as a child. Is there anyone reading this that goes that far back besides me?*

Instructions
1. Ask participants to number their papers.
2. Explain to participants that periodically you will play the first few bars of theme songs from several TV shows. Ask them to find the corresponding number and write down the name of the TV show.
3. Play the cuts from several theme songs, giving participants about five seconds after each to write the name of the show.
4. When finished, replay the theme bars and ask participants to give the name of the show.
5. Do this activity two or three times during a session.

Variations
1. Allow groups or pairs to work the responses.
2. Ask participants to hum themes and ask other participants to guess the show.

Tips
1. Participants really like this one; even if they can't remember the name of the show, the music itself will bring back memories.
2. Experts will often emerge to the delight of everyone else.

Notes
_____
_____
_____
_____
_____

YOU SAID IT!

Purpose
Introducing a topic; Energizing a long, dry presentation; Meeting starter; Pure fun

Group Size
10-20

Level of Physical Activity
Low

Estimated Time
Ongoing

Props
Word cards, one per participant; prizes
    Participants will stay awake since they may win a prize just for listening intently. Introduce this activity in the beginning of a session or prior to a session and then allow it to work throughout the session.

    This activity is about "forced listening." Sometimes the content of a meeting or training session is so dry, people have a tendency to use the time to catch up on some ZZZs. Therefore, it is permissible to use any techniques and gimmicks that will encourage listening and participation—activities such as this one.

Instructions
1. Give each participant a slip of paper with a word on it. Explain that the word pertains to the content of the session (or is relevant to the meeting, company, etc.). Tell them not to tell anyone else what the word is.
2. Explain the rules to the group:
   - Each word was given out twice, so the two people who have the same word are in competition with each other.
   - Each person should listen for another person, such as the speaker, to use their word. When they hear someone say the word, they should yell, "You said it!"
   - You can only call out "You said it!" if the person who speaks the word is not in conversation with you or answering a question from you. (Therefore, you can't coerce them into saying the word.)
3. Give the person who yells "You said it!" first a prize.

Variation
For a small group, use only one person per word.

Tips
1. Use words that relate to the context of the meeting or program; words common to the participants' company, such as departments or the president's name; or fun words from everyday life.
2. The size of the prize doesn't matter; people find reward in the act of winning anything.

ESPECIALLY FOR BIG GROUPS

AT THE FAIR

Purpose	Team building; Physical energizer; Especially for big groups
Group Size	20-200
Level of Physical Activity	High
Estimated Time	10-30 minutes
Props	At the Fair cards, one event per group, one card per participant; lively music

Nobody will be able to resist playing in this exercise since each small group gets to entertain everyone else with their part of the fair. Use this activity midway through or at the end of the program; participants will be less inhibited with their performances after spending some time together.

The Altamont Fair happens once a year on the fairgrounds in Altamont, NY. Residents of the village begin preparation well in advance; groundskeepers ready the stadium, stores stock the shelves, community groups plan their booths, teenagers seek jobs, homeowners increase security, and some knowing people leave for vacation. Two days before opening day, equipment and fair employees arrive in town to set up. For the next week there are non-stop cacophonous music, whirring and clacking of a variety of rides, shouts of frightened—but delighted—riders, noises from a variety of animals, and smells of hay, popcorn, chili dogs, and cotton candy. Then the fair is over for another year, and the only things remaining are peace, quiet, and flies.

Instructions

1. Organize participants into groups of five to twenty.
2. Give each group cards for each person. Explain that each group has the name of a different event that may occur at a county fair.
3. Explain that groups will have five minutes to develop and practice the event shown on their card before performing it for the whole group at "show time."
4. Give the signal to begin planning and practicing.
5. After five minutes, ask the groups to take turns performing their acts in the center of the room.

Variations

1. Ask groups to come up with their own events.
2. Give all groups the same events.
3. Give groups only different rides to mime, for example, roller coaster, ferris wheel, merry-go-round.
4. At the end, call for work analogies, e.g., "The tractor pull is like ..."

Tips

1. This is your chance to run a fair. Enjoy it!
2. Encourage groups to clap for each performance.

AT THE FAIR ACTIVITY SHEET

Tractor Pull	Ferris Wheel
House of Mirrors	Pig Races
Sheep Herding	Livestock Judging
Ring Toss	Pie Eating Contest
Kissing Booth	Stock Car Racing

Balloon Stampede

Purpose
Team building; Physical energizer; Pure fun; Outdoor Activity; Getting to know you; Especially for big groups

Group Size
40-200

Level of Physical Activity
High

Estimated Time
3-10 minutes

Props
One balloon per participant (plus extras)

Use this high energy activity in which pairs in teams compete in a relay race with participants who are willing to loosen up and have fun. It is best used in a forum for activities only, or as an afternoon energizer.

> *I remember Sunday School picnics with three-legged and sack relay races. What fun—but serious competition. The secret to winning the three-legged race was to have a friend as a partner with whom you could practice the week before. Faith Aumack and I were unbeatable. Talk about a bonding experience!*

Instructions

1. Set up in an open space in a room by marking starting and finishing lines about 20 feet apart.
2. Organize participants into groups of twenty to forty behind the starting line.
3. Ask participants to find partners in their groups and organize their groups with partner sets lined up one behind the other.
4. Give each participant one balloon. Instruct them to blow it up and tie it.
5. Explain the rules:
   - This is a relay race. The object is for one group to finish first.
   - As each set of partners moves to the front of their line, they should put the balloons between them and hold them there without using their hands. They are to decide where to hold the balloons (for example, back-to-back, side-to-side, etc.).
   - The set then walks quickly down to the stopping line and back to the starting line without allowing their balloon to drop.
   - When one set is back and crosses the starting line, the next set goes.
   - Each set of partners must participate.
   - If a balloon escapes, the set must stop, reposition the balloon, and continue.
6. Begin the relay.
7. Award a prize to the first group that finishes.

Variations

1. Tell participants they have to hold the balloons in a certain way.
2. Ask participants to break the balloons upon returning.

Tip

This is meant to be fun—not serious competition. Keep it light.

Notes

_____

_____

_____

_____

_____

_____

_____

_____

_____

_____

BUMPER COLLISION

Purpose

Getting to know you; Especially for big groups; Physical energizer; Pure fun

Group Size

20 plus

Level of Physical Activity

High

Estimated Time

5-8 minutes

Props

Music

Participants will get to know each other as they move around and bump into each other while music plays, then introduce themselves to the nearest "cars" whenever a whistle blows. Use Bumper Collision at the beginning of a session. They'll love it!

Bumper cars are great fun: drive—bump—turn—and drive again. For drivers really into the fun of it, the inevitable occurs: drive—bump—uh, oh! Now you're stuck in a bumper collision and it takes time to untangle your bumpers and move out on the track again.

Instructions

1. Ask for a show of hands of people who have ever ridden bumper cars.

2. Invite participants to imagine that they are bumper cars. Describe the scenario of them moving around the floor "bumping into" one another. Give them the analogy we often use when we say: "Guess who I bumped into today?"

3. Explain the following rules:
   - When the music begins, everyone should begin "driving" around.
   - When they hear a whistle, they should move into collision; the number of drivers in each group will be determined by the number of whistle toots. For instance, if they hear three whistle toots, three drivers should collide together; four toots equals four drivers; and so on.
   - When in collision, drivers should introduce themselves, giving names, companies, jobs, etc.
   - When they hear one whistle toot, they should begin driving again.
   - Each time they collide, they should be with people they have not been with in a previous collision.

4. Begin the music.

5. After thirty seconds, blow the whistle three times, stop the music, and give them about thirty seconds to exchange information with each other in groups of three before turning on the music again.

6. After about twenty seconds of people "bumping" around, blow the whistle four times and invite participants to share information.

7. Continue the process through about five whistle blowings—each time blowing a different number of toots.

Variation

Change the name of the game to New York Taxi and use a horn instead of a whistle.

Tip

Model driving a bumper car as you give instructions.

Notes

_____

_____

_____

_____

_____

_____

_____

_____

_____

_____

CREATIVE CONGRATUlATIONS

Purpose
Getting to know you; Physical energizer; Pure fun; Especially for big groups

Group Size
10-500

Level of Physical Activity
High

Estimated Time
2-5 minutes

Props
None

In this activity, participants meet one another and then have fun creating congratulatory comments for each other that, most likely, are not true. Use this quick activity to warm up a group without their having to disclose quickly. It works best with groups that you know enjoy having some fun.

Wouldn't it be great if each time we met a person for the first time we knew something great about that person so we could begin a conversation with that knowledge? Instead, we sometimes walk away from five minutes of small talk, thinking, "I hope I never have to talk with that person again because I have nothing worthwhile to say."

Instructions

1. Gather participants in a space where they can stand and move around.
2. Explain that there is a certain joy we share when we can offer someone genuine congratulations. And what a good feeling for the receiver! But since these participants don't know one another yet, they do not know what congratulations to express. This activity will allow them to capture those good feelings without even knowing anything about one another.
3. Instruct them to take two to three minutes to walk around meeting as many people as they can. After they introduce themselves, they should make up a congratulatory greeting to offer the other person. Some examples might include: "Congratulations on your 30th birthday" or "Congratulations on having your first book published" or a humorous "Congratulations on being the first person to make it into the Olympics without trying out."
4. Explain that after the exchange of names and congratulations, both persons should move on to the next person and do the same.
5. Explain that they may use the same creative congratulations or different ones for each person.
6. After they begin, allow about two to three minutes for the activity.

Variation

Ask participants to write humorous congratulations before they begin the activity to use during the activity.

Tips

1. To model the activity, ask a participant to come to the front of the room. You should congratulate that person using a humorous congratulation. I once congratulated a man in his 20s for receiving the Golden Handshake from the company for 25 years of service in the same position he currently held. The look on his face was worth the entire experience.

2. This activity needs to be combined with laughter.

Notes

_____

_____

_____

_____

_____

_____

_____

_____

_____

_____

Double Take

Purpose	Getting to know you; Physical energizer; Especially for big groups
Group Size	20-500
Level of Physical Activity	High
Estimated Time	3-5 minutes
Props	Upbeat music; Double Take Sheet for leader

In this activity, participants pair up by finding a common ground, whether it be a similar hair color or a passion for pizza. Double Take is a fun, simple way for people to mingle in a nonthreatening way. Use it with an active group of people, whether they know one another or not.

> *I don't know where the phrase "double take" came from, but I have my suspicions. Perhaps "double take" was coined by a teenager coming into the house after school, finding Mom in the middle of mixing chocolate chip cookie dough, taking a taste on the tip of a finger, ignoring Mom's cries of protest, and then taking another.*

Instructions

1. Ask participants to stand and move to a location in the room where they can walk around and mingle freely.
2. Tell participants that when the music begins, they should begin shaking hands with people and introducing or re-introducing themselves.
3. Explain to them that they will have an opportunity to "do a double take" with another participant.
4. Tell them that you will call out a characteristic that they may have in common with another group member. They should immediately find another person who shares that particular characteristic. For instance, if you call out "hair color," they should form a pair with a person who has the same hair color.
5. Explain that you will call out many of these and each time they should "do a double take" with a new person.
6. Begin the activity using the leader sheet provided.

Variations

1. If the group is small, ask participants to think of a way they could form a pair with another person and engage that person. Give them five chances to do this with five different people.
2. Use this to create groups of four to six people and change the name of the activity to Group Grope.

Tips

1. Blow a whistle each time you call out a different word or phrase.
2. Use some words or phrases that are particular to the group.
3. Each time there may be people who have not found a "double take." You might acknowledge that by asking for a show of hands in response to the question: "Who has not found a double take?" Moving on quickly to the next item will allow those individuals to make a "double take."

Notes

_____

_____

_____

_____

_____

_____

_____

_____

_____

_____

DOUBLE TAKE ACTIVITY SHEET
(FOR THE LEADER)

hair color

eye color

shoe size

favorite color

age

pet ownership

same color shirt

favorite pizza topping

height

favorite food

music preference

favorite sport

favorite team

type of car

length of daily commute

Getting the Goods

Purpose
Physical energizer; Getting to know you; Getting to know you better; Especially for big groups

Group Size
10-100

Level of Physical Activity
High

Estimated Time
5-10 minutes

Props
Whistle

Groups will "get the goods" they want on participants from other small groups as they conspire and then ask questions. This is an active, interesting way for groups to get to know about each other and to work together. Use it in the beginning of a session for participants to meet or at another time to energize the group. This is not an activity for executive, highly intellectual, or conservative types (unless, of course, you up the ante).

Unfortunately, getting the goods appears to be a favorite activity of politicians. Success means getting greater goods than the goods obtained by an opponent.

Instructions
1. Organize participants into groups of five to eight people standing in an open space.
2. Explain that the groups will have an opportunity to "get the goods" on people in the other groups.
3. Give these instructions:
   - The goal of the activity is for participants to find out information about people in the other groups.
   - There will be four or five rounds.
   - For each round, each group will decide the information they want from the members of other groups, such as middle names or favorite types of music.
   - When I blow a whistle, the groups will scatter to ask those questions of as many people as they can from the other groups.
   - The correct procedure is for two people to approach each other, exchange names, and then ask each other their questions.
   - When I blow the whistle again, the groups get back together, tell each other the information they gathered, and select another piece of information they want for the next round.
4. Lead them through four to five rounds.
5. When the rounds are completed, ask each group what kinds of information they obtained from the group.

Variations

1. Give each group a sheet of information to gather from which they may choose for each round.

2. Ask groups to make up questions in advance without telling them how they'll be getting answers. Say to them, "Determine what things you would like to find out about other people in the room and write down about five of them."

3. Use this activity to have groups gather information on a topic, or to answer questions they've written about the topic.

Tip

Don't belabor this activity. Sometimes three rounds are enough.

Notes

_____

_____

_____

_____

_____

_____

_____

_____

_____

_____

Good Sports

Purpose

Grouping people; Physical energizer; Outdoor activity; Especially for big groups; Pure fun

Group Size

20-200

Level of Physical Activity

High

Estimated Time

3-5 minutes

Props

Good Sports cards, one per participant

In this activity, people will form groups by finding others who have the same sport card they do. To form groups at any time during a session, use it with groups that are willing to "play."

> *My friends Alice and Betty Allen, sisters who live in a nearby retirement community, are avid football fans—all year long. They follow the games in the fall and winter; the draft and trades in the spring, and training camps in the summer; they know it all. Like music, sports interests are for all; some of us play, some of us watch, and some of us complain about the athletes' salaries. That makes it universal, right?*

Instructions

1. Give each participant a Good Sports card.
2. Organize participants in an open area of the room where they can move about.
3. Tell participants that they will be engaged in an activity called "Good Sports." Explain that there is no room for couch potatoes in this activity.
4. Explain that each person has a Good Sports card with a picture representing a particular sport on the front. They are to find other participants who have the same sport and form a "team."
5. Tell them that the only catch is that they may not show the card or speak any words; they must demonstrate the sport as they move about the room.
6. Explain that when they have found another person or persons who have the same sport, they should huddle together and continue the search for the rest of their team.
7. After three minutes, ask each group to quickly demonstrate their sport for other groups to see and guess.

Variation

Use particular kinds of sports only, such as summer sports, Olympic sports, etc.

Tip

You demonstrate or ask a participant to demonstrate a sport for everyone to see before the activity begins.

Notes

_____

_____

_____

_____

_____

_____

_____

_____

_____

_____

GOOD SPORTS ACTIVITY SHEET

Happy Birthday!

Purpose	Especially for big groups; Getting to know you; Grouping people; Pure fun, Physical energizer; Outdoor activity
Group Size	20-200
Level of Physical Activity	High
Estimated Time	3-6 minutes
Props	None

This activity brings together people born in the same month—possibly on the same day. It works every time, even with people who have done it before. Use this with any group; age and size don't matter.

My father-in-law, Tom Greene, just celebrated his 75th birthday. What a joyous event! We bought him a new computer, complete with all the bells and whistles. That's because Tom is a very talented and creative 75-year-old who spends part of his time producing a church news magazine.

Instructions

1. Explain the importance of celebrating birthdays—remembering and valuing an individual just for existing.
2. Ask participants to walk around and find others who share the same birth month. For example, my birthday is in September, so I would walk around repeating, "September" until I find others with the same birth month.
3. When participants are in "birth month" groups, ask them to yell out their month in order beginning with January.
4. Then ask group members to share their exact birthdays.
5. Ask how many people discovered common birthdays.

Variation

Ask month groups to plan for and then demonstrate, rather than yell out, their month. For example, the May group may play act dancing around a maypole.

Tip

Keep this activity crisp, quick, light, and pleasant.

Notes

_____

_____

_____

_____

_____

How Quickly They Forget

Purpose
Getting to know you; Physical energizer; Especially for big groups; Pure fun

Group Size
8-100

Level of Physical Activity
Medium

Estimated Time
2-5 minutes

Props
How Quickly They Forget cards, one per participant; pencils
Participants will see how difficult it is to recall the details of a face they were introduced to just moments before. This activity works best in the beginning of a session with people who do not know one another.

Recently I had an experience that I've never had before. A person I had been introduced to on two other occasions didn't remember me when standing face-to-face the third time. His apology included, "I forget faces, but never names." With me it's the opposite; I forget names, but not faces. Which is the greater insult?

Instructions
1. Instruct participants to stand and find one participant they do not know and introduce themselves to that person.
2. After about ten seconds, tell them to remain standing and arrange themselves back-to-back with the person they just met. Explain that they are not to look back at their partners.
3. Pass out How Quickly They Forget cards and pencils.
4. Instruct participants to take thirty seconds to write what they remember about their partners on their cards.
5. After thirty seconds, ask them to turn around and see how many of their answers were correct.

Variations
1. Don't use cards. Just ask them to name what they remember about their partner, with the partners letting them know if they are right or not.
2. Give participants blank cards and ask them to write what they remember about their partners.
3. Give participants blank cards and ask them to sketch their partners.

Tip
Keep this one short and snappy. It doesn't have enough value to keep it going for a long time.

HOW QUICKLY THEY FORGET ACTIVITY SHEET

Please complete the following items.

Eye color _____

Hair color _____

Hair length/style _____

Height _____

Description of clothing _____

Wearing glasses? If so, describe _____

Jewelry? If so, describe _____

Job title/position _____

First name _____

Last name _____

Other distinguishing features _____

Marching Orders

Purpose	Physical energizer; Team building; Pure fun; Especially for big groups
Group Size	12-150
Level of Physical Activity	High
Estimated Time	6-12 minutes
Props	Band music

Here is a wonderful chance for participants to experience the thrill of being in a parade. This activity works best with groups of forty or more, and is especially good when participants need a stretch break or when teams need an achievement activity.

> *I love a parade! From the Rose Bowl in California to Mardi Gras in New Orleans to the Mummers Parade in Philadelphia (have you heard of that one?), we all love a parade.*

Instructions

1. Organize participants into groups of five to twenty-five.
2. Encourage participants to practice marching when the music begins. (You may wish to show them some professional moves!)
3. Play band music for two minutes while they practice—"Left, right, left, right!"
4. At the end of three minutes, explain that they are about to enter the marching field. Tell groups that they will now have three minutes to design and practice a marching routine. Explain that when practice time is over, each "band" will perform its routine for the other groups.
5. Play music while the groups practice.
6. After three minutes, invite each "band" to perform its marching routine while you play music.

Variations

1. For a short finale, have the whole group perform a routine with one person or group leading.
2. Do the same activity giving each person a baton and have each group perform a routine using batons. The batons (particularly those with brightly colored streamers flowing from each end) add another level of playfulness, and twirling ineptness allows for lots of humor.
3. Don't give them music; ask them to create their own.

Tips

1. Don't attempt to lead this activity unless you can enjoy the element of play that is associated with it.

2. If you use batons, demonstrate some moves, particularly if you are not a competent twirler; others will see that it is okay to be clumsy.

3. Make sure that the groups applaud as each "band" finishes its routine.

4. I've had groups provide their own music by singing or humming. It adds fun to the routine.

Notes

_____

_____

_____

_____

_____

_____

_____

_____

_____

_____

Motor Mania

Purpose

Team building; Physical energizer; Mental aerobics; Getting closure; Pure fun; Especially for big groups

Group Size

24-160

Level of Physical Activity

High

Estimated Time

10-20 minutes

Props

None

Participants will be on their feet and working together in this activity as they become the motorized objects of their choice. The activity is wonderful for culminating a program or inserting an achievement activity into team building! It always works. Groups love it, particularly engineers!

Have you heard the expression "I have to warm up my motor?" Did you know that came out of a session where participants were engaged in this exact activity? Well, I'm not surprised you didn't know; most people have not heard of this one. You have my permission to use it in trivia contests.

Instructions

1. Organize participants into groups of eight to sixteen.
2. Tell groups that they will have five minutes to truly become a motorized moving object, which means that each individual will physically participate in performing roles necessary for the depiction of that object. Give examples like a blender or a fan.
3. Explain that at the end of five minutes, each group will get to demonstrate its object, while the other groups guess which object they are portraying.
4. Give the signal to begin the planning time.
5. After five minutes, call on each group one at a time to give a demonstration of its motorized moving object, while the other groups guess what the object is. If no one guesses correctly, ask the performing group to reveal the motorized moving object.
6. Make sure the other participants applaud after the object is revealed.

Variations

1. The leader could give the groups the names of the objects they will portray.
2. The leader could give prizes for categories like synchronization, teamwork, and originality.

Tips

1. Open space works best.
2. Use upbeat music while participants are planning.

OCTOPUSES

Purpose

Physical energizer; Team building; Especially for big groups; Getting to know you; Pure fun

Group Size

27-90

Level of Physical Activity

High

Estimated Time

4-6 minutes

Props

None

Participants will form the shape of an octopus to reach out with their "tentacles" and share with others. Use this activity when you have open space and a group that doesn't mind having fun.

A mollusk breed
Having eight extensions
Will pull and suck
With carnivorous intentions
Fascinating these
sea creatures we find.
Formidable to watch,
and fun to mime.
E.W.

Instructions

1. Organize participants into groups of nine.
2. Explain that each group will now become an octopus, meaning that one person will take the form of the body, while the other eight make a circle around and touch the body person.
3. Explain that an octopus uses its tentacles to feel and grasp.
4. Suggest that although their groups resemble octopuses, the purpose of the tentacles has changed. The tentacles in their groups are for spreading pleasant thoughts.
5. Explain the following rules:
   - The Body will tell the tentacles what their task is. Their mission is to take nice thoughts from the Body to other people in the room.
   - The Body will say things like: "Tell someone how pleased you are to make their acquaintance"; "Tell someone you wish them the best of luck in their career"; or "Tell someone you hope they win the Publisher's Clearinghouse Sweepstakes next year."
   - When I say "Tentacles, go," the tentacles will each go find one person in the room, meet that person by shaking hands and ex-

changing names, and then deliver the message from their octo-pus.

- When I say, "Octopuses," the tentacles should return to their octopus.
- Another person in the octopus will then become the Body and choose a message for the tentacles to deliver.

6. Begin the activity. Do three or four rounds.

Variation

Use the activity for tentacles to get, rather than give, information or thoughts.

Tip

Play some fun sea or bubbling music during this activity.

Notes

_____

_____

_____

_____

_____

_____

_____

_____

_____

_____

On All Sides

Purpose	Physical energizer; Getting to know you; Especially for big groups
Group Size	12-200
Level of Physical Activity	High
Estimated Time	3-6 minutes
Props	Whistle

     This is a great way for people to connect and energize at the same time. Use it at the beginning of a session or as an energizer later on. If the group knows each other well, use the variation without words.

> *The main purpose of icebreakers is to establish a safe open environment in which people can interact.*

Instructions

1. Ask participants to stand in an open area where they have room to move about.
2. Explain the rules for On All Sides:
   - When I blow the whistle and call out "On One Side," each participant should find a partner.
   - I will give instructions: side-by-side, back-to-back, face-to-face. The partners should position themselves accordingly.
   - When the partners are positioned side-by-side, they should introduce themselves giving vital statistics (name, where they live or work); when they are back-to-back, they should tell something about their extended selves (family, friends, associations); and when face-to-face, they should tell something about personal interests or hobbies.
   - When I call out "On All Sides," four people should hook up and repeat the process—side-by-side, back-to-back, and face-to-face—without talking.
3. Lead the group through three to four rounds of this, ending with On All Sides.

Variations

1. Do it all without talking.
2. On All Sides, give different numbers like On All Sides 3, On All Sides 6, or On All Sides 4, and instruct the group to come together with as many people. On the last one say, "On All Sides 10" and watch people scramble.

Tips

1. Your calls need to be loud and distinct.
2. Model the activity with four participants before beginning or have the total group slowly walk through a complete series.

SHAKE IT UP

Purpose

Getting to know you; Grouping people; Physical energizer; Especially for big groups

Group Size

20-250

Level of Physical Activity

High

Estimated Time

2-4 minutes

Props

Shake It Up Activity Sheet cut into cards, one card per participant

This icebreaker gets people moving around, shaking hands, and introducing themselves to one another. Use it with people who don't know one another very well or at all, as a way to meet and as a way to group themselves for further small group activities.

> *I learned early in life that a good, firm handshake signaled confidence and directness, so I always acted on that—until I got arthritis in my thumbs. OUCH! I have now tempered my hand-shaking. The impression I give is no longer as important as the other person's physical comfort.*

Instructions

1. Pass out one Shake It Up Activity Card to each participant.
2. Ask participants to pair up with someone they don't know to practice types of handshakes.
3. Describe each type of handshake from the descriptions on the Shake It Up Activity Sheet: The Vise, The Pump, The Grab, The Fish, The Fingerhold, The Sway, The Milker, The Topper, The Flip, and The Thump. As you describe each one, encourage participants to practice with their partners.
4. Explain that each person holds a card with one type of handshake on it. The task is to walk around and shake the hands of other people. When they shake, they will take note of who else uses the same handshake they are using. They should join with those people in walking around shaking hands with others until all persons with the same handshake are grouped together.

Variations

1. Forget the grouping. Encourage participants to walk around shaking hands and to use a variety of the handshakes.
2. Ask people to use their favorite handshake.
3. Just have partners use handshakes and then share which kinds of handshakes they usually use.

Tip

Have fun with modeling the handshakes as you explain each one. Dramatize as much as you dare.

SHAKE IT UP ACTIVITY SHEET

The Vise—Grab that other hand and grip like you mean it. The goal is intimidation.

The Pump—Pump, pump, pump it up. You'll actually get your heart rate up as you shake hands while pumping your partner's hand up and down.

The Grab—Just pull them in nice and close with this "invade their personal space" handshake.

The Fish—Ever heard the expression "like a limp fish?" That's what your partners will think they're holding when they grab hold of this weak handshake.

The Fingerhold—It's at the tip of your fingers with this half-of-a-handshake. Just take their fingertips in yours and go from there. The palms aren't involved at all.

The Sway—When you take another's hand in yours just start swaying it back and forth between you, from left to right, as if you're holding hands or jumping rope.

The Milker—Did you ever have someone get a little too familiar squeezing your hand as if they were milking a cow? Now it's your turn to make someone squirm.

The Topper—This type of handshaker puts a second hand on top of yours to make a hand sandwich. They feel this added touch lets you know that they really mean it. Do you?

The Flip—Even a handshake can be a power trip with this one. When you take this shaker's hand, flip it over so yours is on top.

The Thump—This "good ole' boy" handshake can sometimes be painful. Take your partner's hand, then reach around with your left hand and deliver a resounding thump on the back.

SIGNIFICANT EVENTS

Purpose

Getting to know you; Getting to know you better; Physical energizer; Self-disclosure; Especially for big groups

Group Size

12-500

Level of Physical Activity

High

Estimated Time

3-5 minutes

Props

None

This is charades with a self-disclosure twist—participants will act out the significant events in their lives. This activity works with every group every time as long as there is room for small groups to stand in a circle.

I just recently discovered that not everyone lives their lives waiting for the next event (or, at least they're not aware that they do). I do. I have even figured out ways to make any mindless experience an event, such as grocery shopping, or paying bills. (Caution: It doesn't always work.) The next time you're at a rather dry gathering of people, ask individuals to describe the significant events in their lives; the discoveries are amazing.

Instructions

1. Organize participants into groups of six to twelve and arrange them standing in circles.
2. Explain to participants that to find out important facts about one another, they will participant in Significant Events.
3. Tell them to take turns of twenty seconds each moving into the center of the circle and demonstrating—miming—a significant event from their life, without talking.
4. Explain that as each person does this, the rest of the group gets to guess what the significant event was.
5. Encourage them to make sure each person has twenty seconds to act out a significant event.

Variation

Ask people to describe the circumstances around the event, but not say what the event was. For instance, someone who competed in a marathon could say, "I prepared for months for the event, I was very tired when it was over, I needed to make sure I had plenty of fluids, I wore skimpy clothing," etc.

Tip

When introducing the activity, demonstrate a significant event you had and really play it up (such as winning an award, having a baby, traveling to Africa).

STRINGING US ALONG

Purpose Physical energizer; Getting to know you better; Getting closure; Especially for big groups

Group Size 20-200

Level of Physical Activity Medium

Estimated Time 10-20 minutes

Props Ball of yarn for each group of ten to twenty participants
  This activity plays on the double meaning of the word "yarn" as participants weave the yarn among them and relay a story. This makes a great culminating activity or physical energizer and a way for people to get to know one another better.

> *Balls of yarn elicit images of kittens playing or someone knitting for loved ones. The term yarn may also refer to a wild, elaborately woven story. Since these remembrances evoke positive images, introducing balls of yarn usually brings playful smiles.*

Instructions
1. Organize participants into groups of ten to twenty. Give each group one ball of yarn.
2. Explain to participants that when you give the signal to begin, they are going to form a tightly knit group as they pass the ball of yarn across and around the circle until each person has had it. Explain that as each person gets the ball, he or she should thread the ball through something they are wearing—an article of clothing, a piece of jewelry, etc.—and then pass it on.
3. Give the signal to begin.
4. After the yarn has woven its way completely through each group, explain that the groups will now begin the unthreading process one at time. As each person unthreads, they have to tell a "yarn"—telling a story about how they'll apply what they learned during the session when they get back to work or home.

Variations
1. To emphasize affiliation, have the participants tell "yarns" about their lives.
2. If the exercise is used as an energizer, have participants tell one thing they've learned so far.
3. Use the activity as a timed group competition, weaving the yarn through and then out.

Tips
1. You might begin the process by telling something that you got from the session.
2. The activity works best when participants do not have a barrier, such as a table, between them.
3. Encourage embellishment of stories.

SWING YOUR PARTNER

Purpose

Getting to know you; Physical energizer; Especially for big groups

Group Size

40-200

Level of Physical Activity

High

Estimated Time

2-3 minutes

Props

Country music

In this activity, participants introduce themselves to each other in a light, energizing way as they move through the motions of a traditional square dance step. Use this activity in an evening meeting, or with an open group of people.

This week the local country radio station WMZQ is having a contest that goes like this: Each day they will play a certain song, after which they will name three listeners. If the listeners hear their names, they have 20 minutes to call the station and receive prizes. Now I am not usually a country music listener; but somehow, they got my phone number. They called and asked if I wanted to play. Why not? Any excuse for a game. So, this week I am listening to country music. And I am convinced of one thing: It is next to impossible not to smile, tap, or bounce up and down while listening.

Instructions

1. Organize participants so that they are standing in an open space with room to move around.
2. Remind them of the country dancing step of linking arms at the elbow and circling around. Have them practice with another person, first linking on the left arm and then on the right.
3. Explain that this is an activity to get them to know many people in a short period of time.
4. Tell them that when the music begins, they should move around the room swinging with one person after another, using the right arm then the left. While swinging, they should introduce themselves by their first name only (or nickname) saying "Hi, I'm Susan."
5. Begin the activity.

Variation

Add other movements such as do-si-do and alternate with swing.

Tips

1. This is a lot of fun and high energy.
2. Don't overkill. One minute may be long enough.

The Domino Effect

Purpose
Physical energizer; Pure fun; Team building; Introducing a topic; Especially for big groups; Outdoor activity

Group Size
20-200

Level of Physical Activity
High

Estimated Time
5-10 minutes

Props
None

To get participants up and moving, let them play Dominoes—literally. Use this activity with groups who are willing to participate in a playful activity as an energizer, or with less playful types as an introduction to a more serious discussion of the domino effect.

The game of Dominoes is light, fun, and easy to play for all age groups. We spent many evenings last winter with my father-in-law and his friend (who subsequently became his wife) playing Dominoes—by their rules of course. As I recall, they usually won.

Instructions

1. Organize participants into groups of ten to twenty.
2. Explain the domino effect—those situations that arise when one thing causes another to happen which in turn causes something else, much like a row of falling dominoes each knocking over the next domino in turn.
3. Tell groups that they will each demonstrate the domino effect using the following procedures:
   - Groups will have two minutes to decide what formation to make and practice making it (e.g., from a standing position, one at a time bend down and then stand back up). They may choose a formation that requires more people than are in their own group.
   - With the rest of the group as audience, each group will then make the formation and behave as dominoes.
4. Instruct the groups to begin their strategizing.
5. After two minutes, ask each group one at a time to come to a visible position and create their formation. If they need more people, they may ask other groups to participate with them.

Variation
Ask each group to decide on a formation for the whole group to play out and have the whole group do all of the formations.

Tips

1. Bring dominoes and set them up. Then introduce the activity by pushing down the first domino and let participants watch them all fall.
2. Encourage groups to make formations as intricate as they dare.

The Hummer's Parade

Purpose

Getting into groups; Team building; Especially for big groups; Getting closure

Group Size

20-200

Level of Physical Activity

High

Estimated Time

15-30 minutes

Props

Kazoos for everyone

Although all participants may not know the Mummer's Strut, they each get to make some original noise and formations in this activity by forming their own version of a kazoo parade. This high-energy activity makes a great culminating event for a creativity, stress management, or team building session.

> *Philadelphia has a wonderful tradition on January 1 of each year—The Mummers' Parade. Since my parents were born and raised in South Philadelphia, we were introduced to the "Mummers' Strut" as very young children. The strut is a cross between a dance and a march routine—a march with "swing." What a fine display of teamwork and precision of execution.*

Instructions

1. Organize participants into groups of ten to twenty.
2. Invite participants to imagine a magnificent parade with a fancy division of beautifully clad individuals and floats, garnished in satins, sequins, and feathers; a comic division with individuals or groups of people on stilts, in wagons, or on foot working the crowd, all causing eruptions of smiles and laughter; and a string band division with members clad in beautifully colored and patterned costumes with long, sweeping feathers, playing traditional songs and swaying and performing routines with grace and precision. This describes the Mummer's Parade which takes place in Philadelphia on January 1 each year.
3. Explain that participants probably will not be able to replicate the parade exactly because they lack the precise garb, tools, and steps, but they will be able to have their own parade because they are colorful themselves.
4. Explain that each group will have five minutes to design and practice a routine using a musical instrument that you will provide—the kazoo. (Hence the name, "Hummer's Parade.")
5. Pass out kazoos and tell groups they have five minutes to design and practice a thirty-second routine which they'll perform for the other groups.
6. After five minutes, ask each group to perform its routine.

Variations

1. Forget the kazoos and just have the groups hum.
2. Use the Rose Bowl Parade or some other parade that participants are familiar with as your introductory example, but don't forget to change the name of the activity.

Tips

1. Encourage participants to enjoy themselves by building on the "this is your big chance" theme.
2. For whatever reason, kazoos give people permission to behave with less restraint.
3. Explain how to use a kazoo. The first time I used kazoos, I threw out many that participants said "didn't work" only to discover that participants didn't know how to use them!

Notes

_____

_____

_____

_____

_____

_____

_____

_____

_____

_____

THE LINE UP

Purpose
Physical energizer; Getting to know you better; Energizing a long, dry presentation; Especially for big groups; Team building; Outdoor activities

Group Size
16-200

Level of Physical Activity
High

Estimated Time
5-7 minutes

Props
The Line Up Activity Sheet

Lining up by height order or alphabetically is just the beginning in this activity as participants think of creative ways to line up in order. Use this activity to break monotony or long periods of sitting and you'll find participants finding out about each other, too. Any group is game for this one.

How long do you have to know a person before you discover their shoe size? How about their arm's reach? County of origin? Favorite color? Number of siblings?

Instructions
1. Organize participants into groups of eight to twenty.
2. Tell participants that in The Line Up they will have a chance to learn things about one another they may never think to ask.
3. Give these instructions:
   - This is group competition.
   - I will give the instruction for groups to line up in a particular way.
   - Your groups should get in line as quickly as possible.
   - When your group is lined up appropriately, but not before, all group members should clap to indicate your readiness to me.
4. Do a practice round. Tell the groups to "Line up by height, and clap when you're finished."
5. Begin the activity. After each line-up, determine which group clapped first and then pronounce it the winner of that round.

Variations
1. Use periodically throughout a long session.
2. Ask groups to come up with their own ways of letting you know they're ready. (I've had groups yell something, hum a song, put up their hands, etc.) This adds a lot to the fun.

Tips
1. Keep the tone light; this is a fun competition.
2. Laugh and play with humorous comments from participants; there will be many.
3. Remember political correctness with regard to your own or participants' comments.

THE LINE UP ACTIVITY SHEET (FOR THE LEADER)

1. Line up in order by shoe size.

2. Line up in order by length of arm's reach.

3. Line up in order alphabetically by favorite color.

4. Line up in order by number of siblings you have.

5. Line up in order alphabetically by your county of origin.

6. Line up in order by hair color, lightest to darkest.

7. Line up in order by age, youngest to oldest.

8. Line up in order by length of time with current employer.

9. Line up in order alphabetically by first name.

10. Line up in order alphabetically by last name.

11. Line up in order by number of pets.

12. Line up in order by hair length, longest to shortest.

13. Line up in order by the number of bones you've broken.

14. Line up in order numerically by street address (for example, 1111 Eleventh St., 8327 Oaks Court, 15444 Beachland).

15. Line up in order by the height of your heels, lowest to highest.

The Wink

Purpose	Getting to know you; Pure fun; Physical energizer; Especially for big groups
Group Size	30-300
Level of Physical Activity	High
Estimated Time	2-5 minutes
Props	None

This activity gets people introducing themselves and making contact. It is appropriate for mixed groups when people don't know each other well. Choose an audience that enjoys an element of playfulness.

> *Whether it's a flirtatious gesture or a knowing response, a wink has hidden meaning. And a part of its meaning is the suggestion: "This is our little secret; no one else is included."*

Instructions

1. Before the activity, designate three to fifteen people (depending on the size of the group) to have "the wink"—making them Winkers.
2. Tell participants that the object of the game is to get rid of the wink.
3. Explain the rules:
   - Three to fifteen participants will act as the Winkers, but the rest of the group does not know who they are.
   - The Winkers will get rid of the winks by winking at people they meet. Those persons then have the winks and can only get rid of them by winking at other people.
   - Whenever someone winks at you, you then have the winks and may get rid of them only by meeting someone else and winking at them.
   - When time is called, the persons who have the winks are the losers.
4. Begin the activity.
5. Call time after two to three minutes and ask whoever has the winks to raise their hands.

Variation

If it's a small group, just designate one or two Winkers.

Tips

1. Model the wink for participants, exaggerating the behavior while shaking someone else's hands.
2. Remember that not everyone can wink. If any of the group say they can't wink, believe them! Tell them just to do an exaggerated blink.

FOR NON-ICEBREAKER TYPES

A Contradiction in Terms

Purpose Introducing a topic; For non-icebreaker types; Mental aerobics

Group Size 10-40

Level of Physical Activity Medium

Estimated Time 10 minutes

Props Flip chart; marker

Your participants will become aware of and verbalize the mixed messages sent in their own organization—the sometimes contradictory ideas their company promotes. Use this at any point in a session.

There's an American phrase that refers to "speaking out of both sides of one's mouth." This describes a person who sends two seemingly opposing messages. Sometimes sending opposing messages is appropriate because of the situational context; sometimes it is not. Employees in an organization usually recognize mixed messages when they are sent, but often don't understand the context for them. Another reason to "blame" the organization is born!

Instructions

1. Organize participants into groups of three or four.
2. Give examples of well-known quotes that send mixed messages such as: "Look before you leap" compared to "He who hesitates is lost," or "Out of sight out of mind" paired with "Absence makes the heart grow fonder."
3. Ask participants for other examples and write them on a flip chart.
4. Explain to participants that organizations send mixed messages for a variety of reasons. An example is an organization that insists on "quality at any cost" while giving the message that "every piece of paper wasted means less goal sharing for everyone."
5. Give participants about one minute to share their own mixed messages with the total group.
6. Tell them they have two minutes in their groups to name the mixed messages that their organization sends.
7. When two minutes are up, ask them to report their messages and the incongruity of each pair.
8. Follow up with a general statement about the importance of understanding when those mixed messages are appropriate or when they are destructive to organizational goals.

Variation Give participants mixed messages that are occurring in the organization and ask them to make sense of them.

Tips

1. The tone for this activity will be set by you. It can be very serious if you encourage participants to think about difficulties with organizational communication, or it can be light and fun. You decide.

2. If you're not prepared to deal with company politics, avoid this exercise.

Notes

_____

_____

_____

_____

_____

_____

_____

_____

_____

_____

Best and Worst

Purpose	Getting to know you better; Team building; Meeting starter; For non-icebreaker types
Group Size	8-200
Level of Physical Activity	Medium
Estimated Time	2-4 minutes
Props	Best and Worst cards, one of each per participant

In this activity participants get to share the best and worst of their own experiences with one another. Use this in the beginning of a session with groups who meet together regularly or who know one another fairly well as an icebreaker, or in a team building or organizational development session as a disclosure activity.

There are some people who live and describe their lives in the extremes. The weather is the coldest, the vacation the best they ever had, the flu the most debilitating, the book the most interesting, their job the worst, the party the most fun, their friendship the best.

Instructions

1. Ask participants to think of the best thing and the worst thing that happened to them in the last week and write it on the matching card.
2. Instruct participants to share those aloud with the rest of the group.

Variations

1. Use a specific topic for the best and worst examples, such as the best and worst things about working on this team, or the best and worst things about this organization.
2. For large groups, organize participants into partners and ask them to share.

Tips

1. This activity gives people the chance to swap stories. It can be a lot of fun.
2. Begin the activity by sharing your Best and Worst.

BEST AND WORST ACTIVITY SHEET

Best

Best

Worst

Worst

Good News, Bad News

Purpose

Team building; Getting closure; Meeting starter; Introducing a topic;
For non-icebreaker types

Group Size

5-12

**Level of Physical
Activity**

High

Estimated Time

5-6 minutes

Props

Large sheet of paper, approx. 3′ × 12′; markers or crayons

Good News, Bad News provides a forum for people to see—on paper—a quick assessment of perceptions about a group or organization. Use it with a group of people from the same organization at the beginning of a session in which each participant will be defining strategies for change or solving problems.

> *Many evenings, my husband and I organize our quick-sketch updates of the day around good news, bad news. We usually begin with good news because it is far more fun to share. Interestingly, by the time we get to the bad news, much of the "sting" is gone; the sadness of the bad news is overshadowed by the joy of the good news.*

Instructions

1. Post the paper on the wall or a table and draw a vertical line to create two columns, heading one Good News and the other Bad News.
2. Ask each participant to choose a marker or crayon and step up to the paper.
3. Explain that the object of this activity is to put on paper the perceptions they have about their organization or group. Ask them to think about the positive things going on—the good news—and the negative things happening—the bad news.
4. Explain that they now have three minutes to take turns writing the good news on one side of the line and the bad news on the other.
5. Now ask them to step back and observe by allowing their eyes to sweep the entire sheet, reading the lists on the paper.
6. Ask for general observations.
7. Explain how this activity fits with the agenda.

Variations

1. Ask people to read their own comments aloud.
2. For a meeting or problem solving session, use the issue at hand as the topic for Good News, Bad News.

Tips

1. This is a great way to take the pulse of an organization at staff meetings.
2. For team building, use Good News, Bad News about the team.
3. This is not appropriate for a group of people who are deeply dissatisfied with the organization, unless the overwhelming expression of negatives will meet your purpose for the session.

Notes

_____

_____

_____

_____

_____

_____

_____

_____

_____

In or Out

Purpose

Introducing a topic; Getting closure; Pure fun; For non-icebreaker types

Group Size

4-20

Level of Physical Activity

Low

Estimated Time

4-6 minutes

Props

Flip chart and marker, current "In or Out" list

Participants will prove their knowledge of the topic by creating a list of what's "In" and what's "Out" for behaviors associated with your topic. Use this activity to introduce or review such topics as supervision, communications, customer service, ethics, or just for fun.

> *At the end of each year, I look forward to the Sunday Section of the paper for the trend-watchers' listings of what's "In" and what's "Out." What I find somewhat frustrating is that it takes just about as long for me to accept a new fad as it does for the fad to go out. That's true of clothing, decorating, and hair styles. Just when I began to enjoy short, bouncy, carefree styles ...*

Instructions

1. Read a current "In or Out" list.
2. Explain that some people may have disagreed with the decisions for these categories, but nevertheless, they were printed.
3. Explain to participants that in any given context, there are those universally accepted forms of behavior and those universally unacceptable forms of behavior, and those "some think of them" as acceptable behaviors and those "some think of them" as unacceptable behaviors. There is never universal agreement on all behaviors.
4. Introduce your topic and explain that you want them to think about the ideas presented during the session.
5. Ask them to work with you to generate the what's "In" and what's "Out" list for behaviors associated with your topic.

Variations

1. First ask the group to generate a list of what's "In" and what's "Out" for the organization. Then ask them to generate a list for the topic.
2. Use this as a brainteaser and ask the group to generate what's "In" and what's "Out" for the year.

Tip

Be aware of the fact that some people may want to change this to *who's* "In" and *who's* "Out." If this serves no purpose, don't acknowledge those responses.

Missing Links

Purpose

Getting to know you; Physical energizer; Especially for big groups; For Non-icebreaker types

Group Size

10-400

Level of Physical Activity

High

Estimated Time

5-10 minutes

Props

None

There is no telling what types of connections will turn up when participants begin comparing notes in this exercise. This is a great activity to begin a session; but feel free to use it as an energizer anytime.

My colleague, Carole Anne Turner, told me the story of a time that she and her husband, Roger, decided on a sultry August night to take a moonlight guided ranger's tour into Bryce Canyon in a scenic region of Utah. Four other families also signed up for the tour—an exclusive event since the tour was only offered when there was a full moon. Two families, naturally connected by a distinguishable New York accent, soon became engaged in conversation, comparing notes about life near that metropolis. During their explorative dialogue, they discovered that the younger couple had purchased their home from the older couple a few years earlier. Since all negotiations had taken place long distance, through brokers and attorneys, they had never met. Now what are the chances of that happening? Well, statisticians claim that as the world shrinks in size (thanks to the technology revolution), the chances are one in two that these types of connections will be commonplace. Commonplace or not, these connections are delightful.

Instructions

1. Organize participants into groups of six to twelve.
2. Ask participants if they have stories to tell of discovering connections to people they met for the first time. Encourage participants by telling them one of your own stories or relating the one above.
3. Explain that they will now have an opportunity to discover the connections or "missing links" they have with the people in their groups.
4. Ask participants to stand and form a circle with their group.
5. Instruct them to choose one person in each group who will begin the activity by telling things about themselves, such as places they've lived, jobs they've had, people they've known, vacations they've taken, schools they've attended, and so on.
6. Tell them that the first people to establish a connection with the speakers should identify themselves as a "missing link," move to

the left of the speakers, explain the link, and then proceed to tell things about themselves until another group member makes a connection.

7. Continue the "missing link" process until all members of the group are somehow connected.

Variation

If it is a small group, ten to twenty people, feel free to use the activity with the entire group.

Tip

If there are people who can't make a link, encourage them to feel comfortable using this meeting or workshop as their "link" with the last person.

Notes

_____

_____

_____

_____

_____

_____

_____

_____

_____

_____

Musical Instrument

Purpose
Getting to know you; Getting to know you better; Introducing a topic; Team building; For non-icebreaker types; Especially for big groups

Group Size
12-100

Level of Physical Activity
High

Estimated Time
3-10 minutes

Props
Large posters of four to ten musical instruments (you may use the Musical Instrument Activity Sheet and enlarge the instruments)

People will learn about each other by grouping themselves according to commonalties with instruments. This activity works equally well with large and small groups regardless of position or age. Use it in the beginning of the program for people to assess their own behaviors, to get to know one another, or to get a different perspective on people they already know.

> *If I had to choose one medium for icebreakers and games I would choose music. Participants can remember it, mime it, draw analogies from it, study it, play it, compose it, listen to it, sing it, hum it, write lyrics, clap to it, dance to it, and move to it. Music— the most versatile instrument!*

Instructions
1. Post pictures of musical instruments on the walls.
2. Ask participants to choose the instrument that is most like them and to go stand near that picture.
3. When participants are in those positions, ask them to form a circle with the other people who have chosen the same instrument, introduce themselves, and share with one another the reasons they chose that instrument.
4. When they've done that, ask each group to agree on the three most common reasons people in the group gave for identifying with the instrument, and choose a spokesperson to give that information to the total group.

Variations
1. Instead of instruments, use animals, flowers, etc.
2. Ask participants to perform a musical piece as the instruments they have chosen.
3. Ask participants to compare the instruments to specific ways of behaving: as a supervisor, as a team member, etc.

Tips
1. If your group is small, use four pictures; use more for larger groups so the group activity is manageable.
2. Use instruments that are familiar to the audience.
3. If it's a small group, skip step three.

MUSICAL INSTRUMENT ACTIVITY SHEET

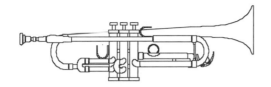

Trumpet

Violin

Cymbals

Drum

Electric
Guitar

Saxophone

Grand
Piano

Horn

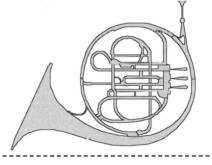

Clarinet

Flute

Road Signs

Purpose
Introducing a topic; Meeting starter; Energizing a long, dry presentation; Mental aerobics; For non-icebreaker types

Group Size
6-30

Level of Physical Activity
Medium

Estimated Time
3-5 minutes

Props
Road Signs Activity Sheet
Use with groups who would enjoy working with analogies since they'll be comparing common road signs with life on the job. Engineers, middle managers, marketing personnel, and executives are examples of groups who might fit into this category.

When I was on a road trip to see a client, I started paying particular attention to road signs. The tedium of the long drive had gotten to me; I needed a diversion. One sign that hit me between the eyes was a simple one that we see frequently: BUMP. BUMP: a raised place in the road that we detour around to avoid, or slow down for to minimize the jarring effect, or speed over to deny the impact. A little like life's BUMPS: There are all different ways of dealing with them.

Instructions
1. Organize participants into groups of two to three.
2. Give each group a different road sign.
3. Instruct groups to look at their road signs and think of an analogy to the organization that helps or discourages them from reaching their goals. Give examples such as: Detour—sometimes we're moving along well, and suddenly we come upon a situation in which we must deviate from our current strategies; or Clearance 12'6"—we like to know parameters before we proceed so we don't get halfway there and have to stop.
4. When groups are finished, ask them to share their analogies aloud with the other groups.

Variations
1. Give each group all road signs and ask them to come up with an analogy for each one.
2. Give each group the same sign and see what different analogies they come up with. Use periodically throughout the session.

Tip
If you do this one early in a session, chances are good that participants will keep referring back to them, or name new ones that relate to other organizational situations.

ROAD SIGN ACTIVITY SHEET

TRIVIA X-O

Purpose

Mental aerobics; Getting closure; Team building; For non-icebreaker types; Energizing a long, dry presentation; Introducing a topic

Group Size

4-20

Level of Physical Activity

Medium

Estimated Time

10-15 minutes

Props

X-O game board drawn on a flip chart; markers

This is a simple, quick way to review information, introduce a concept, or just have fun. It works well with any group as an introductory or review activity.

I recently played about 20 games of Tic-Tac-Toe with my five-year-old nephew, Michael. And he beat me. I remembered back to when I was his age and couldn't get enough of Tic-Tac-Toe, and I wondered why.

Instructions

1. Create a Tic-Tac-Toe game board on your flip chart and position it so everyone can see it.
2. Organize participants into two teams.
3. Flip a coin (or use some other method) to determine which team will go first.
4. Ask the first team to chose a square.
5. Explain that you are going to read questions concerning your topic and that each team will score points for every correct answer given when it is their team's turn.
6. Explain the rules of the game:
   - The first team will choose a square and then listen to a question.
   - The first team has one minute to answer the question. The first response counts, so the team should consider carefully before calling out their answer.
   - If the answer is correct, a representative from the first team places an X in the square chosen by the team. If the answer is incorrect, the second team gets a chance to answer, but they do not get an O if their answer is correct. Each team can only score on their own turn.
   - The second team then selects a square and responds to a question.
   - The game will continue with teams alternating turns until one team gets three in a row or all the squares are filled.

- The winner is the team that gets three in a row. If neither team gets three in a row, the winner is the team with the most squares.

7. Begin the game by reading a question to the first team.

Variations

1. Make the objective getting the most squares, rather than getting three in a row.
2. Use a board with more or fewer squares.
3. Use as an affiliation activity if the members of the group know each other by creating questions about your participants and allowing their colleagues/coworkers to respond.

Tips

1. Play up the competitive spirit of the game.
2. Use startling statistics or facts to wake up participants to the topic.
3. If you use information that the group should know, always repeat the questions and answers.

Notes

YOU ARE WHAT YOU DRIVE

Purpose
Getting to know you; Getting to know you better; For non-icebreaker types

Group Size
5-150

Level of Physical Activity
Low

Estimated Time
5-10 minutes

Props
None

This activity is good for any type of audience, including upper management types, because it is relatively safe and light, and because most people can relate to the concept. The beginning of a program is a great time to use it, although I have successfully used it after lunch.

Have you ever noticed that people tend to dress up in cars that "suit" them? The cars that people choose often divulge clues about the owners' lifestyles, affluence, ages, etc. (Not that we wish to typecast anyone!) Some people meticulously choose cars that match; others drive cars that are hand-me-downs, are affordable, or that represent something they definitely are not (but, in some cases, would like to be).

Instructions

1. Organize participants into groups of two to ten.
2. Ask participants to write down the type of car they drive and why they drive that car.
3. Invite one person in each group who already has an engine revved to be the "Car." The other participants in the group should now take turns guessing what kind of car that person drives and explain why they think that.
4. Explain that once everyone in a group has given their opinions, the "Cars" get to reveal the kinds of car they really drive and explain why.
5. Remind them to allow the opportunity for each person in the group to be the "Car."

Variation
Organize participants by like vehicles and instruct them to collectively decide and then explain to the rest of the group why they drive that car type. You may use categories like: station wagon, sports car, truck, four-wheel drive vehicles, basic sedans, luxury cars, etc.

Tips

1. At break time, listen for such comments as, "So how do you like your Miata?" and "How many miles do you have on your Volvo?"
2. The activity is often a leveler for groups of males and females; each group demonstrates an equal amount of interest.

You're a Poet and Don't Know It

Purpose	Mental aerobics; Getting to know you better; Getting closure; Self-Disclosure; For non-icebreaker types; Introducing a topic; Team building
Group Size	3-30
Level of Physical Activity	Medium
Estimated Time	8-12 minutes
Props	You're a Poet and Don't Know It Activity Sheets, one per participant

In eight to twelve minutes, don't expect the intensity of a master poet, but in this activity participants will strongly focus their creative energies on words that connote images as they write simple haiku. Use this as an affiliation activity, an exercise in creativity, or an illustration of the power of words. Use it with conceptual audiences who enjoy mental challenges.

The first time I discovered haiku, I thought it was the answer to a nonwriter's dream—short, simple, easy-to-write, uninspired poetry. Then I heard a young poet describe his cruel childhood years through haiku. With my heart in my throat, I listened intently to the power and punch of simple words, as if each was followed by an exclamation point. My appreciation for the art form leaped forward.

Instructions

1. Pass out You're a Poet and Don't Know It Activity Sheets and explain haiku.
2. Read examples of haiku from the Activity Sheet.
3. Explain that participants will now have an opportunity to write their own haiku using personal images or experiences and then share them with another person in the group.
4. Give participants five minutes to compose haiku.
5. Ask participants to partner up and share poems.
6. After about five minutes, ask participants to read aloud their partner's poem and explain any circumstances around the writing of the poem or selection of the topic.

Variations

1. Make the writing of haiku a small group activity.
2. Ask participants to post their haiku for others to read at breaks.
3. Provide a list of haiku topics for participants to select from.

Tips

1. Many people are insecure about their ability to write. Encourage participants to feel comfortable with this activity by eliminating any elements of perceived competition.
2. Start the activity by reading one of your own compositions.
3. If you think participants are self-conscious, suggest that they post their poetry without including their name.
4. Encourage participants to write more haiku and post them anytime during the day.

Notes

_____

_____

_____

_____

_____

_____

_____

_____

_____

_____

YOU'RE A POET AND DON'T KNOW IT ACTIVITY SHEET

Haiku

Haiku is a form of unrhymed verse poetry that originated in Japan. Each haiku consists of three lines and usually relies on comparisons and visual images. In pure form, the first and third lines have five syllables each and the middle line has seven syllables. Examples:

The Puppy
Pick-up day is here
Our child, playful pup now home
Then the work begins

Deadlines
First the challenge made
Tempers, chaos, "do this now"
Then the battle won

_____

_____

_____

_____

_____

_____

_____

Getting Closure

Alice's Anthology

Purpose Mental aerobics; Introducing a topic; For non-icebreaker types; Pure fun; Getting closure; Team building

Group Size 4-24

Level of Physical Activity Medium

Estimated Time 4-8 minutes

Props Lines of poetry

In this activity, participants get to work in small groups to write their own poems. Use Alice's Anthology to open creative minds or hearts or to focus on a specific concept or topic. For thinking audiences.

> *The poet Maya Angelou once said, "We are more alike, my friends, than we are unalike." From Shakespeare to Maya Angelou, poetry has gone far beyond the limited reaches of our minds. My friend, Alice Allen, recently referred me to an article in the* Christian Science Monitor *titled "Beowulf in the Boardroom: Executives Ponder Poetry."* The article speaks of management consultant Peter Block introducing poet David Whyte to working in corporate America. Whyte is quoted as saying, "Poetry opens people's thought, removes limits, and allows them to conceive—often for the first time—new and unexpected answers to old problems." Enough said.*

Instructions

1. Choose one line of poetry that has substance or relevance for your group or topic.
2. Explain the universality of poetry—the soul-catching quality of language.
3. Organize participants into groups of two to five.
4. Give each group the same line of poetry.
5. Instruct groups to use the next three to five minutes to create a whole poem using the line given to them. The line may be placed anywhere—the beginning, the ending, or somewhere in between.
6. When time is up, ask groups to read their poems aloud to the rest of the group.
7. If time allows, ask groups to come up with titles for all poems read.

Variations

1. Give each group a different line of poetry to work with.
2. Ask groups to record poems on flip charts.

**Christian Science Monitor,* September 7, 1995.

3. Make the poems working documents throughout the session by encouraging participants to add verses to their poems as the session progresses.

Tips

1. This can be a powerful activity if used to achieve a very specific purpose such as conflict resolution, dealing with change, increasing sensitivity to the needs of others, accepting diversity, team building, etc.
2. When used at the end of a session, people commit lines to mind and heart.
3. Some anthologies of best-loved poems are organized topically.

Notes

_____

_____

_____

_____

_____

_____

_____

_____

_____

_____

Arrivals and Departures

Purpose

Getting closure; Introducing a topic; Meeting starter; For non-ice-breaker types

Group Size

6-12

Level of Physical Activity

Low

Estimated Time

2-5 minutes

Props

Arrivals and Departures Activity Sheet

In Arrivals and Departures participants will list behaviors they would like to adopt or get rid of. Use this activity at the beginning or end of a session in which people have been focusing on behavior change—either procedural or personal. This works very well with management and supervisory, communication, conflict, diversity, motivational, and personal effectiveness sessions.

> *I love airports. There is so much going on. Everyone is engaged. Everyone knows the purpose for being there. Everyone participates. Recently I was in the Greensboro, NC airport waiting for a flight to Washington National Airport. At Gate 20, there was a striking contrast between people waiting to board the flight and those waiting to receive passengers coming off the flight. The flight was delayed about fifteen minutes. Those waiting to board demonstrated emotions from mild complacency to extreme angst and total disgust.* Departures. *In one of the groups waiting for passengers to arrive, excited animation abounded; they had signs, banners, balloons, and flowers. They were chatting excitedly and exchanging greetings as new people kept joining the group. I almost missed the flight because I was so taken with the joy that filled the room when the flight landed and passengers debarked.* Arrivals.

Instructions

1. Copy the Arrivals and Departures Activity Sheet onto a transparency.
2. At the end of a session, put the transparency on the projector for everyone to see.
3. Explain that when we take personal responsibility for our own actions, we take the time to examine our own behaviors and decide whether to keep, modify, or change them to get the results we want.
4. Ask participants to consider the behaviors they choose to keep or would like to implement as arrivals, and the behaviors they would like to get rid of, or change dramatically, as departures.
5. Ask each person to talk with a person next to them about behaviors they have been in touch with during the session and identify

at least one arrival and one departure that they are committed to working on.

Variation

If it is a small group, ask each person to talk about arrivals and departures aloud.

Tip

Ask the group for stories about observations of arrivals and departures.

Notes

_____

_____

_____

_____

_____

_____

_____

_____

_____

_____

ARRIVALS AND DEPARTURES
ACTIVITY SHEET

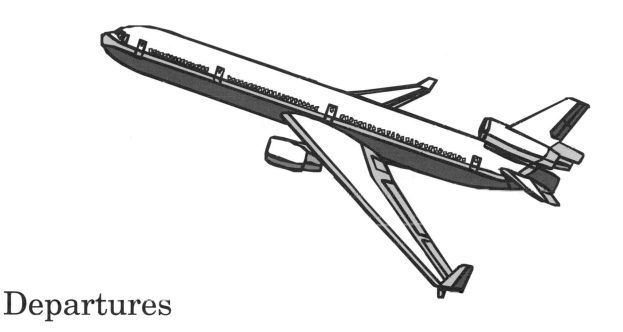

Departures

Arrivals

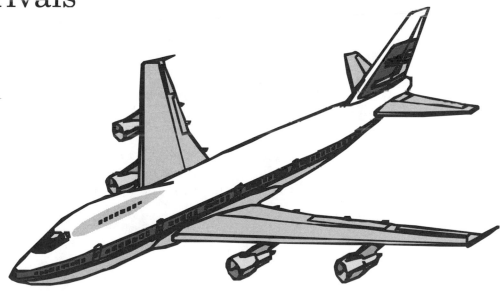

Bloom Where You're Planted

Purpose   Getting closure

Group Size   6-15

**Level of Physical
Activity**   Medium

Estimated Time   2-5 minutes

Props   Small flower pots, one per person; potting soil; seeds
                     Participants will get to walk away from this session with more than ideas; they'll have a plant to nurture and watch grow. This closing activity is particularly powerful if the metaphor of "bloom where you're planted" has been set earlier in the session. You may use this with any group, as long as you have appropriately prepared the soil ...

Bloom where you're planted. Contentment. Commitment. Not a lack of future thinking; not a stunter of growth. Acceptance of the challenge; be all you can be where you are. Eliminates excuses, such as "if only I ..." Bloom where you're planted.

Instructions   1. Explain to participants that when they leave, they will have an opportunity to grow their newly acquired, or enhanced, knowledge and skills. As a symbol or reminder, they will have a chance to plant a seed that can grow along with them.
                     2. Instruct participants to step over to a table that contains the props.
                     3. Ask them to plant a seed.
                     4. While participants are still standing, ask them to share what plans they have for their own future goals.

Variation   If your group is a team, have them plant seeds in one container with name markers by each.

Tip   Even though this can be a thought-provoking and rather serious activity since people will be making decisions about the future, the planting part is light and fun—and should be.

HIT THE DECK

Purpose

Getting closure; Introducing a topic; Team building; Physical energizer; Pure fun

Group Size

12-40

Level of Physical Activity

Medium

Estimated Time

10-15 minutes

Props

Decks of cards; flip chart paper; magic markers; questions and answers; prizes

Straight recall of information can be downright boring, but not when combined with physical movement and light competition. Here's an activity that demonstrates just that.

Use it whenever you would like participants to review information, particularly at the end of a session.

You have probably heard the expression "teaching to the test." Sometimes trainers need the test to help them synthesize concepts and focus on content goals.

Instructions

1. Organize participants into groups of four to six. Arrange each group so that participants are standing around a table. Place a deck of cards in the middle of each table.

2. Give each group a flip chart and marker and instruct them to label the top sheet "Score sheet."

3. Ask each group to select one person from the group to be designated "Hitter."

4. Explain the rules of the game in this manner:
   - Teams will compete to correctly answer questions about the content of the program.
   - I will read a question aloud. Participants should discuss possible answers with their group members.
   - When the group has an answer, the "Hitter" should reach into the middle of the table and "hit the deck."
   - I will acknowledge the first person to "hit the deck," and will give that person a chance to give their group's response aloud.
   - If the answer is right, the "Hitter" gets to draw the top card from the deck. That group then gets to add the value of the card to its column on the score sheet on the flip chart paper.
   - If the first group to "hit the deck" gives the wrong answer, the second person to "hit the deck" gets to give that group's answer.

5. After ten to twelve rounds of questions, ask the groups to tally their scores.

6. Give a prize to each person in the group that has the greatest number of points.

Variations

1. People at tables could have their own competitions. The first person to have an answer at each table gets to "hit the deck" and then answer the question to group members. You then would read the answer aloud for group members to verify. This would allow for a winner at each table.

2. Add bonus questions that are not about the content—preferably humorous questions.

Tips

1. Use both closed and open questions.

2. If one hitter gives an incomplete answer, allow the second hitter to expand on it. In these cases, award each group half of the value on its card.

3. If you use numbered cards, the cards are worth their face value (i.e., one to ten points); if you use playing cards, the leader decides in advance the value of face cards.

Notes

_____

_____

_____

_____

_____

_____

_____

_____

If I Had a Hammer

Purpose   Introducing a topic; Getting closure; For non-icebreaker types

Group Size   6-24

**Level of Physical
Activity**   Medium

Estimated Time   3-5 minutes

Props   If I Had a Hammer Activity Sheets
                       Participants will compare the "tools" they learned in the session to the drawings of real tools on an activity sheet. Use this activity to gain closure after an informative or skill-building session.

> *I'm sure you've heard the story about the man who bought a new chainsaw. After using it for two hours, he returned it to the store claiming that he sawed less wood using it than he had with his manual saw. The store manager looked it over, took it in the back, tried it himself, brought it back out, and told the man to take it home and try it again because it appeared to be working fine. The man went home, used it for two hours again, and returned to the store with the same complaint. The store manager was clearly puzzled so he brought the man in the back with him so the customer could point out exactly where the problem lay. As the store manager turned the saw on, the buyer asked, "What's that noise?" The moral is that a tool is no good unless you know how to use it.*

Instructions

1. Distribute one If I Had a Hammer Activity Sheet to each participant.
2. Ask participants to think of the tools they became acquainted with during the session.
3. Instruct them to use the Tool Boxes to draw analogies between the tools on the sheet and the tools they heard about during the session.
4. When participants are finished, ask them to explain their analogies about each tool to the group.

Variations

1. Ask participants to list tools, then develop analogies.
2. Create a sheet with a column of hardware tools next to a column of business tools and ask participants to match each piece of hardware with a business tool, then explain their matches.
3. Give each group one of the tools to create analogies for.
4. Use the tools for a grouping activity in the beginning of the session.

Tips

1. Bring in some tools to introduce the activity.
2. Tell the story about the chainsaw before or after you do the activity.

IF I HAD A HAMMER
ACTIVITY SHEET

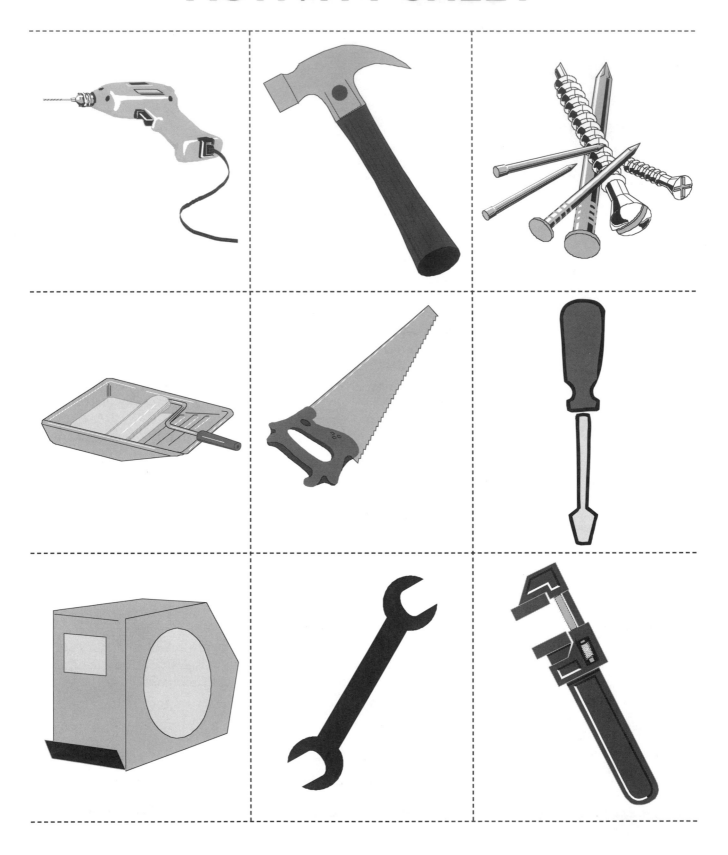

LEAF IT TO ME

Purpose

Team building; Getting closure

Group Size

8-30

Level of Physical Activity

Medium

Estimated Time

15-20 minutes

Props

Tree trunk with bare branches drawn on a large piece of paper; glue stick; brightly colored paper leaves

The tree that participants create in this activity will symbolize teamwork, with each leaf representing an individual contribution. Use this activity to culminate a team session.

> *A tree is a powerful analogy for organizational development. It embodies power, strength, organization, purpose, renewal, changes, and more. And within the analogy lies rare beauty, made clear by Joyce Kilmer's popular line: "I think that I shall never see a poem lovely as a tree."*

Instructions

1. Post tree trunk drawing in a central location.
2. Put leaves in a central place where participants can help themselves to them.
3. Invite participants to think about their greatest behavioral contributions to the team—both those they know are expected and the additional commitments of time, attention, and behavior that will support the attainment of team goals.
4. Instruct participants to write one idea on each leaf, representing contributions they will commit to. Ask them to come forward individually and glue their leaves onto the tree branches.

Variation

If colored leaves are not available, have participants use markers and draw the leaves right on the branches.

Tip

Participants will respond appreciatively to a well-presented tree trunk. It adds importance to the activity.

LEAF IT TO ME ACTIVITY SHEET

LEAVING TIPS

Purpose	Getting closure; For non-icebreaker types
Group Size	6-20
Level of Physical Activity	Medium
Estimated Time	2-5 minutes
Props	Flip chart; marker

Participants get to give advice in this one. The activity helps people put personal closure on the session, and address future thought or action. Use this at the close of meetings or training sessions.

It's always fun to give advice to someone else. Taking advice—now that's a different thing. Some of the experts suggest waiting until a person asks for advice before giving it. Well, that may be fine for the person asking, but it does nothing for the advice giver. After all, we want to give advice at the moment we're listening to or observing a scenario. If we weren't meant to give advice, would the urge be so compelling? I have found a sneaky way to give advice: I say to the person, "If I were going to advise you—which of course I'm not—what do you think I would say?" If the person doesn't respond with the words I had in mind, I can correct them. Correcting is different from advising.

Instructions

1. At the end of a session, explain to participants that we often have parting thoughts, but many times don't get the opportunity to share them. Here's the opportunity.
2. Instruct them to think of tips for the other people in the room as they prepare to leave, that will help them to implement or to think further about the topic.
3. Ask each person to offer one tip for others in the room. Record the tips on a flip chart or board.

Variations

1. Ask small groups to come up with tips and share them with the total group.
2. Ask them to write tips on pieces of paper and silently pass them around the group for all to read.

Tips

1. This is so simple—but it works. Don't minimize it's impact.
2. If you are sending out minutes after the session, include the tips.
3. Make it a fun activity by asking people to leave physical tips as they voice their tips. People will leave pennies, pieces of candy, etc.

NEW! IMPROVED!

Purpose	Getting closure; Introducing a topic; Pure fun
Group Size	12-25
Level of Physical Activity	High
Estimated Time	4-8 minutes
Props	Example commercials for the leader

Participants enjoy writing commercials relevant to their work. This is a great activity for leaving people with a positive impression at the end of a meeting or training session. It's particularly effective with middle managers and other change agents who have to sell ideas to employees or management.

In presentation skills seminars, I challenge participants to think of each presentation as an act of persuasion—persuade to your opinion, persuade to try something new, or persuade to action. Commercials do all three.

Instructions

1. Explain to participants that salespeople quickly learn the difference between presenting features to potential customers and presenting benefits. Explain that features are the characteristics of a product or idea, while benefits are the ways the product or idea will be useful to the customer.
2. Read examples of commercials to participants.
3. Ask them for others.
4. Instruct participants to write short commercials for their audiences on a topic relevant to them, remembering to include features and benefits.
5. Ask participants to read the commercials they wrote out loud.

Variations

1. Have participants work in groups or pairs.
2. If you have time, ask them to draw an illustration to go with the commercial on flip chart paper.
3. If you have time, have each person or group come to the front of the room and deliver the commercial.

Tip

Write a commercial to entice them to write commercials and read it after you explain the activity.

PIE A LA MODE

Purpose   Introducing a topic; Getting closure; Team building

Group Size   6-60

**Level of Physical
Activity**   High

Estimated Time   5-10 minutes

Props   Pie a la Mode Activity Sheets, one piece of pie per person, one color
per group

Pie a la Mode groups people together by colored pie pieces and
reinforces for each participant one significant point of the session. It
is a good closure activity (assuming that people will be eating soon!).
This activity will guarantee that in a successful session, everyone
walks away with a proverbial piece of the pie.

> *Whether the conversation is about wills or shareholding or
backyard space in a condominium complex, everyone wants a piece
of the pie. Many world, national, marital, and sibling conflicts relate to the idea of scarcity and equality. Wouldn't it be easier if we
could all be assured of a piece of the pie—and a la mode at that!*

Instructions   1. Explain to participants that in this next Pie a la Mode activity,
they won't get to sample any strawberries, pecans, or raisins, but
they can be assured that they all will get a piece of the pie.
2. Pass out one piece of pie to each person.
3. Instruct participants to write on their pieces one significant learning point they got from the session and will take away with them.
4. Ask participants to stand and form groups with other people who
have the same kind of pie and make the pie whole by putting the
pieces together.
5. Instruct them to take turns taking their pieces of the pie back
while sharing with their small group the significant learning point
they received from the session.

Variations   1. Leave out the writing on the pieces, and ask people just to tell one
another significant learning points or valuable insights.
2. I like to group people in the beginning with the pie pieces, then
have them take back a piece at the end of the session while sharing what they've learned.

Tips   1. If it is a small group, use one pie.
2. Choose colors that signify types of pie: blue for blueberry; red for
cherry, etc.
3. Participants may put pies together on tables, on the floor, or
standing and holding them together.

PIE A LA MODE
ACTIVITY SHEET 1

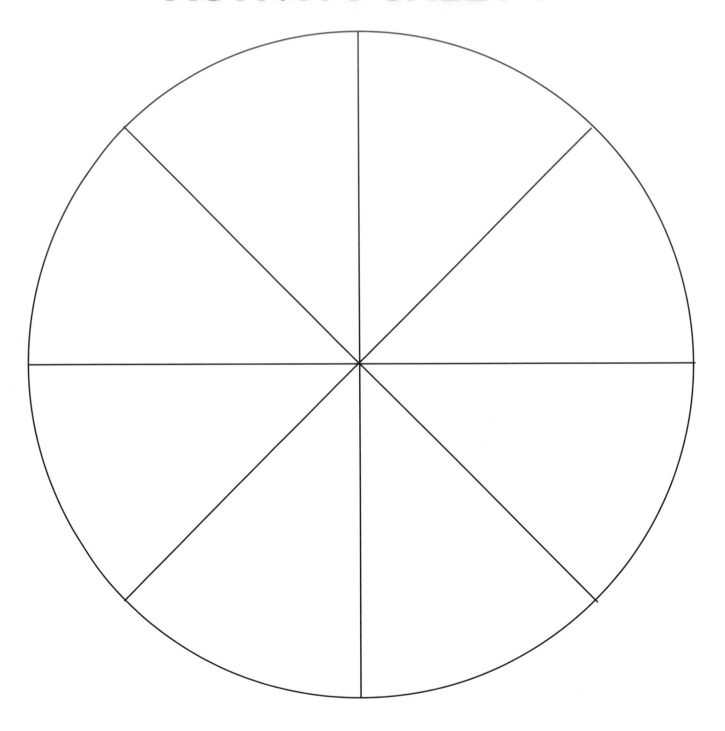

PIE A LA MODE
ACTIVITY SHEET 2

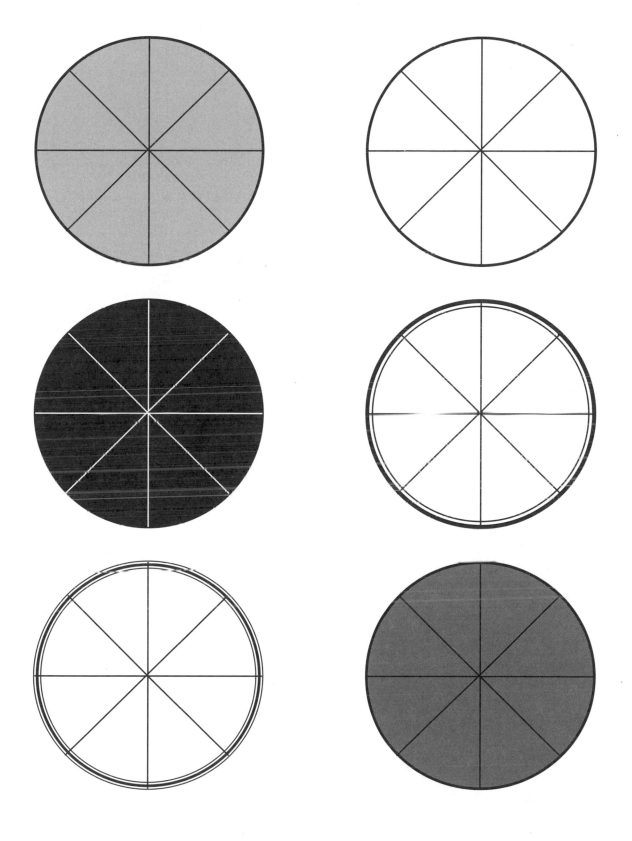

Q & A

Purpose

Mental aerobics; Introducing a topic; Getting closure; Energizing a long, dry presentation; For non-icebreaker types

Group Size

10-40

Level of Physical Activity

High

Estimated Time

15-20 minutes

Props

Question and answer sheets in different colors; 10 or more 8½″ × 11″ sheets per group; 9″ × 12″ envelopes, one per group

Here is a simple way to highlight key material and attend to physical needs. Use this to summarize the conclusion of a topic or to assess prior knowledge at the start of a session.

Training 101: Provide reinforcement and summary of all important concepts and facts.

Instructions

1. Create sets of ten or more Question and Answer Sheets per group by writing one question from your topic area on each 8½″ × 11″ question sheet and its answer on a corresponding answer sheet. Shuffle the Question and Answer sheets and then place 10 or more sets in an envelope for each group.
2. Organize participants into groups of four to six in an area of the room that has open floor space.
3. Give each group an envelope containing ten Question sheets and ten Answer sheets.
4. Instruct participants to distribute sheets among group members.
5. Explain that each group has Question Sheets and Answer Sheets. When you give the signal, groups will have two minutes to open their envelopes and match each Question sheet with its corresponding Answer sheet and then place the matched pair on the floor, with the Question sheet on top.
6. Give the signal for them to begin.
7. After two minutes, say "Stop."
8. Moving from group to group, ask participants to read their questions and then reveal the answers they chose. For each correct pairing of sheets, award one point.
9. Tally points and announce the winning group.

Variation

Use 3″ × 5″ cards and have participants work on table tops.

Tips

1. Use the success of groups as feedback for yourself.
2. Sample question: "What department would you direct someone to if they wanted to set up a credit account?" Sample answer: "Member Services."

Q & A ACTIVITY SHEET

Question Sheet	Answer Sheet

Sculpt-a-Team

Purpose   Team building; Getting closure; Pure fun; Especially for big groups

Group Size   12-36

**Level of Physical
Activity**   Medium

Estimated Time   15-30 minutes

Props   Sculpting balloons

In this hands-on activity, participants actually get to create things with sculpting balloons. It's a wonderful culminating group activity or a great energizer in the middle of a long day. It is totally painless and stress free; everyone enjoys it.

> *Have you ever watched the people who can take long balloons and make animals from them and said to yourself: "I could do that—if I wanted to"? The question I've always wanted to ask is, "Why animals?"*

Instructions

1. Give each participant a sculpting balloon.
2. Ask participants to blow up the balloons (or give them hand pumps) and tie them off, leaving about one inch at the end.
3. Explain that they will be making one large balloon sculpture that will represent the varied contributions of team members to the achievement of team tasks.
4. Ask participants to stand in a circle with their balloons.
5. Invite participants to advance toward the center of the circle one at a time and tell the members the greatest contribution that they bring to the team. As they do so, they should join their balloons with the team sculpture (the balloons already fastened together), thereby creating the essence of value in their team—and a beautiful representation of that in the balloon sculpture itself.

Variations

1. Have partners or small groups fasten their balloons together first, then join them to the other groups' balloon structures.
2. Ask participants to join the balloons in silence while music plays in the background. After the sculpture is made, ask them to share their individual contributions to the team.

Tips

1. The balloon-joining part of the activity can be light or solemn. Choose how you want it to be and lead it in that direction.
2. Try out the balloons before you use them with the group. It is difficult to find sculpting balloons that are easy to inflate by mouth. A pump works best.
3. This is best done with participants standing in a circle or around a table.
4. Use balloons of different colors to signify differences in contributions or teams.

Star Light, Star Bright

Purpose Team building; Getting closure; Meeting starter

Group Size 6-18

Level of Physical Activity Medium

Estimated Time 6-8 minutes

Props Star Light, Star Bright Activity Sheets, one per participant

This activity applies the age-old method of wishing upon a star to improve group communication and set goals. It makes a nice culminating activity for a team building session. Use it any time you want people to think about possibilities rather than impossibilities.

> *Dare to dream. Children make wishes and actually expect them to come true. Adults often make wishes and doubt that they could ever possibly come to pass. Here's a phrase I hear often: "I wish this company could get it together, but I know it never will." We've learned to protect ourselves so we don't get hurt—too much.*

Instructions

1. Ask participants if they have heard the poem, "Star light, star bright, first star I see tonight; I wish I may, I wish I might, have the wish I wish tonight." Explain that children are encouraged to say this and then make a wish when they see the glimmer of the first star in the sky.
2. Encourage participants to think of a wish they have for the team if their time together has shown them a glimmer of hope.
3. Pass out the stars and ask participants to write their wishes for the team on the stars.
4. When they've finished, ask participants to stand in a circle. Explain that their sky is now the floor in front of them.
5. Repeat the rhyme. When you finish, ask participants to come forward one at a time to place a star in the circle on the floor and state a wish.

Variation Have participants place stars in a cluster on the wall.

Tips
1. This activity can be light or serious. Respect the tone.
2. You can buy sky charts that participants can place the stars on.

STAR LIGHT, STAR BRIGHT
ACTIVITY SHEET

SWAN SONG

Purpose   Getting closure; Team building; Physical energizer; Pure fun

Group Size   12-500

**Level of Physical
Activity**   Medium

Estimated Time   2-4 minutes

Props   Swan Song Activity Sheets cut into cards, one card per participant

       In this activity groups of people sing phrases of a common song to create the whole piece. Use this with any group to close a session.

Scenes from summer camp. Rounds around the campfire. Row, Row, Row Your Boat. Frère Jacques, Frère Jacques. Or was that elementary school music class? Anyway, rounds are fun for any group to perform. They're even better if performed with motions.

Instructions
1. Choose a song that is known by the group and/or is appropriate for the topic.
2. Put phrases of the song in the boxes provided on the Swan Song Activity Sheet, then cut along the dotted lines to make cards with each card featuring a different phrase of the song.
3. Give one card to each participant.
4. Explain to the participants that they will sing a song as one body, but that each person has one phrase of the song to be sung at the appropriate time.
5. Conduct the singing of the song twice through.

Variation   For larger groups, give groups specific phrases.

Tip   You must be enthusiastic when you introduce this one; if you are, it will work like a charm. If you aren't, it may be *your* swan song.

SWAN SONG ACTIVITY SHEET

Row, row, row your boat	Gently down the stream
Merrily, merrily, merrily, merrily	Life is but a dream

THIS IS MY COUNTRY

Purpose

Getting to know you; Getting to know you better; Especially for big groups; Team building; Getting closure; Introducing a topic

Group Size

10-200

Level of Physical Activity

Medium

Estimated Time

2-5 minutes

Props

This Is My Country Activity Sheets, one per participant

In this activity participants disclose their thoughts and feelings about their country, organization, or team. Use it in the beginning of a session for affiliation purposes, or at the end of a program or meeting to bring feelings and thoughts to the surface and put closure on the session.

The glory of the Olympics is embedded in the playing of each gold medal winner's national anthem—a touching expression of achievement and patriotism.

Instructions

1. Give each participant a "This Is My _____" card and instruct them to fill in the word you would like them to think about. Examples of topics include country, family, company, or team.
2. Explain that they all have visual images of symbols that define what it means for each person.
3. Instruct them to think of their _____, and below the title draw symbols that represent the entity for them. Give examples.
4. When they finish, ask participants to share with a person sitting near them, explaining the meaning behind their symbols and images.

Variations

1. Ask participants to put any word they'd like in the blank and fill in the pictures.
2. Organize participants into groups and ask them to complete the task as a group on a flip chart or wall chart to share with other groups.

Tips

1. Examples might be: This Is My Country—flag, Statue of Liberty, dollar bill, home; or This Is My Company—computer, pay stub, people, building.
2. This works well as a team building event. The illustrations are usually very meaningful or humorous.

THIS IS MY COUNTRY
ACTIVITY SHEET

This Is My _____

This Is My _____

This Is My _____

This Is My _____

This Is My _____

This Is My _____

YMCA

Purpose
Outdoor activity; Getting closure; Physical energizer; Introducing a topic; Team building; Especially for big groups; Pure fun

Group Size
10-200

Level of Physical Activity
High

Estimated Time
5-8 minutes

Props
None

Groups will use body movements to spell out an acronym, while other groups guess what's being spelled. Use this activity as an energizer, but as a content reinforcer, too! Groups that are open to involvement and arc not self-conscious truly enjoy the physical stimulation.

Acronyms are such an important part of our cultural heritage. Think about it: YMCA; NBA; UCLA; DC; NFL; and OMO. (OMO stands for On My Own and is the name of a beauty parlor in Alexandria, VA. The owner had worked for other salons for many years and finally decided to buy out the owner of this salon. He immediately changed the name to OMO.)

Instructions
1. Organize participants into groups of six to twenty.
2. Explain the group task to participants:
   - I will give each group a word or phrase that has corporate meaning.
   - Each group will physically spell out its word or create an acronym and spell out the letters while saying them out loud.
3. Give groups two minutes to prepare.
4. At the end of two minutes, ask each group in quick succession to spell out its word.

Variation
Ask groups to choose their own words.

Tips
1. Demonstrate enthusiastically how one might form letters with the body.
2. Persons unable to participate may be leaders, directors, or spokespersons for the group.

Getting to Know You

Alliteration Affiliation

Purpose	Getting to know you; Mental aerobics
Group Size	5-25
Level of Physical Activity	Medium
Estimated Time	3-5 minutes
Props	None

Participants will appreciate this activity because it helps them remember each others' names by creating alliterative business names. They may also enjoy the energizing, creative boost to the day. Use this with groups who are not well acquainted with one another for affiliation, or with groups who know each other well for creative energizing.

Alliteration is often used in advertising for effect and recall. Harry's Hamburgers is certainly easier to remember than Cynthia's Brachwurst. Just think how much easier it would be to remember names if first and last started with the same initials, like Edie East, instead of Edie West.

Instructions

1. Explain that it is easier to remember people if we attach significance to their names.
2. Give each participant an index card.
3. Ask participants to create a business with an alliteration that matches one or both of their first and last names. Use your own name as an example, such as Carole's Christmas Candle Shop or Monique's Machinery Warehouse.
4. Instruct them to write the name of the business and a description on an index card.
5. Ask participants to share names, alliterations, and business descriptions with the rest of the group.

Variations

1. If the group knows each other well, ask them to make the alliterations and descriptions for one another, incorporating the characteristics of the other person.
2. Have participants put their businesses and descriptions on tent cards for others to see.
3. Ask participants to draw pictures of their business site.

Tips

1. Make your own alliteration and description to use as an example.
2. If your group is small, have participants post cards for all to read on breaks.

Balloon Bonding

Purpose   Getting to know you better; Getting to know you; Team building; Physical energizer; Pure fun

Group Size   20-200

Level of Physical Activity   High

Estimated Time   5-15 minutes

Props   One balloon per participant, plus extras

This activity allows people to get to know one another in close proximity as they try to keep their balloons off the floor—without using their hands. Use this with any groups that enjoy having some fun.

> One can measure friendships by their bonding power. Some friendships are like elementary paste that goes on easily and has a sickening sweet fragrance, but doesn't stick firmly and eventually dries up and flakes off. Some are like crazy glue—one drop on an object and immediately that object sticks fast and hard to the first object it contacts, whether that object wants it or not. Others are like rubber cement—both sides are coated, and, after a brief period of time, are stuck fast—as long as the materials and conditions are right and remain right. But the best friendships of all are like bonding adhesive: It takes some work to get it on both objects, and you must wait a little while, but, once the objects are stuck, they remain bonded forever.

Instructions

1. Organize participants in an open space into groups of eight to ten people standing in circles.
2. Give each person one balloon to blow up and tie off.
3. Explain the rules:
   - The object of the activity is for participants to introduce themselves to the other group members while the group holds all balloons off the floor—without using their hands.
   - If one balloon touches the floor, the group must again position the balloons so they're not touching the floor, and then continue the activity.
   - Participants should tell their names and three other personal facts about themselves.
   - As people introduce themselves, one balloon should be released outside the circle for each member until all persons have introduced themselves and there are no balloons left in the circle.

4. Give groups the signal to begin.
5. After four to six minutes, stop the activity and ask which groups were able to complete the activity.

Variations

1. Give each group double the amount of balloons.
2. Use one giant balloon per group.

Tips

1. Play with this one. It is best used in an open, friendly environment.
2. Participants will use a variety of ways to keep the balloons up: they may put knees together and balance balloons on them; they may clasp them between themselves in a close balloon hug; they may put feet together and hold the balloons up that way. Encourage them to be creative.
3. Make humorous comments about the ways people choose to keep the balloons off the floor.

Notes

_____

_____

_____

_____

_____

_____

_____

_____

_____

_____

DAYS of OUR LIVES

Purpose   Getting to know you; Getting to know you better; Self-disclosure

Group Size   6-20

**Level of Physical
Activity**   Medium

Estimated Time   4-6 minutes

Props   Sheets of 8½″ × 11″ paper, one per participant

   The results are funny when participants sketch a scene from their lives and then give it to someone else in the group to interpret—no captions included. Use this in the beginning of a session for participants to get to know one another better. I've not used this exercise with executives, and probably wouldn't. Nor have I used it with groups in which I know there have been a lot of negative feelings in the past.

   Soap operas: Vicarious living of events in which we would rarely find ourselves. Are they called soaps because they need to be cleaned up?

Instructions
1. Give each participant a piece of paper.
2. Explain the rules:
   - Draw pictures that tell the story of the "days of your lives" and put your name on it.
   - The drawings will be collected.
   - Drawings will be redistributed randomly. (If you receive your own drawing, you should exchange with someone else or return it to the pile).
   - Then introduce the person whose drawing you have, and tell that person's story by interpreting the drawing.
   - The artist may not interrupt while the speaker is interpreting.
   - After each person finishes the introduction, the artist will have an opportunity to correct misconceptions.
3. Begin the activity by asking for a volunteer to start.

Variations
1. Use some kind of roll paper, such as toilet paper, give participants five sections each, and ask them to highlight the five major parts of their lives.
2. Rather than doing it all in the beginning, spread out the telling of stories throughout the session.

Tips
1. Emphasize that drawing skills are not essential. The fun is in interpretations that are outlandish.
2. After each interpretation, have participants pass around the drawing itself. This adds humor.
3. Post drawings so people can look at them during breaks.

FAVORITE THINGS

Purpose   Getting to know you; Getting to know you better

Group Size   6-200

Level of Physical Activity   Low

Estimated Time   2-5 minutes

Props   Favorite Things Activity Sheets, cut into category cards, one per participant

Participants will enjoy sharing their favorite things with each other. Use this activity with any group at any time during a session.

> *Interested audiences and bright rooms to speak in*
> *Spurts of inspiration and humor abundant*
> *These are a few of my favorite things.*

Instructions

1. Organize participants into pairs.
2. Give each pair a Favorite Things card.
3. Ask participants to share favorite things with their partners.

Variation   If your group is small, ask each participant to share favorite things with the whole group.

Tip   Read a list of your favorite things to set the tone. Keep them light.

Notes

_____

_____

_____

_____

_____

_____

FAVORITE THINGS ACTIVITY SHEET

Favorite Things Card

Thing to do on a rainy day. _____

_____

Thing to do on a sunny day. _____

_____

Task I do at work. _____

_____

Thing my pet does. _____

_____

Thing I like to do most. _____

_____

Thing about my family. _____

_____

Thing about where I live. _____

_____

Thing to wear. _____

_____

Use of my time. _____

_____

Thing to talk about. _____

_____

Party activity. _____

_____

Thing my friend does. _____

_____

Place I most like to be. _____

_____

FOUR OF A KIND

Purpose
Getting to know you; Getting to know you better; Energizing a long, dry presentation

Group Size
10-40

Level of Physical Activity
High

Estimated Time
8 to 10 minutes each time

Props
Playing cards, four of a kind per participant

In this fun activity, the element of chance actually determines when participants have to reveal information about themselves. Use this at the beginning of a training session, and, if participants enjoy it, again after breaks and lunch.

Most people have played a card game where the object is to get pairs or four of a kind. And that's where it stops. But imagine if you took this idea just one step further ...

Instructions
1. Organize participants into groups of five to eight.
2. Distribute four cards of the same kind to each participant.
3. Ask for one person from each group to volunteer to be the dealer.
4. Instruct dealers to collect cards from each group member and shuffle them.
5. Ask the dealers to deal out all of the shuffled cards to the players.
6. Explain the rules of the game:
   - The object of the game is for participants to get four of a kind in their hands.
   - Each time I say "Pass," you should pass one card to the person on the right.
   - When you get four of a kind, say "Four of a kind" and put your cards face down on the table.
   - The person in the group who had that "four of a kind" then shares with the group four things about yourself that the group doesn't already know.
7. Begin the activity and play several rounds.

Variations
1. Play one round before or after each break, so it's a continuous activity.
2. Use this activity for review. Instruct groups to write questions about the content of the session on 3″ × 5″ cards. When a "four of a kind" person is identified, that person gets to either draw a question and answer it or choose a question to answer.

Tip
Keep this activity moving quickly.

GOIN' FISHIN'

Purpose	Getting to know you
Group Size	8-100
Level of Physical Activity	Medium
Estimated Time	5 minutes
Props	Goin' Fishin' Activity Sheet for leader; Bait (fish shaped cards or paper), 3 per participant

Participants will enjoy the comparison between fishing and meeting new people as they fish for the details that will allow for interesting conversation. Use this activity to speed up the affiliation process for any group. It's quick and easy.

> When people meet for the first time, there is usually a superficial exchange that goes something like this:
> "Hi, how are you?"
> "I'm fine. How are you?"
> "I've heard a lot about you."
> "All good, I hope." (Chuckle)
> "Well, most of it." (Chuckle)
> "Susan says you work at the Old Mill."
> "Yeah, I've been there about thirty years."
> And so on.
> If we get beyond the initial testing of the waters, we start to throw out the real bait and fish for relevance:
> "Did I notice a Redskins sticker on your car?"
> "Yes, I've been a fan for years. Do you follow football?"
> "Not really, but my daughter, Jennifer, loves the Redskins. She wouldn't miss a game."
> "Oh, you have a daughter, too."
> And so on.

Instructions

1. Explain to participants that the quickest way to find out some things about another person is to ask them significant questions.
2. Pass out the three pieces of Bait to each participant.
3. Ask participants to choose a partner who is someone they don't know or don't know well.
4. Once partnered, ask participants to take one minute to write down three questions—conversation starters—that they would like to ask their partners.
5. Now tell them they have four minutes to have partner conversations, taking turns with questions and answers.

Variations

1. Use groups instead of partners.
2. Fill in the questions rather than having participants choose them.

Tips

1. Tell a fish story, particularly about the one who got away.
2. Ask how many anglers there are in the room. Ask them to explain about different bait.

Notes

_____

_____

_____

_____

_____

_____

_____

_____

_____

_____

GOIN' FISHIN' ACTIVITY SHEET

Examples of conversation starters:

1. What are some of your favorite movies?

2. What's your idea of a perfect night out?

3. What activities were you involved in during high school?

4. What kind of vehicles do you use and why?

5. What types of vacations do you enjoy most?

6. What regular kinds of exercise do you enjoy?

7. What sports team do you root for?

8. What's your favorite hobby?

9. Where's your favorite place to eat out?

10. What are your favorite TV shows?

Jack-in-the-Box

Purpose Getting to know you; Getting to know you better; Physical energizer

Group Size 12-30

Level of Physical Activity High

Estimated Time 4-5 minutes

Props Jack-in-the-Box Activity Sheet for leader

In this activity participants get energized while creating a truly unsophisticated, very physical chart of demographics. Jack-in-the-Box is definitely not for stuffy types. It serves to physically energize and elicits smiles from all who dare to play.

> *If you've ever watched a child with a jack-in-the-box, you will recall this delightful sequence: turning the handle with anticipation; slowing down near the end of the song; pausing very briefly before the explosion—then turning the handle quickly; physically jerking the head and torso back with the popping out of jack with a look of disarmament; then laughing, sometimes raucously, at the self-inflicted joke while tucking jack back in the box. And it begins again.*

Instructions

1. Ask participants to stand and move to an open area in the room where they can mingle freely.

2. Ask for a volunteer to come to the front and demonstrate a jack-in-the-box with you. (You turn the handle and sing or hum Pop Goes the Weasel; the volunteer jumps up on the word "Pop.")

3. Explain the rules of the game to participants:
   - The purpose of this activity is for groups to compile demographics on habits of the group.
   - I will ask a question. Each participant should think of a response. For instance, I might ask, "What sport do you participate in most?"
   - After I ask the question I will say "Jack-in-the-Box," at which point you all shout your responses repeatedly.
   - People who shout the same response should form groups.
   - The largest group is the leading "Jack-in-the-Box" for that round.

4. Ask the first question.

5. Pause for a slow mental count of two, then yell "Jack-in-the-Box."

6. After people have gotten into groups, ask them to count how many are in each group. Ask all groups beginning with the largest group to repeat their answer for the other participants.

7. Now ask the other questions and repeat the process.

Variation

Give choices of responses. For example: What sport do you participate in most often? Running, swimming, walking, tennis.

Tip

This activity can be very noisy.

Notes

_____

_____

_____

_____

_____

_____

_____

_____

_____

_____

JACK-IN-THE-BOX
ACTIVITY SHEET

Sample Questions:

1. What sport do you participate in most?

2. What is your favorite food?

3. Where do you spend your vacation?

4. How do you get to work?

5. What do you do on Friday nights?

6. What is your favorite holiday?

7. Where do you shop the most?

8. What do you do in your free time?

9. What is your favorite color?

Know-It-All

Purpose Getting to know you

Group Size 6-12

Level of Physical Activity Medium

Estimated Time 10-15 minutes

Props Name tents; Know-It-All sheets listing the names of each participant with blank spaces for comments, one for each participant; prizes

Participants will get to know one another and have a few laughs as they take turns creating fun names for each other based on individual interests. This is best used at the beginning of a program for participants to meet each other.

How many times have you heard someone say, "I can't remember names, but I remember faces and things about people." I've heard it many times—coming out of my own mouth. This phenomenon would be okay if we could call people by what we remember about them, such as: "Hello, Mrs. Red Hair Who Just Came Back from a Trip to the Islands" or "Hi, Mr. Never Misses Star Trek."

Instructions

1. Explain to participants that they will have an opportunity to get to know one another and compete for prizes at the same time.
2. Ask participants to complete the back of their name tents with the following information: current address, favorite job, most admired person, best personal quality, and favorite movie or TV show.
3. Ask participants to introduce themselves and share the information they have on the back of their name tents.
4. When all participants have shared, distribute one Know-It-All sheet to each participant.
5. Explain that they now have three minutes to write down everything they remember about each person in the space provided by that person's name.
6. After three minutes, ask people to walk around the room and check the back of other participants' name tents for the accuracy of their information.
7. Tell participants to score their sheets in the following way: five points for each person they remembered something about and two points for each fact they remembered correctly.
8. Award prizes to the two people who could be classified as the Mr. and Ms. Know-It-All of the group.

Variations

1. If participants know each other, encourage them to write things that other participants do not know about them.
2. Make the activity noncompetitive.
3. To shorten the activity, ask each participant for two facts only.

Tip

Notice when these facts emerge during the course of the session and play on it.

Notes

_____

_____

_____

_____

_____

_____

_____

_____

_____

_____

KNOW-IT-ALL ACTIVITY SHEET

Cut along solid lines and fold along dotted line. Each page makes one table tent card. This works best if you reproduce this page on cardstock or a heavier stock paper.

MAKE YOUR POINTS

Purpose

Getting to know you; Introducing a topic; Physical energizer; Pure fun

Group Size

10-40

Level of Physical Activity

High

Estimated Time

4-6 minutes

Props

Eight point cards per person

This activity gives people a purpose for interacting—a nonsensical purpose maybe, but a purpose nonetheless. Used as an activity, the purpose is just to get to know each other. However, the activity could also be used to introduce a session on negotiating or at a time when you want to make a point about using others as resources.

I think that the point at which human interaction becomes worthwhile is when at least one person gets something of value from the exchange. Take teas, or cocktail parties, for instance. People who truly enjoy them tend to know what they want from the experience; people who don't, find them a bore.

Instructions

1. Distribute eight point cards, numbered from one to ten, to each participant.
2. Explain to participants that the numbers in their hands represent points. Tell them that they have three minutes to swap points with other participants until they each have exactly forty points total. The following rules apply:
   - They may negotiate with other participants to swap number cards.
   - A participant may not refuse to make a swap, but may select which card to exchange.
   - To begin the swap, participants must exchange names.
   - When the swap is completed, participants must shake hands.
   - When participants reach forty points, they may sit down.
3. After three minutes, announce that time is up. Recognize the people who have gotten the required forty points.

Variation

Change the rules so people draw points from another participant's "hand." The first person to arrive at forty points and yell out "Made my point!" is the winner. Play then ceases.

Tips

1. Ask participants to stand and move around while swapping points.
2. This works best when you copy the activity page onto card stock.

3. Since you have ten card values but are only passing eight to each participant, you will only pass out equal quantities of each type of card if your group is a multiple of ten—ten, twenty, thirty, etc. When your group size is not a multiple of ten, it's best to hand out all of the larger numbers and leave out some of the smaller numbers.

Notes

_____

_____

_____

_____

_____

_____

_____

_____

_____

_____

MAKE YOUR POINTS
ACTIVITY SHEET

1

2

3

4

5

6

7

8

9

10

NAME THAT TEAM

Purpose
Getting to know you; Getting to know you better; Creativity; Team building; Meeting starter

Group Size
15-36

Level of Physical Activity
High

Estimated Time
3-5 minutes

Props
None

This is a good, simple way to get people to create a name for the group they're in. Use it at the beginning of a session with groups who will be familiar with the same songs.

There is a teenager in the townhouse next to ours who turns on his stereo every day when he gets home from school, before his parents get home. How do I know he turns on his stereo? Because our walls vibrate from 3:00 p.m. until 6:00 p.m. on weekdays. How do I know his parents aren't home? Trust me on this one. If music is such a universal language, why can't parents and children stay in the same room with each other while listening to music?

Instructions

1. Organize participants into groups of five or six.
2. Explain that they'll now be playing Name That Team. Like the more familiar Name That Tune, they will be using music.
3. Explain the rules:
   - Each team will briefly talk among themselves, sharing things about themselves until they hit on a common theme.
   - Once they hit on a common theme, they should think of a song that demonstrates the theme that they all can hum or sing. For instance, if they are all older, they may choose the song "September Song," or if they were all born in April, they may choose "Singing In the Rain."
4. When each team has a name, ask each to stand and hum or sing their name.

Variation
Tell participants they may add instruments to accompany them (drumming on table, combs, etc.)

Tips

1. Play on group names for the remainder of the session.
2. Don't play music while doing this activity.

PERSONAL Ads

Purpose   Getting to know you; Team building; Introducing a topic

Group Size   10-40

**Level of Physical
Activity**   Medium

Estimated Time   20 minutes

Props   Personal Ad Activity Sheets

Need a real-time, here-and-now, in-your-face activity for introducing Baby Boomers or a Generation X crowd? This may be a best bet. Use this activity for participants to get to know one another, as an introduction to assessment/personality profiles (such as Meyers-Briggs), in a Valuing Diversity session, for pairing people, or in building teams.

Personal ad dating services—an interesting concept. Meet a person with interests you share or admire and you may find a partner for life. I wonder when we'll extend that concept to friendships or business relationships. What about the notion of personal ads at work? For example, an ad might read: John Smith, avid ideas generator, brainstorming bazooka (you give me the context—I'll think of a million creative possibilities), looking for individuals who share my passion for continuous change and disruption, unfettered by concern for ultimate outcome or accomplishments. Or consider this one. Elizabeth Bentley, historian, educator, and avid researcher of quality improvement processes, seeks reliable coworker with a passion for finding holes in processes and systems that need immediate examination and extensive plans for improvement.

Instructions
1. Give participants Personal Ad Activity Sheets and ask them to fill in their own information.
2. When they've finished, post the ads on the wall for reading. Each person should then choose an ad and attempt to locate the person who wrote it. That person will then be their partner for the next activity.

Variations
1. If the group is small enough, each person could read a selected ad and the person who wrote it could step forward.
2. The group could guess who wrote each ad.
3. Participants could write each other's ads.

Tip   Use a portion of the wall to post real Personal Ads from your local paper to stimulate interest before the activity.

PERSONAL AD ACTIVITY SHEET

Personal Ad Examples:

Gender / race:	Married black male Age: 48
Desire:	Looking for man or woman to discuss books, carpool downtown and/or play racquet ball
Hobbies / Interests:	Athletic and loves to cook
Special qualifications:	Nonsmoker, loves mysteries, has three children
Point of contact:	Downtown area gyms, bookshop cafes

MBM, mid-40s, looking for M/F to talk books, commute and/or play racquetball (lunch or early mornings). Nonsmoker; lover of mystery novels, good food and coffee; children a must. Can meet in downtown health clubs, bookshop cafes.

Gender / race:	Single white female Age: 22
Desire:	Looking for roommate
Hobbies / Interests:	Works a lot; loves Chinese food, incense, plants, rap music, café au lait, surfing the "Net"
Special qualifications:	Nonsmoker, dog lover
Point of contact:	Spacious apartment, lower West Side

SWF, 22, looking for person to share spacious, lower West Side office space; nonsmokers only; love Chinese food, incense burning, monstrous plants, rap background music, café au lait, surfing the "Net"; dog lives here too.

PERSONAL AD

Gender / race: _____

_____

Desire: _____

_____

Hobbies / Interests: _____

_____

Special qualifications: _____

_____

Point of contact: _____

_____

_____

Pick Pocket

Purpose

Team building; Getting to know you; Getting to know you better; Pure fun

Group Size

8-24

Level of Physical Activity

Medium

Estimated Time

3-5 minutes

Props

Pick Pocket Activity Sheets, one per participant

This activity is the adult version of the scavenger hunt; participants get to "scavenge" through their pockets, wallets, purses, and briefcases to find the items on their lists. Use this at the beginning of a session for people to get to know one another or midway through as an energizer.

> *My purse stores my life: identification, make-up, pictures, Tic Tacs™, pens, credit cards, tissues, business cards, checkbook, and so on. Last year my friend Suzanne and I attended a conference together. One afternoon she came back from a session very distraught; she had lost her glasses, which had fallen out of her purse. Now Suzanne had always carried a purse the size of a small overnight bag. But another friend had recently made the comment to her that her professional image would be enhanced if she would carry a smaller purse. So, kicking and screaming, she bought the small purse that she brought to the conference. The only glitch was that her friend must have forgotten to warn her that a smaller purse would hold fewer things. So, she stuffed her new purse with the contents of her former purse. Well, she eventually did locate her glasses, and the last time I saw her she was using her large purse. We do have our priorities.*

Instructions

1. Organize participants into groups of five to ten.
2. Give each participant a Pick Pocket Activity Sheet.
3. Tell groups they have two minutes to come up with as many items from the list as they can. Tell them that each item is worth two points.
4. Explain that they may make a reasonable substitution, but if they do, that item will only be worth one point. For example, someone may have an Avis Preferred Renter Card rather than a Hertz #1 Club Gold Card.
5. After two minutes, tell groups to count their points.
6. Ask groups to share what items they got from the list and what substitutions they made.

Variation

Give groups blank sheets of paper and ask them to list things they have in their pockets or purses that they think other groups might not have.

Tip

Give prizes to the group that has the most points.

Notes

_____

_____

_____

_____

_____

_____

_____

_____

_____

PICK POCKET ACTIVITY SHEET

Pick Pocket List

_____ Picture of a close relative

_____ Credit card without a signature

_____ AAA card

_____ dry cleaner receipt

_____ grocery list

_____ original Social Security card

_____ voter registration card for a registered Democrat

_____ Hertz #1 Club Gold Card

_____ buffalo nickel, wheat penny, or steel dime

_____ black comb

_____ electronic pager (beeper)

_____ Swiss army knife

_____ money clip

_____ fitness club card

_____ Sam's Club card with photo

_____ coupon for any food/restaurant item

_____ a mint

_____ contact lens case

_____ matches from a restaurant in another state

_____ cloth handkerchief

PICK UP TICKS

Purpose

Getting to know you; Physical energizer; Energizing a long, dry presentation

Group Size

12-30

Level of Physical Activity

High

Estimated Time

5-10 minutes

Props

Pick Up Ticks Activity Sheets, cut into cards for each category, one card per participant; overhead projector; projector pen; Pick Up Ticks transparency

    Participants will get points for the number of people they can find who have done the things listed on their Pick Up Ticks Activity Sheets. Use this activity at the beginning of a meeting or program for people to get to know one another, or at another time to get people physically energized.

This one's a favorite with dogs (a little humor).

Instructions

1. Prepare a transparency with each Pick Up Ticks category listed and space to fill in tally totals.
2. Give each participant one of the Pick Up Ticks category cards.
3. Tell participants they have three minutes to walk around the room and ask other participants the questions on the cards, placing a tick mark next to a question each time it gets a positive response.
4. After three minutes, tell participants to be seated.
5. Ask participants to report the total number of positive responses they received for each question.
6. Record totals on the transparency.
7. Before or after the next break, distribute the next card.

Variations

1. Ask participants to yell out "Pick Up Ticks" when they get ten ticks by one question. Reward them with a candy or trinket.
2. Ask groups to tally and give totals. Reward members of the group that gets the most ticks in any one category.

Tip

Play off the items on the sheet for the rest of the workshop or meeting.

Notes

_____

_____

_____

PICK UP TICKS ACTIVITY SHEET

Pick Up Ticks Category I

Do you drink espresso?
Do you like country music?
Do you have an Aunt Mary or an Aunt Helen?
Can you recite the *Pledge of Allegiance*?
Have you ever skied in the Alps?

Pick Up Ticks Category II

Do you own a pick-up truck?
Have you ever run a marathon?
Have you ever sipped coffee in a Paris café?
Do you like lima beans?
Can you whistle the tune to *Take Me Out to the Ball Game*?

Pick Up Ticks Category III

Do you own a CD player?
Have you ever been on an African safari?
Can you name four characters from the TV series *M*A*S*H*?
Have you been to a gym/pool this week?
Have you ever seen John Wayne in *The Alamo*?

Pick Up Ticks Category IV

Are you originally from a country outside of the U.S.?
Do you play the piano?
Can you name the Seven Dwarfs?
Do you own cowboy boots?
Have you ever sipped tropical drinks on a sunny, Caribbean beach?

Pick Up Ticks Category V

Do you own a lawnmower?
Can you hum the theme song to *The Brady Bunch*?
Do you own a leather jacket?
Have you ever been to a rodeo?
Do you like guacamole?

Pick Up Ticks Category VI

Have you ever eaten frog legs?
Have you ever attended a Monster Truck show?
Do you own a video camera?
Have you ever hiked in the Grand Canyon?
Can you name a national anthem?

ShareWear

Purpose
Getting to know you; Getting to know you better; Team building; Self-disclosure; Especially for big groups

Group Size
12-500

Level of Physical Activity
Medium

Estimated Time
10-12 minutes

Props
None

This activity is a great way for people to share something somewhat, but not too, personal; to find out something about others; and to share a sense of belonging. Participants truly enjoy this one.

One of the interesting byproducts of our time is shareware: Someone creates software that may be interesting, helpful, or useful and offers it free on the Internet for others to try and adapt. This Sharewear icebreaker gives people the chance to share a story which may—or may not—be of interest, help, or use to someone else. But as with shareware, you needn't buy until you have sampled.

Instructions

1. Organize participants into groups of six to twelve.
2. Explain the concept of shareware. Tell them that the name of this activity is sharewear—emphasizing the variation in spelling—a similar concept but they won't need to create a product.
3. Explain that in their groups, each person will have a chance to tell a story about something that they are currently wearing. For example, they may tell a story about a belt or a suit that they bought recently, or a watch or other piece of jewelry.
4. Give an example of a story about something you are wearing.
5. Explain that they will have eight minutes to tell their stories. They should make sure that each one in the group is heard.
6. When eight minutes are up, ask for examples of the pieces of clothing they used.

Variations

1. Ask participants to make up stories about something they are wearing.
2. Instruct them to try to sell something they are wearing to the other members of the group.

Tips

1. So you can set the stage well, make sure you wear something that you have a good story about.
2. This is a good icebreaker for getting the groups to share work experiences.

3. An example of a sharewear item I used one time is the watch my husband gave me for my 50th birthday. The story is that he served it to me on a tray with coffee in a cup that reads "On a scale of 1-10, I'm a perfect 50." I told the group that every time I look at my watch, I think "I'm a perfect 50."

Notes

_____

_____

_____

_____

_____

_____

_____

_____

_____

THE NAME GAME

Purpose   Getting to know you; Mental aerobics

Group Size   10-40

**Level of Physical
Activity**   Low

Estimated Time   3-5 minutes

Props   Lists of participants' names, one per participant

This is a chance for participants to have fun with names by grouping their own names according to common meanings or famous pairs. Since this helps people remember names, it's great at the beginning of a session.

Whenever we hear a name, we have a tendency to make an association with another name, person, or object. For example, my maiden name was Edie Sink. You can't imagine how often I heard: "Oh, like Steve and Edie?" or "Oh, like the kitchen?" and the ever-popular "Sink or swim?" (My sister Fran Sink once dated a man named Vern Tub. Really; it's a true story!)

Instructions
1. Give each participant a list of names of people in the class.
2. Organize participants into groups of two to four.
3. Instruct them to "play" with the names by linking them together with another person or thing to create a known combination. For example, Edie West could be paired with Donna North, while Ron Greene is paired with Judy Brown. Ben Cohen and Kim Gentle could become Gentle Ben, while Sandy Lund and Dianne Shore become Sandy Shore. Marvin Levy and Herman Strauss would be perfect for "Levy Strauss."
4. Tell them they now have three minutes to play with the names.
5. After three minutes, ask each group to report their name pairings.

Variations
1. Have groups brainstorm names of people they know, then create links from this list.
2. List names of famous people—scientists, philosophers, business people, etc.—and ask them to make associations.

Tip   You could use this activity to introduce any subject in which there will be a play on words.

Notes   _____

_____

_____

TIME CAPSULE

Purpose
Getting to know you; Getting to know you better; Team building; Self-disclosure

Group Size
6-20

Level of Physical Activity
Medium

Estimated Time
5-10 minutes

Props
Time Capsule Activity Sheets, one per participant; shoe boxes, one per group

This activity gets participants sharing real things about themselves because they bring treasures with them to the session to create their own personal time capsules.

Carole Turner told me that one of her junior high school teachers had the students create time capsules, which they filled with memorabilia and then buried. I guess the goal was to help archeologists in the future understand the interests and habits of twentieth-century junior high school children. I sure hope they can; nobody else has been able to.

Instructions
1. Send out Time Capsule Activity Sheets to participants about one week before the session.
2. When participants arrive, organize them into groups of four to six.
3. Explain that the shoe box will represent a time capsule and give one to each group.
4. Ask people to put their treasures in the Time Capsule.
5. Periodically during the session, ask each group to open its Time Capsule and withdraw one participant's treasure from it.
6. Ask that participant to explain the treasure to group members.

Variation
If the session has fewer than nine participants, place all objects in the same Time Capsule. Each time you need an icebreaker, choose an item, ask whose it is, and have the owner describe it.

Tips
1. Be prepared with bags for people who do not come with their treasures. Ask them to choose objects from their wallets, purses, briefcases, or cars to include in their treasures bag.
2. If it is a small group, include your own items in the box.

Notes
_____
_____
_____
_____

TIME CAPSULE
ACTIVITY SHEET
(FOR THE LEADER)

Note to the leader: Use this as a sample to send to participants at least one week prior to the session. You may wish to incorporate it in a letter stating logistics about the session.

On _____, you will be joining us for the following

session: _____. As part of this session, you will be

engaged in an icebreaker activity that involves sharing memorabilia to give

others an encapsulated view of your life. Please bring six pieces of

memorabilia (articles that describe your life such as pictures, plaques,

written articles, clothing, books, etc.) to the session. We will share these

articles, hence, pieces of our lives, with others at the session. You will take

the items with you after the session.

Two to Tango

Purpose Getting to know you; Grouping people

Group Size 10-40

Level of Physical Activity Medium

Estimated Time 5-15 minutes

Props Name slips listing famous pairs of people

This activity is a great way for pairing people with a smile by encouraging participants to ham it up a bit—and consequently, have fun. It's a wonderful energizer since it may be used at any time during a program.

We've all heard the adages "It takes two to tango" and "Two heads are better than one." Forget the one that says "If you want something done right, do it yourself."

Instructions

1. Give each participant a card with one half of a famous pair on it. For example, one person might get Hansel, while another gets Gretel. Explain that they are not to reveal their person to anyone else.

2. Ask the group to move to an empty space in the room and remain standing.

3. Explain to them that somebody in the room got the card naming the other half of their famous pair. The task is to find that other person, but explain that it's not as easy as it sounds. They are not to say their character names out loud. Tell them they will address each person individually and say something—without using names—that their person would say or do. They should do this with each person until they find their partner. For example, the participant holding Hansel's card might walk around saying "I wonder how we could get out of this forest" until Gretel is found.

4. Give the signal for them to begin circulating.

5. When it looks as if all of the partners have found one another, tell each pair to introduce themselves to the rest of the group using their fictitious names and relating what they said to find one another.

Variations

1. Ask participants to act out their roles without talking.

2. Give half the group both cards and have them choose a person to be their partner.

3. If you have a small group, have them sit in a circle and say their pieces one at a time until they have partnered up.

Tips

1. Let participants know this is an energizer. Keep it light and quick.

2. If you have some real hams in the group, let them act it out.

TWO TO TANGO
ACTIVITY SHEET

Hansel	Gretel
Winnie the Pooh	Tigger
MickeyMouse	Minnie Mouse
Rhett Butler	Scarlett O'Hara
Batman	Robin
Antony	Cleopatra
Abbott	Costello
George Burns	Gracie Allen
Timmy	Lassie
Kermit	Miss Piggy
Calvin	Hobbes
Tom	Jerry
Professor Higgins	Eliza Doolittle
FDR	Eleanor
Laverne	Shirley
Siskel	Ebert
Lewis	Clark
Roy Rogers	Dale Evans
Donny Osmond	Marie Osmond
Sonny	Cher

VANITY PLATES

Purpose

Getting to know you; Getting to know you better; Pure fun; For non-icebreaker types

Group Size

6-24

Level of Physical Activity

Medium

Estimated Time

2-4 minutes

Props

Blank table tent cards, one per participant

This activity will be a dream come true for many participants because they'll finally be able to create their own vanity plates (car not included). This activity has two benefits: You don't have to make up tent cards for every participant, and they get to share something about themselves.

> I've never paid the extra money to have special words on my license plates. Part of the reason is that I don't want to be saddled with the same handle for a whole year, and the other part is my need to be at least somewhat anonymous. The idea of people driving through the Shopper's Club parking lot and saying, "Oh, Edie West shops here," is not exactly to my liking.

Instructions

1. Give each participant a table tent card.
2. Explain that this is their chance to have the vanity plates they may have thought about or dreamed of in the past.
3. Give them examples of vanity plates you've seen and ask them for other examples.
4. Instruct them to think of a way to identify themselves on a license plate and to put that on the tent card they've been given. They may use eight spaces—all letters, numbers, or a combination—with no blank spaces between.
5. Tell them they may add other decorative touches (e.g., the cardinal on Virginia plates).
6. When they've finished, ask them to introduce themselves and explain their vanity plates.

Variations

1. Have them partner and then introduce one another to the rest of the group by their vanity plates.
2. Use this as a topic extension and ask them to create plates on the theme; for example, team plates or customer service plates.
3. Rather than tent cards, offer poster board the size of regular plates.

Tips

1. Set the tone you want by creating your own license plate and using it for an example.
2. Ask participants for examples of vanity plates they have seen.

Whodunit

Purpose

Getting to know you; Getting to know you better; Physical energizer; Energizing a long, dry presentation

Group Size

10-20

Level of Physical Activity

High

Estimated Time

3-6 minutes

Props

Questionnaire, one per participant; matrix of participant information, one blank and one filled in per participant

Use Whodunit with any group of people to uncover interesting hobbies, facts, and experiences about each other. This works best at the beginning of a program to get people warmed up.

> *Part of our job as human beings is to speculate about other human beings—what have they done, what are they thinking, where did they come from, where are they going, and what will they do next? And with some people, whatever will they do next??*

Instructions

1. Give or send out a copy of the questionnaire to all participants and ask them to return it in ample time for you to fill in the Whodunit Activity Sheet with interesting facts from participant information. Make sure to include equal numbers of facts about each participant.

2. Prepare Whodunit Activity Sheet and make copies for all participants.

3. Organize the group in a space where people can walk around freely.

4. Give each participant a copy of the Whodunit Activity Sheet and explain that the sheet contains facts about the people in the room.

5. Tell participants that they will have three minutes to walk around the room and confront people with the information, according to the following rules:

   - The object is to get as many signatures as possible in the boxes on the sheet.

   - You may not ask people which of the facts are theirs.

   - You may guess three times with each individual. If any of your guesses are right, you may ask the person to sign in that box.

   - If the three guesses are inaccurate, the person should sign on the back of the sheet and you should move on to another person.

   - You may only give three guesses for any one person.

6. At the end of three minutes, call time and ask participants how many correct responses they had.

7. Award prizes to the person or persons who had the most correct guesses, and consequently, the most signatures.

Variation

In small groups, have participants guess which boxes are applicable to group members.

Tip

Use some humorous information on the Activity Sheet, or include information that will lead to the telling of great participant stories.

Notes

_____

_____

_____

_____

_____

_____

_____

_____

_____

WHODUNIT ACTIVITY SHEET I

Name: _____

Nickname(s): _____

Company: _____

Job title: _____

Sibling Information (how many/type): _____
_____

Pet Information (how many/types/breeds): _____
_____

Favorite article of clothing: _____
_____

Favorite song: _____
_____

Year of high school graduation: _____

College attended: _____

Type of car: _____

Favorite weekend pastime: _____
_____

Names and ages of children: _____
_____
_____

Favorite team: _____

Best feature: _____
_____

Worst feature: _____
_____

Embarrassing moment: _____
_____
_____
_____

Best vacation: _____
_____

Favorite quote: _____
_____

WHODUNIT ACTIVITY SHEET 2

Getting to Know You Better

A Star Is Born

Purpose   Team building; Getting to know you better

Group Size   6-20

**Level of Physical
Activity**   Medium

Estimated Time   15 minutes

Props   Eight-inch gold star for each person

Everyone gets to be a star in this activity when coworkers or teammates list the five best qualities of each participant. This activity is best used for people who have worked together to complete a project—whether it's working at an office or taking part in a session activity. It may be used anytime during a program.

At some point in a lifetime, almost everyone dreams of being the "star of the show" or the "star of the game." That's mainly due to the recognition our society showers on stars. On a team, however, it's important that everyone receives recognition.

Instructions

1. Give each participant a star.
2. Explain to participants that each person on the team plays a starring role that allows the team to successfully attain its goals.
3. Give participants ten minutes to find five people who will vouch for their star qualities with these instructions:
   - Ask five teammates to each name one of your best, or "star," qualities.
   - The five teammates should write the qualities on your star and then sign it.
   - A star is born each time a participant gets five teammates to list a best quality and sign the star.
4. When ten minutes are up, post the stars where everyone can read them at breaks.

Variations

1. Ask participants to add additional comments to the stars as they remember contributions their team members have made!
2. Give each participant three stars. Instruct them to ask three other participants to write a "star" contribution they've made to the team.

Tip   The purpose of this activity is not to choose "stars" of the team. Make sure you place the same emphasis on all contributions and everyone in the group will do likewise.

A STAR IS BORN
ACTIVITY SHEET

ASSOCIATIONS

Purpose

Getting to know you; Getting to know you better; Self-disclosure; Pure fun

Group Size

6-100

Level of Physical Activity

Medium

Estimated Time

5-8 minutes

Props

Associations Activity Sheets, one per participant

In this energizing activity, participants will discover the associations people make with certain words, numbers, or pictures. Unlike Freud, participants will not use information to psychoanalyze one another; this one is just for fun. Participants enjoy their own data in addition to hearing that of others.

Number 4. That's the number I insisted on wearing when I played high school basketball. The reason was simple; my brother had worn that number and was a star. My hero.

Instructions

1. Explain to participants that this activity gets them sharing things about themselves by association.
2. Organize participants into groups of three.
3. Pass out the Associations Activity Sheets.
4. Give participants one minute to complete the sheets. In each of the three blank sections of the sheet, write one or two associations for each category of numbers, pictures, and words.
5. Explain to participants that they will now have three minutes to share their sheets in their groups. Of course, they should begin by introducing themselves.

Variations

1. If the group is small, have everyone share with the whole group.
2. Organize participants into small groups for sharing.

Tip

To begin the activity, share one association of your own.

ASSOCIATIONS
ACTIVITY SHEET

Numbers
: 16
: 40
: 100
: 1,000,000

Pictures

Words
: childbirth
: graduation
: chocolate
: patriotism

Numbers

Pictures

Pictures

BAGGAGE CLAIM

Purpose	Getting to know you; Getting to know you better
Group Size	12-40
Level of Physical Activity	Medium
Estimated Time	5-10 minutes
Props	Baggage cards, one per participant

In this activity, people will find things out about each other before putting faces to names. It's best used with people who don't know one another well because this gets them moving around and meeting each other.

> *Most of us have used the airlines to travel either for business or pleasure and are quite comfortable checking our luggage (or not at all comfortable, but have no other alternative since it's better than toting 85 lbs. of dead weight through ten-mile-long airports in eight minutes). Upon our return, however, many of us have stood patiently (or not so patiently, but again, what is the alternative?) at the baggage claim area, eyes glued to the belt, and watched our luggage slowly turn the corner on the belt only to be snatched up by someone who mistakenly thought the bag was theirs. Usually, a bag snatcher, upon discovering the mistake, will toss the bag back on the belt—to our audible sigh of relief. But what if they vanished from sight with our bags? Wouldn't it be strange to run into a person wearing our clothes, our shoes, our hats, our toiletries?*

Instructions

1. Pass out cards to participants and ask them to "pack their bags" by filling in the blanks.
2. Explain that they will now experience going to the baggage claim and accidentally picking up someone else's bag.
3. Ask participants to walk around the room, shaking hands and introducing themselves to other participants in the following way:
   - The first time each person shakes hands with another person, both participants will introduce themselves and tell each other what is in their bags (based on the information they wrote on the card).
   - The pair will then exchange "bags" and move on to greet other participants.
   - As they greet other participants, they will shake hands and introduce themselves but explain that they have the wrong "bags." They will then proceed to tell each other who their

"bags" belong to and what's in them, using the information on the cards they have in their hands.

- After each meeting, they will "trade bags" and then move on to another participant.

4. At the end of three minutes, ask participants to stop.
5. If the group has twenty or fewer participants, you can ask participants to read the name of the person whose card they are holding, introduce that person by what's in their bag, and return the card to that person so that everyone will eventually be holding their own "baggage" again.

Variations

1. Ask the participants to draw their own luggage on cards.
2. If it is a small group, have participants "guess who" as each card is read.

Tips

1. If you collect the cards, you may use them for drawings and door prizes.
2. Decorate the room with maps or travel posters.

Notes

_____

_____

_____

_____

_____

_____

_____

_____

_____

_____

BAGGAGE CLAIM
ACTIVITY SHEET

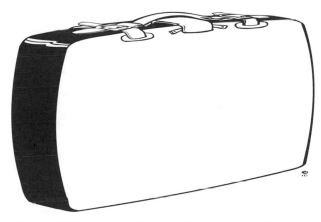

Please "fill the bag" with five interesting facts about your life.

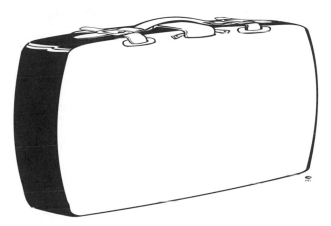

Please "fill the bag" with five interesting facts about your life.

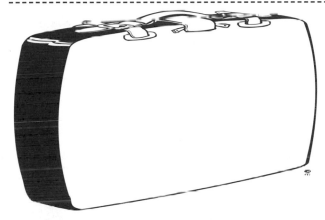

Please "fill the bag" with five interesting facts about your life.

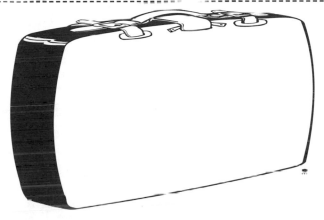

Please "fill the bag" with five interesting facts about your life.

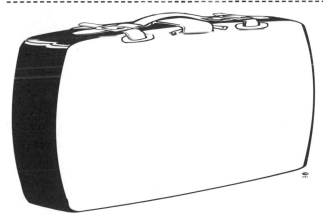

Please "fill the bag" with five interesting facts about your life.

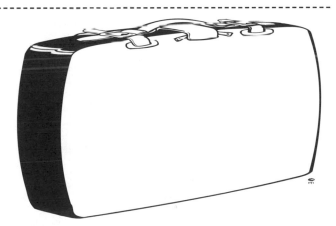

Please "fill the bag" with five interesting facts about your life.

Birth Right

Purpose   Grouping people; Getting to know you better; Physical energizer

Group Size   15-50

Level of Physical Activity   High

Estimated Time   5-7 minutes

Props   None

      Grouping participants by birth order is a fun way for people to relate to one another—whether they already know each other or not. Use Birth Right at the beginning of a session to affiliate or after lunch to energize.

      They say ("they" refers to the professors who teach courses in birth order counseling and the authors of such books as The Birth Order Book, *Dr. Kevin Leman*) that there are some recognizable patterns of behavior in people that are partially due to the order of their placement in the family. It is a fascinating field of study, and certainly worth exploring if one works with children and families.*

Instructions

1. Explain to participants that:
   - birth order plays a role in our childhood development;
   - there are often common experiences and feelings shared by people of the same birth order;
   - this is an opportunity for them to discover those commonalties.

2. Ask participants to group themselves into four corners of the room by the following birth orders: oldest, youngest, middle, and only child. Explain that middle means anyone who is not an oldest, youngest, or only child.

3. After participants are grouped, tell them they have two minutes to answer and record their agreed-upon responses to the following questions:
   - What were the advantages of being a _____ child?
   - What were the disadvantages of being a _____ child?

4. After two minutes, ask the spokesperson in each group to read the lists aloud.

Variations

1. Before Step 2, have people list the advantages of being a _____ child on one side of a 3″ × 5″ card and on the other side, the disadvantages of that position. Then when they move to

*Leman, Kevin (1985) *The Birth Order Book.* New York: Dell Publishing.

Step 3, encourage them to share cards and come to agreement on a few in each category.

2. Ask each group simply to demonstrate one advantage and one disadvantage which the other groups will guess.

3. Rather than birth order, ask participants to think of their order in the organization: new hire; been here one to two years; been here a while; been here forever (or at least it seems that way).

Tips

1. Have fun playing with this one. You'll find that participants will refer back to it often during the session.

2. If you know nothing about birth order, get a book from the library, or purchase a book to help with your understanding of the power of this activity.

Notes

_____

_____

_____

_____

_____

_____

_____

_____

_____

_____

Flake to Flake

Purpose
Getting to know you; Getting to know you better; Introducing a topic; Especially for big groups; Team building; Physical energizer

Group Size
12-500

Level of Physical Activity
Medium

Estimated Time
2-5 minutes

Props
One piece of white paper (about 4″ × 4″) per participant

This activity works best in the winter for any group. It's a quick conversation starter—great for the beginning of a session when participants don't know each other well.

> *In Virginia we shoveled our way out of the Blizzard of '96 very slowly. There are a variety of ways people here deal with the snow: some people (mostly displaced Northerners) jump out their doors, shovel in hand, and attack the snow with vigor as soon as an inch has fallen; others wait until it has crusted and turned to ice around footsteps and tire tracks; and the third group steps through, over, and around the snow while waiting for the spring thaw. We have some of each in my neighborhood. (I must admit, I fit in the first category; I lived in Vermont for thirteen years.)*

Instructions

1. Pass out one piece of white paper to each participant.
2. Instruct them to make a snowflake by folding and tearing their papers.
3. Explain to participants that one of the beauties of winter is snow. Ask them what is true about snowflakes. (They'll respond that they are all different.) Reinforce that truism.
4. Explain that the next activity is called Flake to Flake because like snowflakes, they'll have a chance to discover ways in which they are different.
5. Ask participants to stand.
6. Explain that they will now have two minutes to meet as many people as they can.
7. Instruct them to meet one person at a time, shaking hands and telling some things about themselves that they think may be different from the other person.
8. Explain that when they finish exchanging information, the two people should exchange snowflakes and move on to the next person.
9. After two or three minutes, ask participants to share aloud some of the differences they heard.

Variations

1. Don't use snowflakes. Use stars or sunbeams.
2. Ask participants to write things about themselves on the snowflake first.
3. Take it one step further; ask participants to find the person whose snowflake they hold last and get more in-depth information about that person.

Tip

Demonstrate how to fold and tear paper to make a snowflake.

Notes

_____

_____

_____

_____

_____

_____

_____

_____

_____

_____

GENERATION GAP

Purpose   Getting to know you better; Introducing a topic; Grouping people

Group Size   10-50

**Level of Physical
Activity**   High

Estimated Time   5-8 minutes

Props   Generation Gap Activity Sheets, one per group; decade signs to place
                       around the room
                       By dividing your group along generational lines, you'll discover the
                       differences in attitudes toward the work environment. Use this activity
                       as an energizer, to discover differences, or to gain a sense of belonging
                       within groups. Use it with groups who will benefit from the information
                       or insight.

> *I purchased a book many years ago entitled* The Corporate
> Steeplechase: Predictable Crises in a Business Career, *by Dr.
> Srully Blotnik.* In this book, Dr. Blotnik presents examples of the
> ways people in different age decades may think about and carry
> out their careers. The point Blotnik makes is "that the crises peo-
> ple face in the course of their business careers are largely pre-
> dictable. Each person's experience of them will be unique…. Nev-
> ertheless, there are enough similarities present to allow people in
> business to foresee and prevail over the most important obstacles
> they will encounter" (Blotnik, p. 268). I thought it was an inter-
> esting concept from a career development, motivation, diversity,
> or change management perspective.*

Instructions
1. Explain that often people in different age groups have different
   thoughts about work and careers. This activity will group people
   by age decades and allow them to tell others their opinions and
   ideas.
2. Ask participants to group themselves by birth decades near the
   corresponding signs.
3. Once groups are together, ask each group to select a Scribe and a
   Spokesperson.
4. Give each Spokesperson a copy of the Generation Gap Question
   List.
5. Explain to groups that they have three minutes to brainstorm the
   questions on the activity sheet and agree on the top answers for
   each. The Scribe should record the answers on the sheet.

*Blotnik, S. (1984) *The Corporate Steeplechase: Predictable Crises in a Business
Career.* New York: Facts On File, Inc.

6. Tell them that after three minutes, each Spokesperson will be called upon to give its group's top three answers for everyone to hear.

7. Give the signal to begin.

8. After three minutes, ask each Generation Gap group, beginning with the youngest and ending with the oldest, to report their responses to the questions.

Variations

1. After all groups have reported, ask the total group to analyze commonalities and differences.

2. Ask Scribes to list responses on flip chart paper and post on the wall for all to see. Then ask participants to walk around and read the different responses.

Tips

1. Don't challenge the appropriateness of a grouping choice; some people don't like to reveal their ages and should not be forced or teased into doing so.

2. This activity can be light and fun; or it can be more serious with an important information exchange. Decide in advance and set the stage; or read the audience and go with their mood.

3. Remember and validate unique responses in each grouping.

Notes

_____

_____

_____

_____

_____

_____

_____

GENERATION GAP
ACTIVITY SHEET

1. Do you attribute your job success to your personality skills, product or on-the-job-skills, or to skills you gained through educational programs?

2. The most important thing to you in your career is: money, job stability, or personal on-the-job satisfaction.

3. If you felt you weren't being paid appropriately, would you look for another job, cut back on the amount of work you do, or push your case with the boss?

4. If you don't agree with the boss do you: say so, keep your mouth shut, or go over the boss's head to a higher level?

5. Would you rather stand out at work or blend in with the masses?

6. Would you rather work as part of a team on a project, handle a portion of the project individually, or handle the whole project yourself?

7. Do you feel your current skills are enough to ensure your job success or are you constantly seeking to enhance your skills through classes and on-the-job programs?

8. Do you enjoy training newcomers to your area, easily befriending them, or would you prefer they learn by doing?

HI. HOW ARE YA'?

Purpose

Getting to know you; Getting to know you better; Especially for big groups; Physical energizer

Group Size

15-500

Level of Physical Activity

Medium

Estimated Time

2-5 minutes

Props

None

In this activity, participants greet and meet one another. Use it with any group as a quick opener, or later in a session to highlight the importance of connections.

Sometimes we take people so lightly—people who live each day facing challenges, disappointments, successes, pleasures, sacrifices, pain, joy. When I was in New Zealand, I learned a few things about the Maori culture. One thing I was truly impressed with was the importance given to greetings. When one enters a Maori homestead, one enters into rituals that demonstrate intentions of mutual respect and acceptance.

Instructions

1. Set the stage for participants by explaining that in the U.S. when people meet they often ask questions like, "Hi, how are you?" or "What's happening?" or What's new?"

2. Ask the audience to tell you what might be expected responses. (They'll often say things like, "Fine. How are you?" or "Not too much. How about you?")

3. Suggest to participants that these tend to be noncommittal questions and answers. There must be other ways of greeting people with more meaning, rather than the standard "Good to see you."

4. Tell participants they will now engage in an activity that allows them to put sincerity and honesty into their greetings.

5. Ask them to think of statements to make or questions to ask that would engage them in sincere dialogue.

6. Provide an example, such as: "Hello. I am happy that we have the chance to talk. Tell me, what are the most important things you are doing in your life right now?"

7. Give participants two to four minutes to mingle and ask *real* questions.

Variations

1. Give them a list from which to choose questions to ask.
2. Use this as a small group activity.

Tip

Participants really enjoy this activity. Don't minimize it's effect.

If You Could Be...

Purpose   Physical energizer; Getting to know you better; Introducing a topic;
                   For non-icebreaker types; Energizing a long, dry presentation; Team
                   building; Pure fun

Group Size   16-88

**Level of Physical
Activity**   High

Estimated Time 3-5 minutes

Props   If You Could Be ... Activity Sheet for leader
                   Participants will compare themselves to everything from cookies to
                   corporate departments in this fun way of getting self-disclosure. Use the
                   questions provided for energizing participants anytime during a session,
                   but for thinking types and executives, add the questions that get at the
                   heart of issues. They'll find the responses to these most interesting.

> *The role of cookies in society has been one of celebrating and
> caring: grandmothers keeping cookies in the cookie jar for special
> visits from grandchildren; friends taking cookies to friends in
> need; parents baking cookies for children coming home from
> school; and baking cookies for holidays, like Christmas and
> Valentine's Day, school parties and cookie exchanges. In March
> 1996,* Cooking Light *magazine* pointed out the findings of a re-
> cent national survey showing that Americans consume more than
> 1.5 billion pounds of cookies each year.*

Instructions
1. Organize participants so that they are standing with empty space
   in the corners of the room.
2. Explain the rules:
   - I will ask a question with four possible choices for answers.
   - I will designate which corner stands for which answer.
   - When I have finished asking each question, participants should
     move to the corner of the room that corresponds with the an-
     swer they chose.
   - Participants will then tell others in their corner why they chose
     that answer.
3. Begin the activity.

Variations
1. Have participants seated and raise hands to indicate responses.
2. Use this method to take an organizational forced choice survey.

Tips
1. When the activity is over, ask participants to share some reasons
   for their choices.
2. To add to the fun, predict on a flip chart in advance where you expect
   the most people to be; then show the group after they've answered.
3. Add your own questions that are relevant for the group. They will
   find the responses interesting.
   *Linda Strom, "Smart Cookies." *Cooking Light,* March, 1996.

IF YOU COULD BE ACTIVITY SHEET (FOR LEADER)

Sample Questions:

1. If you could be a cookie, what kind would you be? (examples: chocolate chip, oatmeal, peanut butter, sugar)
2. If you could be a dancer, what kind would you be? (examples: ballet, tap, country, modern)
3. If you could be a pasta, what kind would you be?
4. If you could be CEO of Hershey Foods, what candy would you make more of?
5. If you could be in any department you wanted to be in within your company, where would you be?
6. If you could be stranded on a deserted island with one famous person, who would it be?
7. If you could be a bird, what kind would you be?
8. If you could be an animal, what kind would you be?
9. If you could be an instrument, what kind would you be?
10. If you could be in one place in the world, free of charge, where would it be?
11. If you could be a tree, what kind would you be?
12. If you could be a drink, what kind would you be?
13. If you could be CEO of any company in the world, what company would it be?
14. If you could be a famous person from history, who would you be?
15. If you could be a piece of furniture, what would you be?

LET THE GOOD TIMES ROLL

Purpose Getting to know you; Team building; Getting to know you better; Physical energizer

Group Size 5-20

Level of Physical Activity High

Estimated Time 5-8 minutes

Props Roll of paper (such as a tablecloth); brightly colored markers or crayons

In this activity, participants will describe through pictures their "good times" outside of work. Use it at the beginning of a session for participants to get to know one another, or midway through as an energizer. I've also used it with groups to make a point about consciously bringing their "better selves" to work.

> *Recently in a session I was facilitating, one person said, "We need to have more parties so we can really get to know one another; we all know we're very different people outside of work." The inference was that we're "better people" outside of work. What gets in the way of bringing the "better persons" to work?*

Instructions

1. Post a long, horizontal sheet of paper on a wall with the title listed at the top, "Let the Good Times Roll."
2. Ask participants to think of a time outside of work within the last six to twelve months that they have had a really good time. Perhaps it was a family reunion, party, or camping experience.
3. Invite all participants to approach the paper on the wall and pick a spot to illustrate their good times using no words, only pictures. Explain that they will have three minutes to draw their "good times."
4. After three minutes, ask participants to come forward one at a time, stand by their pictures, and describe their good times.

Variations

1. If participants are dressed casually, put the paper on the floor and invite them to sit on the floor and draw.
2. Use fax paper rolls and position them on a table.

Tips

1. The more colorful, the better.
2. Encourage participants to make large pictures so they will be recognizable from a distance.
3. Participants will have fun as they refer back to the illustrations throughout the session.

Life's Little Suitcase

Purpose
Getting to know you; Getting to know you better; Pure fun; For non-icebreaker types

Group Size
6-12

Level of Physical Activity
Medium

Estimated Time
3-5 minutes

Props
None

Participants bring everything they need with them for this activity. They'll be looking through their wallets for three to five objects which represent their lives that they'll share with the group. Use with groups that are reluctant to do "silly" activities.

A wallet is a standard safe gift to give. It's not too personal, basically generic, affordable, not something that needs to fit or match, easy to send in the mail, and predictable in generating a classic response, "Oh, thanks. A nice, leather wallet." I guess that's why most people have one they use and two in a drawer.

Instructions
1. Ask participants to look through their wallets and find three to five objects they are willing to share with the group that will help the group learn more about them.
2. Ask participants to begin sharing, one at a time.

Variation
Ask participants to choose two things from their wallets without identification and put them in the middle of the table. Have each participant choose two and guess who the owner is.

Tips
1. If any participants don't have wallets, allow them to choose items from their pockets, briefcases, etc.
2. If you have people put items on the table, don't leave the room with the items displayed.

ME, MYSELF, AND I

Purpose
Getting to know you; Getting to know you better; Team building; Self-disclosure

Group Size
6-16

Level of Physical Activity
Medium

Estimated Time
4-8 minutes

Props
Magazines; glue, paste, or transparent tape; one human shape per participant

Participants will get to cut and paste their way to a representation of themselves as they use cutouts from magazines and papers to fill in human body shapes that represent them. This is an activity that helps people define more clearly who they and others are.

This is who I think I am. This is who others think I am. This, then, is who I am.

Instructions
1. Give each person a human shape.
2. Distribute magazines around the room.
3. Instruct participants to cut out pictures and words from magazines that are representative of themselves and attach them to the human shape. And to add to the fun, tell them to feel free to contribute to one another's shapes as well.
4. After the human shapes are completed, pass them around the room and then post them for all to see.

Variations
1. Have participants guess which shape belongs to each person.
2. Have them complete the activity for one another, rather than for themselves.
3. Instead of personal shapes, give each person a silhouette of a group of people and ask them to fill in pictures and words for the team, or use one shape and make it a team project.

Tips
1. This is a good activity for people to engage in when they first come to the room and are waiting for the session to begin.
2. Choose a wide variety of magazines.

Notes
_____
_____
_____
_____

ME, MYSELF, AND I
ACTIVITY SHEET

MOST LIKE ME

Purpose

Getting to know you; Getting to know you better; Self-disclosure; Pure fun

Group Size

10-100

Level of Physical Activity

Low

Estimated Time

3-5 minutes

Props

Most Like Me Activity Sheets, one per participant

Participants will compare themselves to characters in humorous illustrations as a way of finding out more about one another. This activity works well for any group to get to know one another, to find out more about one another, or to encourage self-disclosure.

> *"Look-alikes." At a conference social a couple of years ago, we could pay to have our pictures taken standing next to one of many look-alikes: Tom Selleck, Dolly Parton, and a number of others. I signed up because everyone else was doing it; but when the conference was over, I couldn't decide what to do with the picture. I didn't want to hang it in my home amid the numerous wonderful pictures of family and friends. But if I put it in the office, visitors would notice the picture and say one of two things: "Did you really see ——?" to which I would have to reply, "No, not really, I just posed with a look-alike"; or, "Oh, I see you had a picture taken with a look-alike; I had that same opportunity but turned it down," at which point I would feel compelled to say, "Well, I didn't really want to do it, but everyone else was ..." I threw the picture away.*

Instructions

1. Distribute Most Like Me Activity Sheets.
2. Ask participants to look at the pictures on the sheet and place an X in the corners of the pictures that are most like them.
3. When they've selected, ask them to form triads and share with those people the selections they've made and why they chose them.

Variation

Ask groups or a team to make a composite sheet of everyone in the group and share that sheet with other groups.

Tip

If your group is small, ask participants to share with the total group.

MOST LIKE ME ACTIVITY SHEET

MY HERO!

Purpose   Getting to know you; Team building; Getting to know you better

Group Size   10-15

Level of Physical Activity   Medium

Estimated Time   4-5 minutes

Props   None

This is a way for participants to get to know one another and have someone else extol their virtues. Use with all groups except executive types.

> *When I was growing up my father always told me not to look to a human being as an example of perfection because, if I did, I would invariably be disappointed. He said to choose what you like from many people, but look only to God as your perfect example; that way you would never be disappointed.*

Instructions

1. Organize participants into pairs.
2. Ask partners to find out about the professional roles and responsibilities of their partners.
3. Tell them that after two minutes of discovery time (one minute each), they will have one minute to present their partners to the rest of the group as if they were championing them for a position in the company. Explain that each person may sing the praises of the partner to whatever extent they would like.
4. Begin the activity, asking for a volunteer to go first.

Variation

For larger groups, organize participants into small groups and have them do the activity in small groups.

Tips

1. Although exaggerating for presentation effect, people truly begin to appreciate the value and contributions of others.
2. If done at the beginning of a long session, participants will comment on the information disclosed at various times during the session—often humorously.

Notes

_____

_____

_____

_____

_____

Notebook of Lists

Purpose
Getting to know you better; Energizing a long, dry presentation

Group Size
6-60

Level of Physical Activity
Low

Estimated Time
2-3 minutes each time

Props
Notebook of Lists Activity Sheet for leader; notebook paper; three-ring binder

Participants will enjoy creating lists that help define their group. Use this quick activity with small groups to encourage quick discussion and getting to know one another. Good for any group, any time during the session.

> When my sons were living with me, I spent many evenings listening to interesting and bizarre lists from a book of lists. One such book, The Book Of Lists: The 90s Edition by David Wallechinsky and Amy Wallace,* lists topics like "Twenty Prominent Respectacled Sports Figures" and "The Post-Music Careers of Ten Rock-and-Roll One-Hit Wonders."

Instructions
1. Explain to participants that they will go on record creating lists that somewhat characterize the group.
2. Organize participants into groups.
3. Give each group a sheet of filler paper.
4. Choose one of the list titles; instruct groups to put the list title at the top of the paper and create a list of information gathered from participants in their group.
5. When they've completed the lists, collect them and put them in the notebook.

Variations
1. Create your own lists with company-specific themes such as length of time in the company.
2. If time allows, hear the lists from each group.
3. Let groups choose topics to create lists.

Tips
1. Keep the lists, copy and distribute them to participants following the session.
2. Begin the activity by reading examples of lists from *The Book Of Lists* or another source.
3. Make the notebook available for participants to read during breaks.
4. Repeat the activity each hour or so using a different list.

*Wallechinsky, David and Wallace, Amy (1993) *The Book Of Lists: The 90s Edition*. Boston: Little, Brown, and Company.

NOTEBOOK OF LISTS ACTIVITY SHEET (FOR LEADER)

1. List of vehicles in family

2. List of pets in a lifetime

3. List of collectibles

4. List of collectibles in possession

5. List of nicknames

6. List of musical instruments in possession

7. List of musical instruments played anytime in life

8. List of team sports group members have played

9. List of favorite songs

10. List of favorite movies

11. List of grandparents' names

12. List of breakfast foods eaten that day

13. List of favorite vacation spots

14. List of favorite football teams

15. List of the last movie seen at a movie theater

16. List of places people have traveled

17. List of magazines subscribed to

18. List of all-time favorite TV shows

19. List of first concerts attended

20. List of happiest days of life

Pickle Barrel

Purpose   Team building; Getting to know you better; Getting closure

Group Size   5-15

**Level of Physical
Activity**   Low

Estimated Time   15-30 minutes

Props   Pickle cards (green cards), one for each participant
                     In this activity, participants receive recognition for the little things they do on the job—the "condiments" that make the work day better for everyone.

> *My daughter-in-law Kim stayed at our home last night so my son could work without interruption on a lengthy law school assignment. We decided to have dinner and rent a movie, and my husband was given the task of choosing a movie we would all enjoy and feel good about. He chose one he had seen many years ago—Crossing Delancey, a delightful story of love and pickles. If you're anything like me, you capitalize on any available metaphor when designing an icebreaker. So, here it is: the Pickle Barrel.*

Instructions

1. Explain to participants that often when you hear people mention pickles, it is with reference to a feeling of extreme delight or pleasure—exclamations such as "I love pickles," or "Subs aren't subs without a good dill pickle alongside them." (Maybe this is a northeastern phenomenon?) The beauty of pickles is that they are so highly appreciated, but are only condiments—accompaniments to the real meal.

2. Give each participant a pickle card.

3. Explain to participants that credit or recognition is often given to them for the entrée of their jobs, but often the "condiments"—though highly important—are overlooked. Tell them that today they will think about the "condiment" portion of their roles at work.

4. Ask participants to make a list on pickle cards of the ways they function as "condiments" on the job.

5. Now tell them to choose partners and describe to their partners the value these "condiments" add to coworkers' jobs, task completion, or goal attainment.

6. When partners have had a chance to share information, ask partners to choose one example from their partners' pickle cards and share that example with the whole group.

| **Variations** | 1. | Use the dessert, rather than the condiment, analogy. |
| | 2. | Rather than distributing pickle cards, brainstorm about condiments with participants and ask them to choose one for themselves. |

Variations

1. Use the dessert, rather than the condiment, analogy.
2. Rather than distributing pickle cards, brainstorm about condiments with participants and ask them to choose one for themselves.

Tips

1. If participants indicate that they don't like pickles, invite them to chose their own condiment.
2. I don't advise doing this before lunch unless it directly precedes lunch.

Notes

_____

_____

_____

_____

_____

_____

_____

_____

_____

_____

QUICK QUOTES

Purpose   Getting to know you better; Self-disclosure; Introducing a topic; Getting closure

Group Size   4-20

Level of Physical Activity   Medium

Estimated Time   3-5 minutes

Props   Quick Quotes Activity Sheets, one per participant

In this activity, people will express thoughts and feelings by explaining how a particular quote from a given list appeals to them. Use this anytime during a session to give people the floor.

> *A quote that I came across years ago keeps recurring in my mind. The quote was included in* Mind Traps *by Tom Rusk, M.D.* It appears as the opening to Chapter 4, "The Self-Doubt Trap": "What we must decide is perhaps how we are valuable rather than how valuable we are."*

Instructions
1. Create a Quick Quotes Activity Sheet and copy for participants.
2. Pass out a Quick Quotes Activity Sheet to each participant.
3. Explain that there are times in each of our lives when a quotation provides the "Aha" or concept for awareness of our own context of living.
4. Ask participants to choose one quote and highlight on the page or write a quote of their own that fits the context of their own life experience at the moment.
5. Instruct them to write a few words for themselves that helps them explain the relevance of their quote.
6. Ask each participant to share aloud the chosen quote and explain the relevance.

Variations
1. Do the activity in groups or pairs.
2. If you're going to see the group more than once, ask them to bring in a quote to share.
3. Bring in quotes related to your topic; ask participants to choose favorites and explain why they like them.

Tips
1. If you want to use this as an energizer, bring in quotes that are somewhat humorous.
2. Some serious issues may be brought out during this time.
3. To create the Quick Quotes Activity Sheet, list a variety of quotations that your audience will relate to.

*Rusk, Tom (1988) *Mind Traps.* Los Angeles: Price Stern Sloan, Inc.

REFRIGERATOR MAGNETISM

Purpose   Getting to know you; Getting to know you better

Group Size   6-30

**Level of Physical
Activity**   Medium

Estimated Time   5-10 minutes

Props   Refrigerator Magnetism Activity Sheets
                     Participants will find it easy to exchange personal information just by explaining what's hanging on their refrigerators. Use this activity at the beginning of a session for people to get to know one another, or in the middle of a long session as an energizer.

> *In our kitchen, there are two spots designated for important people and events. One is our refrigerator and the other is a dry erase board where we have our changing prayer list. If you hit the prayer list or the refrigerator, you know you are special to us. Naturally, members of our family are on both in name and picture. After our youngest son's last visit, we discovered an addition to the dry erase board—the Boston Bruins had mysteriously made their way onto the prayer list. One glance at the '96 NHL standings will tell you why.*

Instructions

1. Organize participants into groups of four to five.
2. Give each participant a Refrigerator Magnetism Activity Sheet.
3. Explain to participants that one can often tell a lot about a person or family by the items on the outside of their refrigerator. Show participants some things you brought from your refrigerator.
4. Tell participants their task is to draw on their sheets the items that are on their refrigerators and/or the items they would put on there if they thought about it and made decisions accordingly.
5. When they've finished, ask them to share their drawings with group members and explain why they've included certain items.

Variations

1. Use this with teams. Have them create a collective refrigerator.
2. If it's a small group, have them use large sheets of paper, draw refrigerators and their magnetically attached stuff on them, and then share their drawings with the group.
3. In advance of the session, ask participants to bring five things from their refrigerator to share with the group.

Tips

1. If participants say, "I hate things on my refrigerator," tell them to think of a bulletin board instead.
2. If participants say, "I never noticed what's on the refrigerator," tell them that you are giving them a virtual refrigerator and to put on it what they'd like.

REFRIGERATOR MAGNETISM
ACTIVITY SHEET

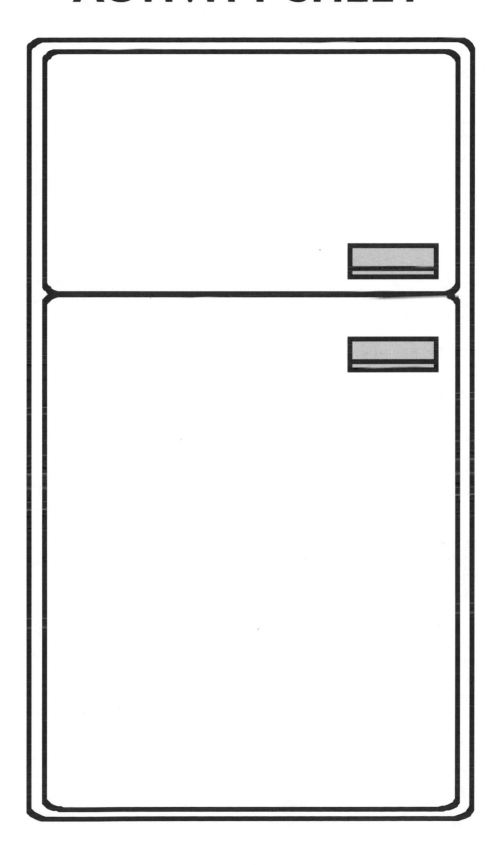

Role Call

Purpose Getting to know you better; Introducing a topic; Team building

Group Size 4-40

Level of Physical Activity Low

Estimated Time 5-10 minutes

Props None

This activity gives participants the one-minute chance to take on the role of another person in the company. Use it during a session to get understanding around the difficulties in making tough decisions, or to highlight that there are different perspectives to each situation or decision.

How many times a week do you hear someone utter the words, "If I were so and so, I would have ..." (and I'm not just referring to politicians in an election year).

Instructions

1. Organize participants into groups of three.
2. Ask participants to take on the role of any position in the company or organization they would like and introduce themselves to group members as such.
3. Explain that as each "Role Player" is introduced, group members may ask one question each of that person. The "Role Player" will then respond from the newly assumed position.
4. After about 5 minutes, ask each group to report what roles they played, and what questions were posed.
5. Make the point that we all have a tendency to be armchair quarterbacks (observers who claim to know better than the person involved what decision to make). However, without having the same information and experience as the person we portrayed, our responses are merely speculative—worthy of further research, but certainly not grounded.

Variations

1. Give participants slips of paper with titles on them and ask them to role play with these positions.
2. Provide a list of questions relevant to the topic and have each "Role Player" respond to the same questions from this list.
3. For team building, ask each person to act the role of someone else on the team.

Tips

1. If it's a small group, have people introduce themselves to the entire group.

2. This activity will be light and humorous or serious (and perhaps, cynical). It's up to you to set the appropriate tone.

3. This may bring up some negative issues about boss and management roles. If you're not prepared to deal with company politics, you may want to avoid this activity; or, prior to the activity, emphasize that some of the responses will be coming from a different perspective which does not necessarily mean better—just different.

Notes

_____

_____

_____

_____

_____

_____

_____

_____

_____

_____

Shaping Up!

Purpose

Getting to know you; Getting to know you better; Self-disclosure; Team building

Group Size

6-12

Level of Physical Activity

Low

Estimated Time

2-5 minutes

Props

Shaping Up! Activity Sheets, one per participant

This is an activity for getting people to divulge information about themselves in a fun way. Use with groups to open a session and get people talking about themselves, or in creating small groups or teams.

There's a very short training video that features a Ziggy-like character who starts out in a box. He first pushes his way out of the box and, once on the outside, longs to be back in the box, so he pushes his way back in. The video has no words, just animation. It is meaningful on many levels. I've used it for organizational change and problem solving.

Instructions

1. Pass out a Shaping Up! Activity Sheet to each participant.
2. Suggest to participants that different shapes have different appeal to different people. Explain that the purpose of this activity is for them to share something about themselves. The shapes will provide a unique way for them to do that.
3. Instruct participants to choose a shape that is most like them or that they are most like and write down the comparisons.
4. Ask participants to share the shapes they chose and tell the group how they are like these shapes.

Variations

1. Don't use the sheet. Instead ask participants to come up with their own shapes, draw them, and tell how they're like them.
2. Ask participants to think of the times they are like each shape. For example, you might say, "I'm like a square when I'm sitting reviewing my bank statement; I'm like a circle when I'm making the rounds at a party; I'm like a triangle when I have a decision to make with a few clear-cut choices."

Tip

Encourage participants to draw symbols on the shapes that represent them. For example, a mustache, curly hair, bow-tie, pencil in the ear, etc.

SHAPING UP! ACTIVITY SHEET

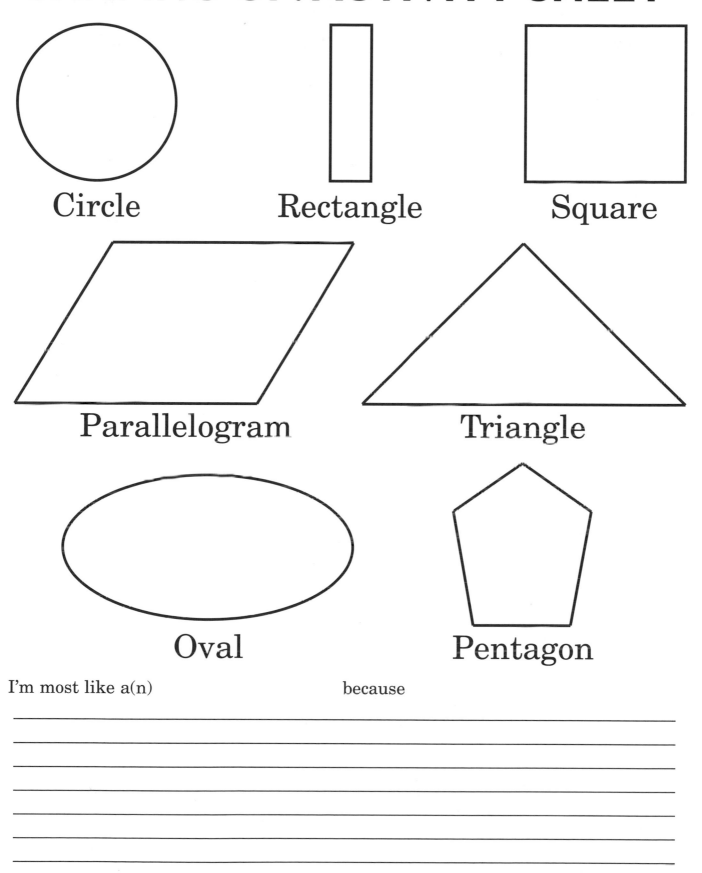

Circle

Rectangle

Square

Parallelogram

Triangle

Oval

Pentagon

I'm most like a(n)   because

Spanning the Globe

Purpose
Getting to know you; Getting to know you better; Physical energizer; Introducing a topic

Group Size
12-48

Level of Physical Activity
High

Estimated Time
15 minutes

Props
World maps, one per group; push pins, about 10 per person

This activity will allow participants to discover just how well traveled they are by encouraging them to share their travels with their fellow participants. Use this activity at the beginning of a session for affiliation, after a break or lunch as an energizer, or to introduce a topic related to globalization or diversity.

> *Isn't it wonderful that we live in an age in which traveling is the norm rather than the exception? My 78-year-old father-in-law still makes the drive across the U.S.A., coast to coast, about once a year.*

Instructions

1. Organize participants into groups of five to eight, standing in front of a map on the wall.
2. Give groups containers of push pins.
3. Instruct participants to put push pins in every part of the world they have visited at some point in their lives.
4. Remind them that the experience of being in a different environment often allows us to broaden our own depth of understanding.
5. Ask them to choose one of the places they visited or lived and share with their group members a true story—including a moral or insight they got from that experience.

Variations

1. Use states or cities instead of countries.
2. Use markers or tacks rather than push pins.
3. If there are only eight to twelve participants, use one map.
4. Give a prize to the person who has traveled to the most countries, states, or cities.

Tip
If you give each participant push pins of one color, others will easily identify their travels.

SUPERLATIVES

Purpose

Getting to know you; Getting to know you better; Self-disclosure; Team building

Group Size

6-60

Level of Physical Activity

Medium

Estimated Time

5-10 minutes

Props

Superlatives Activity Sheets, one per participant

In this activity, participants will write down superlative things about themselves and share them with others. This is a good activity for team building or for people to get to know one another better. Use it at the beginning of a session, or at the beginning of a section that leads into roles or understanding interdependence.

I spoke with a young man last week who told me he wanted to be the best he could possibly be at his job. Wise fellow. Not "I want to be better than anybody else," or "I want to be the best in the company," but "I want to be the best I can be." It's what most of us want from our speaking, teaching, training, or coaching, but many people (dare I say most?) can't help mix it up with comparisons to others—and comparisons can be devastating.

Instructions

1. Organize participants into groups of four to six.
2. Explain that many U.S. high schools in the 60s, 70s, and 80s had a "Superlatives" selection in the senior year. Those superlatives often included "Most Intellectual," "Best Looking," "Class Clown," and "Most Likely to Succeed." The difficulty with that method is the comparing that takes place between students to come up with one winner. To take a developmental approach means to look at oneself and ask, "When am I most likely to succeed," and "How am I most talented?"
3. Pass out Superlatives Activity Sheets to participants and ask them to take one minute to complete them.
4. After one minute, ask participants to partner up and take another minute to share their sheets (each person having thirty seconds).
5. After one minute, ask them to introduce their partners to the rest of their small groups, including the information on their sheets.

Variation

Rather than using the categories on the sheet, ask participants to come up with their own superlatives about themselves.

Tips

1. You might want to play some music from the 60s, 70s, or 80s before or during this activity.
2. This activity is meant to be kept light. Encourage participant humor through examples of your own.
3. Fill out a sheet for yourself and use some of your answers for examples. You might say, "I am best dressed when I am in my old blue comfortable sweats and my new Nike sneakers."

Notes

_____

_____

_____

_____

_____

_____

_____

_____

_____

SUPERLATIVES ACTIVITY SHEET

Fill in the space after each statement.

1. I am "most talented" when I am:

2. I am "most likely to succeed" when I am:

3. I am "most versatile" when I am:

4. I am "best looking" when I am:

5. I am "class clown" when I am:

6. I am "best dressed" when I am:

7. I am the "best dancer" when I am:

8. I am "most friendly" when I am:

9. I like myself "best" when I am:

Used Car Lot

Purpose　　　　　Getting to know you; Getting to know you better; Team building; Self disclosure

Group Size　　　5-50

Level of Physical Activity　Low

Estimated Time　5-10 minutes

Props　　　　　None

This is a great opening activity to get participants to disclose carefully selected information about themselves by comparing themselves to cars. It doesn't seem to matter if participants know each other or not; it works either way.

Everyone can name a car they like, but can everyone name a car that is like them? Just like people who look like their dogs, or couples who grow old together and begin to look alike, people truly do develop characteristics like their cars. Just take notice— you'll see.

Instructions
1. Organize participants into groups of four to six.
2. Ask participants to think of a car that is most like them.
3. Ask for one volunteer in each group to be the first "Car" in the lot. Invite group members to guess what kind of car that person chose and why. When all have guessed, the person should reveal the chosen car and explain the reasons for the choice.
4. If time permits, ask each group to report the makes of cars in their car lots.
5. If the total group is twenty or fewer, ask each group to describe their car lot for the other groups.

Variations
1. If participants know each other well, have participants choose cars for each other and describe the reasons for the choices. (Sometimes they do this anyway following the other activity without your suggesting it.)
2. Instruct participants to hawk their cars—features, benefits, etc.
3. Have groups draw pictures of their cars with pronounced features and show them to the other groups.

Tips
1. This activity works well with a variety of groups from all levels in an organization.
2. Participants will often play with the concept for the remainder of the workshop, bringing an element of fun to the day.

WORDY CONNECTIONS

Purpose
Getting to know you better; Self-disclosure; Introducing a topic; Team building; Pure fun

Group Size
6-20

Level of Physical Activity
Medium

Estimated Time
2-5 minutes

Props
Wordy Connections Activity Sheet for leader

Participants will love this twist on the standard word association game. Use this activity anytime during a session for groups to focus on the topic, get to know one another better, or just for fun as an energizer. Use it at the end of a session to reinforce information and concepts.

On one of my recent flights, I had a conversation with the man sitting next to me. He was telling me about his corporation's change to a new group work structure. He said with sarcasm in his voice, "It's really teamwork with a new name. When we tried teamwork two years ago, it failed miserably because we weren't equipped to handle it. Now they've renamed it group work and they're shoving it down our throats again." I asked, "How do you feel about them doing the same thing, but renaming it?"

His response was interesting. He thought for a moment and then said, "I guess it's okay; at least they realize that teamwork didn't work, and if they have the sense to rename it, I guess they have the sense to learn from the mistakes they made when they tried it before."

Instructions

1. Before the session begins, create a list of ten words to use for the activity, choosing three to five words from the list on the Wordy Connections Activity Sheet and adding five to seven words related to the content of your program.

2. Explain to participants that we've all played word association games before and that's what this is—with a twist.

3. Ask participants to number a paper 1 to 10 and create three columns.

4. Explain that you will read a word and they should write down the first object that comes to their minds in the first column.

5. Read all of the words, one after another.

6. Now tell them you will read a word and they should write down the first feeling that comes to them in the second column.

7. Read the same list through again.

8. Now tell them you'll read a list of words again and they should write down the first action word (verb) they think of when they hear the word.

9. Read the same list through again.

10. Now say each word aloud and allow participants to voice their objects (nouns), feelings, and action words aloud.

Variations

1. Use program or content words only.

2. Ask each person to report only on one of the word connections.

Tip

Listen with both ears and mind for attitudes and feelings about the topic.

Notes

_____

_____

_____

_____

_____

_____

_____

_____

_____

_____

WORDY CONNECTION
ACTIVITY SHEET (FOR LEADER)

Sample Lists:

Ten Words List

1. Electricity
2. Snowstorm
3. Conflict
4. Talk Shows
5. Laughter
6. Holiday
7. Airport
8. Computer
9. Poetry
10. Racehorse

Team Building List

1. Independence
2. Recognition
3. Conflict
4. Team
5. Creativity
6. Partners
7. Feedback
8. Systems
9. Alone
10. Dependence

Just for Fun List

1. Play
2. Howdy Doody
3. 1967 Ford Mustang
4. Entertainment
5. Picnic
6. First Toy
7. Puppy
8. Pizza
9. The Wizard of Oz
10. Teddy bear

GROUPING PEOPLE

CANINE KIBITZING

Purpose Grouping people; Physical energizer

Group Size 24-60

Level of Physical Activity High

Estimated Time 3-5 minutes

Props Canine Kibitzing Activity Sheets with six sounds on cards, one card per participant

In this activity, participants are assigned a sound to make, and then use this sound to bark their way into groups as they seek out other people making the same noise. Use this at any point in a session when you want to group and physically energize participants.

> *Recently, my husband and I were visiting my mother in New Jersey. Suddenly, her dog Jody began to bark at an arriving stranger. My husband listened curiously and then exclaimed, "Jody says 'Bark, bark!'" At which point our dog, Jordan, began to "Woof, woof." I must admit I had never paid attention to the distinct sounds dogs make, but Peter Spier has. One of his children's books is all about dog sounds. Whatever your age, you must read Peter Spier's books.*

Instructions

1. Give each participant a card with a dog sound on it.
2. Tell them that in this activity they will be forming smaller groups. To do that you would like to introduce the languages of the canine community. Explain that many languages are represented in the group.
3. Instruct participants to begin their canine kibitzing by making the sound on their cards. When they hear a bark, yap, or woof similar to their own, they should form a group with those canines and wait for others to do likewise.
4. When groups are formed, ask each to give their sound for the rest of the groups to hear.

Variation Any sounds work for this familiar activity.

Tips

1. The spin on this is the idea of different "canine" sounds. Play on that in your introduction.
2. Choose your group and activity carefully for this one. I only use those groups that are playful or less into self-importance.
3. Never refer to the participants as "dogs." ┆
4. For a small group, use four sounds.

CANINE KIBITZING
ACTIVITY SHEET

Growl

Ruff

Woof

Arf

Bark

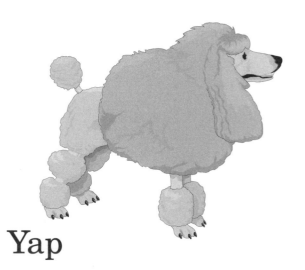

Yap

Easy Money

Purpose   Getting to know you; Grouping people; Physical energizer

Group Size   24-72

Level of Physical Activity   High

Estimated Time   5-10 minutes

Props   Pennies, from 1-6 per participant

In this activity, participants get themselves into groups of six and then meet and find out about each other. Use it at the beginning of a session with groups who don't know each other well and who would like an easy way to meet.

After all these years, you would think I could resist the temptation, but once in a while I can't. A letter comes in the mail: "Open Immediately—Dated Material. Edie West, you have won $_____." Now I know full well that the sentence continues with "if you ..." But, who knows? This really might be my big chance ...

Instructions
1. Give each participant one to six cents.
2. Explain that they will now form groups by participating in an activity called Easy Money.
3. Give these instructions:
   - Each person in the room has from one to six cents.
   - The object of the activity is to form groups of people who have one to six cents; in other words, each group will contain a member with one cent, a member with two cents, etc. This is an easy way for you to mix and get to know each other.
   - To do that, you will mingle, approach each other, and let each other know how many pennies you have by saying one of the following:

     if one cent, you would say "A penny for your thoughts";

     if two pennies, "This activity isn't worth two cents";

     if three cents, "It's as easy as one, two, three";

     if four cents, "One cent, two cents, three cents, four";

     if five cents, "Don't take any wooden nickels";

     if six pennies, "I have sixth cents."

- As you meet, stay together with the people who will form your group and look for those who will complete the group.

4. Begin the activity.

5. When groups are formed, instruct them to form a circle. Participants will introduce themselves and tell a number of things about themselves that corresponds to the number of pennies they have.

Variation

Have people organize into groups having the same number of pennies.

Tip

You may use cards or paper with pennies on them, but the real ones work the best. When the activity is over, you can remark that they can't leave saying they didn't get anything out of the session.

Notes

_____

_____

_____

_____

_____

_____

_____

_____

_____

_____

Going Nuts

Purpose

Grouping people; Getting to know you; Getting to know you better; Especially for big groups

Group Size

10-100

Level of Physical Activity

Medium

Estimated Time

5-10 minutes

Props

Nut cards, one per participant, one type per group; fast, upbeat music
   Participants will find out who is the nuttiest person in their session as they get into groups and share their nutty experiences. Use this activity anytime during a session when you want to get participants into groups and energize them.

> *"Play" is an essential part of a child's development. I am convinced that the same is true for adults. During play, people get in touch with who they are. So if we wax philosophic about this, maybe, just maybe, we can use our funny, outrageous, or nutty experiences to reach inside and pull out a valuable piece of ourselves. Aha!*

Instructions

1. Create groups of four to ten participants by passing out nut cards and explaining that when the music begins, they should group themselves by "like nuts." In other words, a filbert should find all other filberts and form a group.
2. When groups are formed, explain that we all have had "nutty" experiences. Provide an example of a nutty experience you have had.
3. Instruct participants to share nutty stories with one another, beginning with one "nut" in each group.

Variations

1. When they've finished, ask each group to choose the nuttiest story.
2. If the total group has sixteen participants or fewer, ask each group to report their nuttiest story.

Tips

1. Refer to groups by their nut names for the remainder of the session. For example, one group might be "the walnuts."
2. Give prizes (perhaps a bag of mixed nuts?) to the "nuts" that had the nuttiest stories.

Notes

_____

_____

_____

GOING NUTS ACTIVITY SHEET

filbert	macadamia
pistachio	peanut
Brazil nut	almond
walnut	pecan
hazelnut	cashew

LET'S FACE IT

Purpose	Grouping people; Getting to know you; Pure fun
Group Size	12-40
Level of Physical Activity	Medium
Estimated Time	2-4 minutes
Props	8″ white paper circles, one per table; pictures of facial parts, one per person; transparent tape, one roll per table.

Participants will form groups as they form faces out of the facial parts they are each given when entering the session. Use this activity to group people at tables without a prescribed seating arrangement. This works particularly well if you're mixing people from departments or organizations.

This year I bought my husband a video of My Fair Lady. *I watched it once with him (although he would say I slept through most of it), and again last week with my mother. One of my favorite parts is when Henry Higgins sings, "I've Grown Accustomed to Your Face." The human face is a reflector of the heart.*

Instructions

1. Before participants arrive, put one round circle on each table.
2. As participants enter the room, give each of them one of the facial part pictures.
3. Explain that their task is to find a table in need of their facial part to make a face on the circle. When they find the table, they should tape their facial part to the circle, and sit at that table.
4. Instruct table groups to name their faces when all parts have been filled in.

Variations

1. Give each participant a facial part and ask them to form a group with others who have different parts to create a face—all without talking.
2. Give participants facial parts and ask them to form a group with other people with the same part by walking around the room and pointing to the part.

Tips

1. If you want to mix people from different departments or organizations, give the same facial part, such as a mouth, to each person from a department so they will join different tables.
2. Follow this activity with Create-a-Character.
3. Put the circle at the top of a page or newsprint and instruct groups to fill in bodies.

LET'S FACE IT
ACTIVITY SHEET I

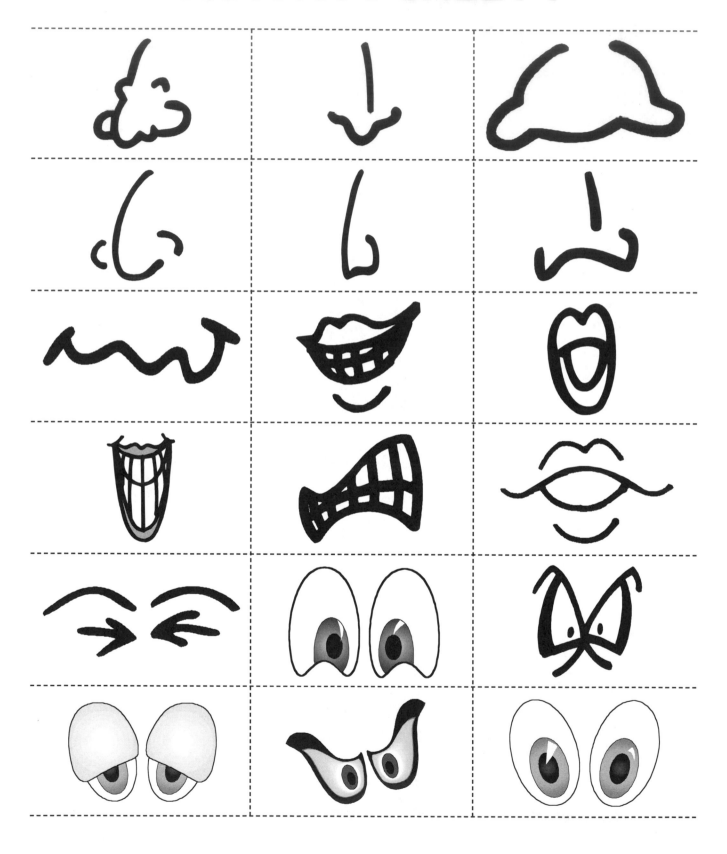

LET'S FACE IT
ACTIVITY SHEET II

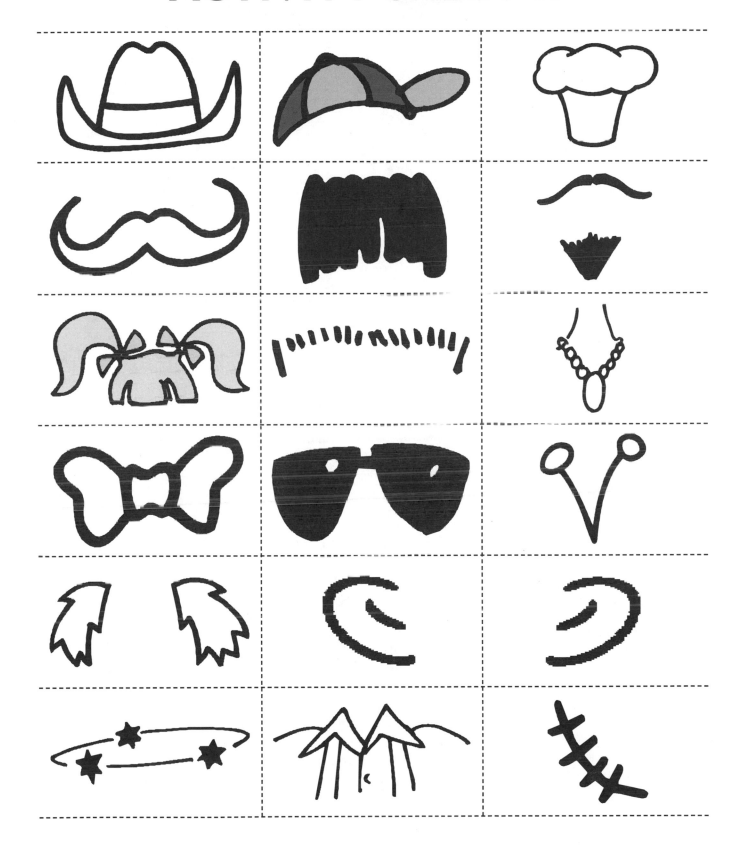

P.A.N.I.C. Club

Purpose   Team building; Grouping people; Getting to know you; Getting to know you better; Introducing a topic; Especially for big groups

Group Size   5-200

Level of Physical Activity   Low

Estimated Time   4-7 minutes

Props   P.A.N.I.C. Club Activity Sheets, one card per participant

This is a way for people to get to know one another by exploring the differences they have. Use it with groups of people who don't know one another, or with those who do for added insight and understanding, or as an introduction to team building or a diversity topic.

> *Have you had the experience of going to a special event or party where you know no one or only one or two people? Welcome to the P.A.N.I.C. Club, where people have absolutely nothing in common! Shortly after we were married, my husband and I attended a dinner at which he was the only person I knew. I became an observer of group behavior for that evening. Here's what happened: Immediately people who knew one another from work began connecting and formed one little group; people who knew each other from a particular neighborhood formed another little group; people who knew each other from past dinner events formed another group; and me and two other individuals moved quickly to the hors d'oeuvres table searching frantically for something to talk about. We were members of the P.A.N.I.C. Club—people with absolutely nothing in common. It worked; at the hors d'oeuvres table we could each contribute a comment about the lavish spread before us and the refreshing tartness of the punch. Voilà!*

Instructions

1. Tell participants to organize themselves into groups of six by finding five other people who have different cards than they do and then standing with them in a circle.
2. Explain that they have all joined the P.A.N.I.C. Club—people with absolutely nothing in common—as noted by the different cards they have.
3. Instruct the group to think of unique characteristics, interests, and experiences, and then take turns sharing those with other members of their group. The goal is to share only characteristics or experiences they think are unique to them.
4. Tell them to take twenty seconds each to describe their uniqueness.

Variations

1. Combine this activity with commonalities and ask people to name one difference and one commonality they have with other members of their group.
2. Ask groups to list names of group members and their unique qualities on a flip chart, and report at the end of the activity.

I often follow this activity with Missing Links.

Tip

Notes

_____

_____

_____

_____

_____

_____

_____

_____

_____

P.A.N.I.C. CLUB
ACTIVITY SHEET

STREET GANGS

Purpose
Grouping people; Introducing a topic; Mental aerobics; Team building; Pure fun

Group Size
10-50

Level of Physical Activity
Medium

Estimated Time
5-10 minutes

Props
Street Gangs Activity Sheets, one card per participant
   This activity groups people into gangs by common street names. The gangs will then be able to make up their own identities. Use this one to group participants and to inspire creativity.

> *Do you think people choose streets to live on because they think the name suits them? Are there really Main Street kinds of people? Or Fiddler's Alley kinds of people? Is Church Street Tavern an oxymoron? How about Maple Terrace Refuse?*

Instructions
1. Give each participant a street name card.
2. Explain to participants that this activity will get them into groups by streets creating "street gangs." For example, there will be a Maple Street Gang and a Church Street Gang.
3. Instruct them to find other participants who are in the same gang and be seated at tables together.
4. Ask each gang to think about their street name, then describe the characteristics of their gang, and design a symbol for it.
5. When groups are finished, ask them to share results with other groups.

Variations
1. Once people are in groups, suggest that they decide on a new street name that better characterizes their group.
2. Use only steps 1 and 2.

Tip
Describe some streets you have lived on or visited.

STREET GANGS
ACTIVITY SHEET

42nd Street	Buena Vista Way
Rodeo Drive	Main Street
Pennsylvania Avenue	Maple Street
Church Street	Buckboard Street
River Road	Fiddler's Alley

THE BIG DIPPER

Purpose   Physical energizer; Grouping people; Team building

Group Size   20-140

**Level of Physical
Activity**   High

Estimated Time   5-10 minutes

Props   The Big Dipper Activity Sheets, one card per participant

   This stellar activity is good for any group as a way for people to connect at the beginning of a program, or to rejuvenate after lunch. Everyone gets a "starring" role as they group together to form constellations.

> *I had wondered why we call family groups "family constellations" until I read the dictionary definition of a constellation: "Any of 88 stellar groups considered to resemble and be named after various mythological characters, inanimate objects, and animals." Just kidding.*

Instructions

1. As people come in, pass out one constellation card to each participant.
2. When all have cards, explain to participants that currently everyone is a star without a formation.
3. Explain that this activity will get people into groups—constellations.
4. Instruct participants to move about the room introducing themselves to people and looking for other participants who share a constellation with them. They may find these people by saying anything other than the name of the constellation. For instance, if they are part of the Big Dipper, they may say, "I'm also found in some punch bowls." They may not use any of the words found in the name of the constellation.
5. Explain that when they find other participants who share their constellation, they should band together.
6. After about two minutes (or when most people have formed groups), explain to participants that groups will now have an opportunity to display their constellations.
7. Ask groups to take turns forming their constellations for the other participants. When they have done so, ask other groups to guess the constellation.

Variations

1. Give participants time to practice their star formations before showing other groups.

2. Put people into groups and ask them to decide on the constellation they want to represent.

Tips

1. Play music with a star or heavenly theme while people are grouping and again when they are forming constellations.
2. Keep participants standing throughout the activity.
3. Part of the humor in this activity comes when participants don't exactly remember the constellation, and so create their own version.
4. Play on their "star" natures.

Notes

_____

_____

_____

_____

_____

_____

_____

_____

_____

THE BIG DIPPER
ACTIVITY SHEET

The Big Dipper

The Little Dipper

Great Bear

Seven Sisters

Leo the Lion

Orion the Hunter

TRAFFIC NOISE

Purpose Grouping people; Physical energizer

Group Size 18-40

Level of Physical Activity Medium

Estimated Time 2-5 minutes

Props Traffic Noise Activity Sheets, one card per person/one vehicle per group

I have found this activity to be a high-energy, fun way to get people into groups at any point during a session when participants are open to a playful moment.

In case you hadn't noticed, different types of vehicles make distinct sounds. Have you ever watched children as they play "driving," moving about making engine noises? They've noticed the difference in sounds. Would you recognize a vehicle by the sound it makes?

Instructions

1. Explain that you are introducing an activity that will organize participants into groups—an activity called Traffic Noise. Tell them that they will be creating traffic in the room.

2. Give each participant a small picture of a type of vehicle. (The number of vehicle types you have should match the number of groups you wish to form.)

3. Invite participants to group themselves by their vehicles' sounds. In other words they should "drive through" the group, imitating the sounds their vehicles make.

4. Explain that when they find other participants who have the same vehicle (because hopefully, they'll be making a similar sound), they should join together, continue "driving around," and listen for other vehicles who are speaking the same language.

5. When all participants are in their vehicle groups, ask each group to make its vehicle sound collectively for the other groups to hear.

Variation If participants in the vehicle group don't know each other well, invite them to introduce themselves, saying where they are from, what they do, etc. If they already know each other well, ask them to talk about the topic of the session or their reasons for participating in the session.

Tip While the groups are making their collective sounds, encourage them to truly get into gear and move like their vehicles move.

TRAFFIC NOISE ACTIVITY SHEET

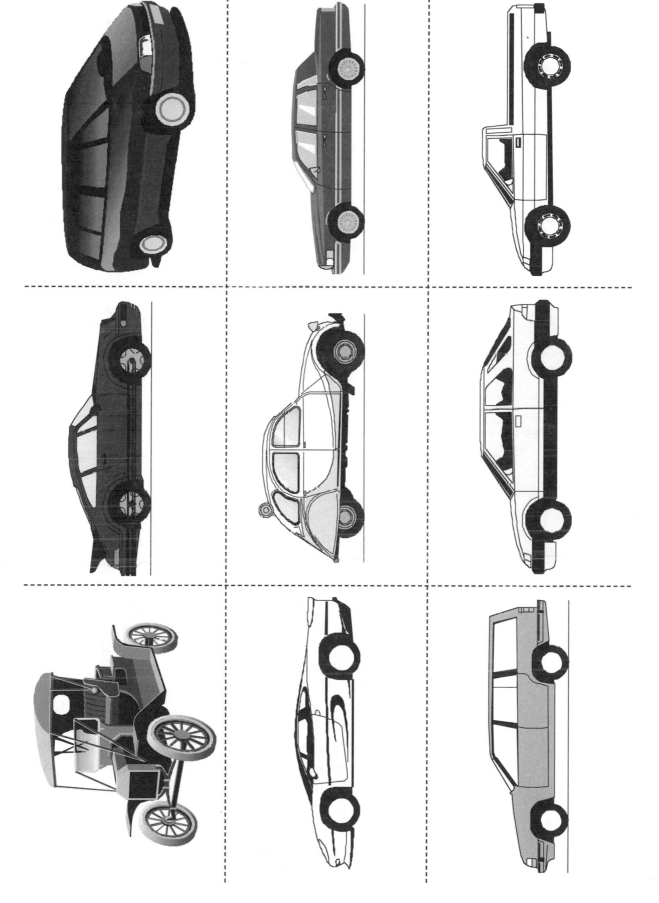

Upset the Fruit Basket

Purpose   Physical energizer; Pure fun; Grouping people; Getting to know you

Group Size   20-60

Level of Physical Activity   High

Estimated Time   3-6 minutes

Props   Upset the Fruit Basket Activity Sheets, one card per participant

Participants will group and regroup themselves according to fruit cards they are given. This is a grouping activity which also serves as an energizer. Use it with groups that enjoy having some fun and that want to spend time mingling.

The original Upset the Fruit Basket is a childhood favorite. Many of you may remember two other favorites: Kick the Can and Spring the Lever. For the benefit of those who don't recognize them, these were the games played before "Dungeons and Dragons" and video games.

Instructions

1. Distribute fruit cards to participants.
2. Organize them so that they are standing in an open area.
3. Explain that the name of this activity is Upset the Fruit Basket.
4. Tell them that there are six kinds of fruit represented in the room.
5. Explain the rules:

   - I will say "Upset the Fruit Basket" and name certain fruits. One person from each of those fruit groups should come together and introduce themselves.
   - The remainder of the participants may form their own groups with the same number of people. For instance, if I say "Upset the Fruit Basket, lemon and banana," all the lemons and bananas should form pairs and introduce themselves. All the other fruits should make random pairs and introduce themselves. If I say, "apples, grapes, pears" those three types of fruits should form groups of three and introduce themselves, while the lemons, strawberries, and bananas get together.

6. Begin the activity using the following categories:
   (1) lemon and banana.
   (2) pear and pear.
   (3) apple, grape, and strawberry.
   (4) lemon, banana, apple, grape, pear, and strawberry.

Variations

1. Ask participants to discuss a certain topic or issue rather than just introducing themselves.
2. Use more exotic fruits such as pomegranate, kiwi, pineapple, coconut, and papaya.

Tips

1. People will group themselves by yelling the name of their fruits or showing their cards.
2. If you want a quieter activity, tell them to group themselves only by holding up their cards and looking for group members.

Notes

_____

_____

_____

_____

_____

_____

_____

_____

_____

UPSET THE FRUIT BASKET
ACTIVITY SHEET

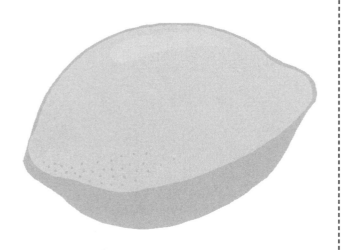
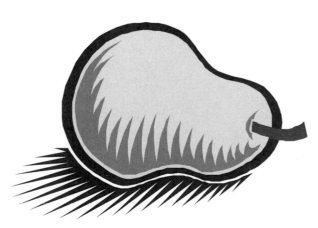

Introducing a Topic

Blockbuster

Purpose   Introducing a topic; Getting closure; Meeting starter

Group Size   6-12

Level of Physical Activity   Medium

Estimated Time   3-10 minutes

Props   Blockbuster Activity Sheet

In this activity participants will describe work situations in different ways using familiar video store categorizing techniques. Use Blockbuster with a small group of people to introduce change or the implementation of a process, for working through a process or issue, or in analyzing supervisory or management situations.

> *"What video do you want?" Can you imagine how many times that question is asked every week in households around the world? Speaking of videos, I'm surprised someone hasn't yet designed a video store/coffee shop. Picture this: Videos are playing in small lounges throughout the coffee shop area. Get your coffee and biscotti and watch a video. Choose the appropriate section to sit in based on your video taste: sections for suspense would be equipped with leaning bars—no need to sit down; horror sections could have grasping bars; the history section would need straight, hard-backed chairs so viewers stay awake; the autobiography section could be lined with mirrors; the biography section could have tables for two or four; drama would require stuffed, formal couches; comedy would have bean bag chairs (no chance of falling off of them); and the juvenile section would have just a carpet, pillows, and stuffed animals to hold. Any ideas for names for these places? How about* Home Video *or* Coffee Couch?

Instructions

1. Organize participants into pairs.
2. Ask how many people frequent video stores to rent videos. Ask them to name the sections.
3. Explain that many programs, situations, or experiences in the workplace could be analyzed using similar categories.
4. Ask them to participate in an example. Choose some organizational event that occurred recently. Ask volunteers to describe briefly the horror that did or could have happened; the drama of the situation; the history that led to the situation; the suspense; the autobiographical angle (as in how it affected them); the biographical angle (how it affected others); and the comedy of the situation. (You may choose to avoid the juvenile aspect, unless someone volunteers it.)

5. Explain that they'll now have an opportunity to do the same with _____.

6. Give each pair one of the video topics and a copy of the Blockbuster Activity Sheet.

7. Tell them they have three minutes to explain the situation within their category.

8. Hear responses from all pairs.

Variations

1. For a larger group, put people in groups of four or five.

2. Ask participants (or groups) to list situations that have occurred at work; then decide which category they best fit into.

Tips

1. This works well for train-the-trainer sessions. Have participants think of the learning experience their participants will have and have them equate it to types of movies.

2. This can be quite humorous or serious business. Know what you're getting into. Set the mood accordingly.

Notes

_____

_____

_____

_____

_____

_____

_____

_____

_____

BLOCKBUSTER ACTIVITY SHEET

Event:

Describe the horror:

Event:

Describe the drama:

Event:

Describe the action:

Event:

Describe the suspense:

Event:

Describe the comedy:

Event:

Describe the sci-fi quality:

BOUNCING BACK

Purpose	Physical energizer; Introducing a topic
Group Size	6-30
Level of Physical Activity	High
Estimated Time	2-3 minutes
Props	One ping-pong ball per table

In this activity, participants bounce a ball back and forth between them, spelling out a word, letter by letter, that relates to your topic each time they hit the ball. Used at the beginning of a program, it stimulates interest; in the middle, it's an energizer; and near the end, it's a reinforcer.

Want a quick, easy, fun, and light-traveling activity for after lunch, before a break, or mid-discussion? Bouncing Back may be just what you need.

Instructions

1. Organize participants at rectangular or round tables of five to ten participants.
2. Give each group a ping-pong ball which will be in their possession for the duration of the meeting or training session.
3. If there is more than one group, instruct them to mark their balls so they don't mix them with the balls of other groups.
4. Explain that they will be using their tables as ping-pong tables and hitting the ball back and forth around the table. To do that each person will need to have a book, pamphlet, or similar item to use as a paddle.
5. If using the activity as an introduction to a topic, explain that you will give them a word that introduces a topic or concept. They then should spell out the word until someone misses, with each hit coinciding with the hitter saying a letter. For example, the hitters might spell out T-E-A-M-W-O-R-K. Play stops and starts over when the ball is missed by a player.
6. Instruct groups to work for a personal group best within a two-minute time frame by seeing how many times they can spell the word before missing the ball.
7. Tell them when to begin.
8. After two minutes, ask each group to report its group best.

Variations

1. Make the activity a group competition: Whichever group spells out the word the most times before dropping the ball wins the game.
2. Use sentences or phrases instead of word spellings.

Tips

1. Use balls of different colors.
2. Use sponge balls or balloons.

CONSTRUCTIVE FEEdback

Purpose   Introducing a topic; Team building

Group Size   6-12

Level of Physical Activity   Medium

Estimated Time   3-6 minutes

Props   Box; 30 pieces of wadded paper

Your participants will value the benefits of constructive feedback as they try to accomplish a goal not possible without feedback from their peers. This activity works best with a small group of people so all can participate. Use it at any time in a program to introduce the value of feedback. Conceptual thinkers will make the most of the activity if you ask them to draw conclusions; concrete thinkers will appreciate the experiential demonstration.

My colleague, Kirby Edmonds, demonstrated this activity for me with a group of six corporate executives. They got more from the experience than we could ever have taught them. Experiences do speak louder than words.

Instructions

1. Ask for one volunteer.
2. Position the volunteer in a standing position and place an empty cardboard box somewhere behind the person, but at some distance.
3. Place the thirty pieces of wadded paper within reach of the volunteer.
4. Explain to the group that their job is to give clues to the volunteer that will help him or her to throw the wads into the cardboard box without turning around. Give examples of clues such as, "A little further to the left."
5. Begin the activity.
6. About halfway through the activity, remind the volunteer of some of the clues given. Ask which ones were actually helpful and why.
7. Keep the activity going until the volunteer has successfully thrown three wads into the cardboard box.
8. Ask the group to describe what is true about feedback based on what occurred in the exercise.

Variation   If you have fewer than seven people and more than five minutes, ask them all to stand in a square and do the activity for each person, one at a time.

Tip

Points to make if they don't come from the group:

- In this situation, feedback was expected and welcome.
- One person could not make the goal in a timely manner without other perspectives and suggestions.
- When the goal was accomplished, everyone participated in enjoying the success.

Notes

_____

_____

_____

_____

_____

_____

_____

_____

_____

CREATE-A-CHARACTER

Purpose   Team building; Getting to know you better; Introducing a topic

Group Size   12-40

Level of Physical Activity   Medium

Estimated Time   3-5 minutes

Props   Flip chart paper, 1 page per group; markers

Use this activity as one way for participants to think about desirable character traits while working with one other person or a group of people. Use it for team building, as an individual activity for personal development, or for pairs or groups to get to know one another better.

> *We've all known people who we would classify as "real characters." That is usually an affectionate term for people who behave outside of expectations, who insert humor in unexpected places, or who seem to add something to the environment that no one else does. What a gift!*

Instructions

1. Organize participants into pairs or small groups.
2. Ask participants to call out some character traits that they truly admire. Record them on a flip chart or chalkboard.
3. Explain that although we cannot make significant changes to some physical characteristics we have, we can make choices about the character traits that we would like to have and display.
4. Tell each group to create the kind of character they would admire by listing six traits this character would have.
5. Ask partners or groups to share their characters.

Variations

1. If the group is small, have participants work individually.
2. Ask participants to tell stories about the "characters" they've met and determine what traits made them "characters."
3. Ask groups to create their own character silhouette on flip chart paper and fill it in with traits.

Tips

1. Good to follow Let's Face It.
2. When I take this a step further, I explore the behaviors that match; for example, the answer to "How do we know if someone is loyal or strong?"

DOGGONE IT

Purpose	Introducing a topic
Group Size	8-30
Level of Physical Activity	Medium
Estimated Time	5 minutes
Props	Flip charts; markers

By drawing on their own experiences with supervisors or bosses, participants in this activity will create a list of behaviors that discourage communication. It is best used at any time during a supervisor or manager training session.

"His bark is bigger than his bite" is a common expression often applied to mammals of the two-legged variety to mean "He's not to be feared." The expression probably came from careful observation of canines. Dogs bark for a variety of reasons, but we often focus on the warning bark: "Stay clear until you prove yourself friendly!" Much like canines, we send signals with clear messages—sometimes even when we don't intend to.

Instructions

1. Organize participants into groups of two to six.
2. Explain to participants that dogs often make noises and gestures that scare people or other animals off; hence the expression, "His bark is bigger than his bite." Explain that supervisors sometimes say or do things that scare employees or other supervisors off—often unintentionally. People then become reluctant to communicate with them.
3. Instruct groups to brainstorm together to create a list of behaviors supervisors use that may often discourage further communication. Ask each group to write its list on its flip chart.
4. After ten minutes, ask each group to report its list of behaviors.

Variations

1. Use for communication skills training.
2. Use for an introduction to programs on establishing behavioral ground rules.
3. Ask for volunteers to act out behaviors.
4. Ask for a list of other animals and their warning behaviors; then ask who else, other than supervisors, need to be aware of their body signals.

Tips

1. Although there is an element of fun in the beginning of this activity, the atmosphere will become more solemn as people discuss specific behaviors.
2. Ignore references from participants who compare their own supervisors to dogs.

Doom & Gloom

Purpose   Introducing a topic; Meeting starter

Group Size   4-40

**Level of Physical
Activity**   Low

Estimated Time 4-5 minutes

Props   Flip chart; markers

Participants identify with this activity as they consider the things they want in life and the reasons they don't have them. Used as an introductory parenthetical, this activity may stave off some negative responses to a new idea, process, or program. Used at the end of a program or meeting, it may inspire open-mindedness or, at the very least, awareness of "prophet of doom and gloom" statements.

> *Don't you hate it when you enthusiastically introduce an idea to someone who immediately (usually before you've even finished) jumps into a "sixteen reasons why it won't work" routine? It happens everywhere. For example, at home: "Do you want to go to a movie tonight?" Spouse's response: "Oh no, it's the first showing; it will be so crowded we won't get a good seat; we don't have a baby-sitter, I forgot to bake the cookies for the PTA meeting tomorrow night, and …" Or at work: "Why don't we create a new system to respond to customer complaints?" Coworker's response: "We tried that before; it won't do any good anyway; why bother when management is the real problem and …"*

Instructions

1. Ask participants to take one minute to think of something that they really want to do. Give examples such as "Build a boat and sail around the world" or "Learn to fly an airplane."
2. Ask for a few examples and write them on a flip chart.
3. Read the examples to the group one at a time.
4. As each example is read, encourage participants to become prophets of "Doom & Gloom" by giving a statement that predicts failure for that idea. For example, if someone suggests learning to fly, a prophet of doom and gloom might respond, "You're too old; it's expensive; and don't forget the insurance hassles!"
5. Make the point that a doom and gloom mentality often inhibits personal and organizational gain.

Variation   Form groups of four and have group members act as prophets of doom and gloom for each other's ideas.

Tips

1. Encourage prophets to be creative with their answers.
2. Follow this activity with Look on the Bright Side.

Fifty Ways

Purpose	Introducing a topic; Pure fun; Getting closure
Group Size	6-20
Level of Physical Activity	Medium
Estimated Time	8-10 minutes
Props	A copy of *The King's Trousers,* a children's book by Robert Kraus (1981. NY: Windmill Books, Simon & Schuster.)

Participants will come up with creative solutions as they think of all the ways to answer a question from a simple children's book. This activity is a great opener or closer to use with leaders and supervisors and with any group for thinking out of the box and for considering all possibilities before closing on one.

I think that sons and daughters, nephews and nieces, grandchildren, and friends' children were given to us so that we can have a second opportunity to read children's books. I find that my favorites in adulthood are not my favorites from childhood. I'm sure there are many reasons for this, but one of the greatest is a matured sense of humor. The books with subtle (and not so subtle) humor are my favorites. Life experiences enhance understanding and grinning.

Instructions

1. Explain to participants that you will read a story that will encourage them to think about alternative patterns of behavior, and what traits separate them from others.
2. Read the story of *The King's Trousers* up to the part where the King says to his servant "Let's think of a new way for me to get into my trousers."
3. Ask participants to partner up and spend two minutes thinking of new ways the king might get into his trousers.
4. After two minutes, ask for all responses.
5. Continue with the story.
6. At the end, ask the group how the king solved the problem.
7. Now ask them how the story relates to their own situation.

Variations

1. Ask a participant to read the story.
2. Ask participants to describe ways they are treated differently because of their position.
3. For supervisors, read the story from beginning to end; ask participants the following question and listen to the responses:

"What makes you different from the people you supervise?" Make the point that you may not be different as a person, but your role is distinctive.

Tip

Have fun with this.

Notes

_____

_____

_____

_____

_____

_____

_____

_____

_____

_____

FIRST THINGS FIRST

Purpose   Self-disclosure; Introducing a topic; Getting closure

Group Size   6-600

Level of Physical Activity   Medium

Estimated Time   4-6 minutes

Props   First Things First Activity Sheets, one per participant

Use this activity in a session where the emphasis is on personal effectiveness, efficiency, or time management. It works particularly well with professionals who feel overextended or stressed by personal or professional commitments.

> *So many of my colleagues regularly express dissatisfaction with the stress and overextension of their professional lives. Is this wrong? Is there an answer? Is there even a question? I'm not sure, but I do agree with many who believe that much of our time is spent* reacting to the expectations *rather than* planning for the importance *in our lives.*

Instructions   1. Ask participants to raise their hands if they feel they work too hard or too much.

2. Ask participants to raise hands if they think that their time is not always spent taking care of priorities first. Ask for examples.

3. Explain to participants that they will now take just a few minutes to highlight priorities by taking a quick check on time usage.

4. Pass out the First Things First Activity Sheets.

5. Ask participants to spend two minutes filling out the sheets, then spend two minutes sharing their sheets with a person sitting near them.

Variation   If it is a small group, ask participants to share with the total group the things they would like to change. Make the observation, if it is the case, that many of them appear to be the same.

Tip   This is not meant to solve problems, just highlight priorities.

FIRST THINGS FIRST
ACTIVITY SHEET

INSTRUCTIONS: Please complete the sheet below by listing your ordinary work activities such as answering correspondence, answering the phone, or managing the budget, as well as your ordinary household activities like making dinner, walking the dog, or folding laundry. Then indicate whether each is a daily, weekly, monthly, or annual activity and assign an estimated time. Finally, place a check under either the Too Much column or the Too Little column. Use this information to help you complete the plan for change section at the bottom of the page.

Personal Data

Name: _____

Role: _____

_____

Date: _____

Activities	% of Time	Too Much	Too Little
Daily			

Activities	% of Time	Too Much	Too Little

Weekly

_____

_____

_____

_____

_____

_____

_____

Monthly

_____

_____

_____

_____

_____

_____

_____

Activities	% of Time	Too Much	Too Little

Yearly

_____

_____

_____

_____

_____

_____

_____

_____

Plan for changes I would like to make:

Personal:

_____

_____

_____

_____

_____

Full Plate

Purpose   Introducing a topic; Getting closure

Group Size   4-20

Level of Physical Activity   Medium

Estimated Time   3-5 minutes each time

Props   One 6″ paper plate per participant; 1/2″ stickers—3 of each color per participant

You'll build on the "full plate" analogy in this activity as participants fill their plates with representative stickers and highlight important information or insights. Use this as a way for people to stay on track during the program, and to concentrate on significant learning points.

> *Yesterday my son sent me an ad for a Daystar Turbo 601: 66MHz with 256K cache for the Mac IIsi, IIci, IIvx, IIva and Performa 600. I asked him why the price was reduced. He told me that it is now half as fast as current upgrades. Symbolic of life in the 90s. My friend, Marty, is visiting with us this weekend while she is attending a conference in Washington. Each day she returns to our house feeling brain-dead. Someone needs to invent a way for us to increase the MHz and K in our brains.*

Instructions

1. Give each participant a plate with dividers for each topic or major point in the session.
2. Give each participant three differently colored stickers that represent each topic.
3. Ask participants to write the topics or major points for the day in each section on the plate.
4. Tell them to assign one sticker color to each category.
5. Give participants the following directions:
   - During the course of the session, you will hear information or gain insights related to each of the topics. When you hear or think of them, place a colored sticker in that section of the plate with one to three words beside it that will trigger that thought for you.
   - When we complete discussion of each topic, you will be asked to share the information or insights with two other people. That will allow you to hear important information or ideas that others experienced, and will reinforce the learning for you.
   - If you hear information that you find relevant, add a sticker or write one to three trigger words in that section on your plate.

- At the end of the session, you will walk away with a Full Plate of understanding related to our topic today.

6. Begin the activity, remembering to stop after each key point; ask participants to find two other people to share with; and give them three minutes to review plates.

Variations

1. Ask them to share discoveries with one other person or a small group
2. Rather than colored stickers, choose picture stickers that are representative of each topic or key point.

Tips

1. Some participants will say they need larger plates or more stickers. Provide additional stickers if it makes sense to do so.
2. You may add an incentive by giving a prize for completed plates.

Notes

_____

_____

_____

_____

_____

_____

_____

_____

_____

LETTERS TO THE EDITOR

Purpose   Introducing a topic; Getting to know you better

Group Size   6-12

**Level of Physical
Activity**   Medium

Estimated Time 3-5 minutes

Props   Paper and pens for participants

        Participants will each draft a letter to the editor on a given topic. This is a great but somewhat risky activity that can add substance to the group's functioning or presentation—or it could open a Pandora's box. Choose a topic that will achieve the purpose you want. I've used this at the beginning of a program, but it may work midway through or at the end as well.

> *Letters to the Editor—a wonderful opportunity to give feedback and defuse hostility, as well as provide a forum for agreement and thanks giving.*

Instructions

1. Explain the topic of the meeting to participants.
2. Explain to them that they may already have some opinions or reactions to the topic and that it is important to share them with others in the group.
3. Ask them to imagine that they've been given an opportunity to write a response to the "editor" of the program or idea.
4. Instruct them to write one-paragraph Letters to the Editor that they would be willing to share with the group. Explain that the letters should reveal their current thoughts and feelings about the topic.
5. Begin the activity.
6. After two minutes, ask them to take turns sharing their letters with the group.

Variations

1. When the letter writing is completed, ask participants to pass the letters around for everyone to read.
2. Choose a topic that relates to the community or the group.

Tips

1. During the sharing time, don't allow for rebuttal or refuting. Establish up front that all will just be listening because they'll be getting more information during the session that may reframe concepts differently for them.
2. Use this to give people the permission they need to be heard, and then to change their minds.

Look on the Bright Side

Purpose   Meeting starter; Introducing a topic

Group Size   4-20

Level of Physical Activity   Low

Estimated Time   5-10 minutes

Props   Flip chart or overhead projector, markers

This activity will be easy for some, difficult for others—depending on your outlook on life. But it opens the brighter side of us all. Use it at the beginning of a program to get buy-in or when introducing a new policy, program, or process.

> *I am an optimistic realist. (Is that an oxymoron?) My husband is an optimistic romanticist. (No incongruity there.) So, 6:00 a.m. in our home goes something like this:*
> *"Good morning sweetheart. Welcome to the day."*
> *"It's raining. I wanted to walk today."*
> *"But this rain will help our roses. Besides, you've been wanting to go to the health club this week."*
> *"I know, but not today; I have other things scheduled. How about your day?"*
> *"It should be a good day. I have a department head meeting first; then a meeting to resolve a dispute with an employee; then regulations to read and a policy to write for tomorrow; plus the start of the budgeting process, a report for the Board to finish, lunch with the board chair, and a resident council meeting to re-examine parking policy and restrictions ..."*

Instructions

1. Explain to participants that this activity is called Look on the Bright Side. They will have an opportunity to take a negative situation and articulate possible positive outcomes.

2. Give an example such as "It's raining, damp, and miserable today."

3. Encourage participants to think and say all the *possible* good that could come from that. (Notice I didn't say *probable*.)

4. Write their responses on the flip chart.

5. Write "I Hate It When" on a blank flip chart page and ask for appropriate examples to record under the heading.

6. When you've gotten several examples, read them aloud one at a time and ask participants to "look on the bright side" by verbalizing possible positive outcomes.

7. When finished, introduce your topic or start your meeting. Good luck!

Variations

1. Ask small groups to do the activity.
2. Have partners do the activity.

Tips

1. Don't just use the topic you want them to buy into.
2. Don't present an overly optimistic front; it may turn some people off.

Notes

_____

_____

_____

_____

_____

_____

_____

_____

_____

_____

ORANGE YOU SMART

Purpose
Team building; Introducing a topic; Getting closure; Physical energizer; Mental aerobics; For non-icebreaker types

Group Size
18-60

Level of Physical Activity
High

Estimated Time
5-8 minutes

Props
Orange You Smart Activity Sheets with letters on them, one set per group. One set includes:

A-3	F-1	K-1	P-1	U-2
B-1	G-2	L-2	R-2	V-1
C-2	H-1	M-2	S-2	W-1
D-1	I-3	N-2	T-3	Y-1
E-4	J-1	O-3		

This activity works like Scrabble with a twist—the words must relate to the topic. When introducing a program or discussion, Orange You Smart gets participants interested and gives you an idea about participant knowledge of the topic. Used at the end of a program, the activity reinforces words and concepts; in the middle of a program, it reinforces and acts as an energizer.

Most of us have played Scrabble or Boggle at some point in our lives. Usually we were alone in thinking of words. [Except, of course, when someone walked by and added their advice. (Why didn't we think of that word?)]

Instructions

1. Organize participants into groups of four to ten.
2. Explain to groups that they will have three minutes to recall words related to the content and arrange the orange disks in Scrabble-like fashion.
3. Explain that when all groups have finished, they will score their arrangements in the following way: *one point* for each letter used (where the letter is used as part of two words, it is counted twice); *two points* for words of five to six letters; and *four points* for words of seven or more letters.
4. Remind them that all words must be related to the content (knowing full well that participants will stretch these parameters to the limit!).
5. Give the signal for them to begin.
6. After three minutes, ask groups to tally the results.
7. Ask each group to report its words (reinforcement) and its scores.

Variations

1. Using magic marker, write letters on oranges—yes, the fruit! They're fun, they roll around, and they smell great!
2. Give them a second chance at another point during the program.
3. For better results, increase the time allotted.

Tips

1. Build on the intellectual prowess and competitive drive of participants in your introduction.
2. Sometimes I have participants work on tables, sometimes on the floor.

Notes

_____

_____

_____

_____

_____

_____

_____

_____

_____

_____

ORANGE YOU SMART ACTIVITY SHEET

Pictures Don't Lie

Purpose   Introducing a topic; Team building

Group Size   2-40

**Level of Physical
Activity**   Low

Estimated Time   3-5 minutes

Props   One picture for each group (preferably a humorous picture that includes people interacting)

In this activity, participants realize the role *assumptions* play in our lives. They will individually analyze a picture, then compare their assumptions with those of the other group members. I've used it with any type of group and at any point during a program. It's simple in concept and works every time.

> *Is this familiar: "Oh, I'm sorry. I thought you meant ..."? Or how's this one: "Oh, I'm sorry. I thought you were going to ..."? Whether we're dealing with situations or people, we all have a tendency to use prior knowledge and experience to form assumptions that may not be accurate. The good news is, we have many successful lawyers in this country. The bad news is ... well, you figure it out.*

Instructions

1. Organize participants into groups of two to six.
2. Give each group a picture.
3. Tell groups they will have one minute to list the things they see happening in the picture.
4. When the lists are completed, explain that we all have a tendency to make assumptions about people and situations rather than sticking to facts. Some of the time, this is helpful; at other times, it creates difficulties.
5. Instruct each group to read each statement on its combined list and determine whether it is a statement of fact or an assumption, marking each statement with an F for fact or an A for assumption.
6. When groups have finished or after about two minutes, ask participants for observations about the activity.

Variations

1. Give all participants the same picture and let the groups react to each others' lists.
2. If your total group has fifteen participants or fewer, have them complete the activity as one group.
3. Use a written description of an incident instead of a picture.

Tips

1. This is a great icebreaker for topics like interviewing, investigating, and supervisory coaching and training.
2. Encourage participants to engage in light argument about which are statements of fact and which are assumptions.

Notes

_____

_____

_____

_____

_____

_____

_____

_____

_____

_____

PIECE BY PIECE

Purpose
Introducing a topic; Team building; Pure fun; Getting closure; Grouping people

Group Size
8-40

Level of Physical Activity
High

Estimated Time
6-10 minutes

Props
One 50-piece puzzle per group of four
    Participants enjoy this activity because it engages them in cooperation quickly. Use it at any time to make a point about interdependence, the necessity of everyone's input, or the importance of regular communication; as an activity of competition; or just for the fun of it.

> *At a garage sale recently we put about twenty-two jigsaw puzzles on the block. I hated to do it; puzzles are like books—they're easy to love. About ten puzzles are still on the shelf. You know, the ones with meaning: the puzzle with the picture of a water wheel from my college alma mater; the Monet puzzle that is a remembrance of a trip to Paris; the music puzzle given to my son who played trumpet in the band; and on and on.*

Instructions
1. Divide the pieces from each puzzle into four small bags.
2. Put one complete puzzle—four bags—on each table.
3. Organize participants into groups of four.
4. Tell each participant to take a bag.
5. Explain that they are going to put a puzzle together with their tablemates but they have to follow these instructions closely :
   - In your groups, you each have pieces that make up one puzzle.
   - Begin by putting your puzzle pieces together by alternating turns. One person should put down one piece, then the next person should put down the next, etc. You should do this without talking or touching one another's pieces.
6. After one minute, give these instructions:
   - Continue taking turns putting down pieces in silence, but you now may touch one another's pieces.
7. After one more minute, give this instruction:
   - You will have two minutes to finish putting the puzzle together any way you choose. Talking is permitted during this last two minutes.
8. After the final two minutes, stop the puzzle-making.

9. Ask participants for observations and insights they gained from the activity.

Variations

1. Have groups put puzzles together without restrictions. Ask participants to explain how they cooperated and collaborated.
2. Give groups the same puzzles and make completion of the activity competitive.
3. Allow groups to finish their puzzles before beginning the discussion, or after the discussion.

Tips

1. After asking for participant insights, include these points if they've been left out:
   - We often work in isolation without involving others whose pieces need to fit into the puzzle.
   - We often use only one mode of communication to get something done.
   - When we involve one another, using all of the pieces and communicating in many different ways, we have a greater chance for successful completion of the project.
2. Choose puzzles that have messages or pictures that relate to the content of the program or to the group in some way.

Notes

_____

_____

_____

_____

_____

QUESTIONABLE CONVERSATION

Purpose Getting to know you; Getting to know you better; Introducing a topic

Group Size 8-40

Level of Physical Activity Medium

Estimated Time 10-20 minutes

Props Questionable Conversation Activity Sheets, one card per participant

Participants will use questions they have chosen to gain information about partners. Used for introductions, this activity works best at the beginning of a session to provide structure for conversations. Used as an introduction to questioning skills or open and closed questions, this activity focuses participants on types of questions and the importance of structuring questions before asking.

Philosophers are respected because they ask questions; politicians are respected because they give answers.

Instructions
1. Organize participants into duos.
2. Explain to participants that they will now have an opportunity to find out about their partners by asking both closed and open-ended questions.
3. Give each person a Questions Card. Explain that each card contains two kinds of sample questions; one is a closed question; the other is open.
4. Explain that the task is to write down two more of each type of question. The challenge is to use questions that will give them the kind of information they would like to know about their partners.
5. Tell them they have one minute to complete the questions.
6. After one minute, explain that they will now have two minutes to ask their partners the questions. Caution them to allow for each partner to ask questions and get answers during those two minutes.

Variation Ask participants to write down questions they would like to be asked, and instruct them to exchange cards with their partners to do the activity.

Tips
1. Use this with groups who know one another well and ask them to think of questions that they could ask to get additional information about a person.
2. Begin the activity by bringing one participant to the front of the room and allowing other participants to ask open and closed questions to get information. (Or, if you are trusting, ask participants to ask you questions.)

QUESTIONABLE CONVERSATION ACTIVITY SHEET

OPEN QUESTION

An open question is one that encourages divergent, thoughtful responses. Answers would necessarily be several sentences in length and would generally encourage discussion. Example of an open question:

1. What aspects of your job give you the most satisfaction?

CLOSED QUESTION

A closed question is one that only requires a one-word or yes or no answer. Example of a closed question:

2. Do you enjoy your current job? (Yes or No answer only)

RECIPE FOR TEAMWORK

Purpose   Team building; Introducing a topic; Getting closure

Group Size   8-40

Level of Physical Activity   High

Estimated Time   15-20 minutes

Props   Recipe sheets, one per participant

Participants will love the idea of creating a recipe for success, particularly if you position the activity before a morning or afternoon break.

> *We're always looking for a recipe for success—a clean, clear, specific set of instructions that will lead to achievement, money, fame, and benevolence, every time, without fail. Well, it worked for Mrs. Fields, Ben and Jerry, and Paul Newman didn't it? So why not us?*

Instructions

1. Organize participants into groups.
2. Explain that there are elements to team building that are essential to success—just as there are key ingredients in _____ (list the recipe of your choice). One of the reasons teams fail is that they have not identified, measured, and folded in the ingredients for success.
3. Give participants recipes for _____.
4. Ask them to notice each ingredient, the qualities it possesses that add to the finished product, and the order and way it is added.
5. Instruct them to play on the "recipe for success" analogy by substituting ingredients for teamwork, naming the ingredient, its quantity, the value it adds to the mix, the time when it's added, and the manner of insertion. Tell them they'll have five minutes.
6. After five minutes, ask groups to read their "recipes for success" aloud.

Variations

1. Assign ingredients to individuals or groups.
2. Offer a dietetic version or fruit substitute version and have the groups compare the differences. Then use the analogy of regular and fat-free desserts—different ingredients bringing different results.
3. Use another analogy such as a "blueprint for success."

Tip   Give each student a tasty sample from whatever recipe you used as an example, such as homemade cookies.

SENSORY EXPRESSION

Purpose   Introducing a topic; Getting closure; Pure fun

Group Size   8-20

**Level of Physical
Activity**   Low

Estimated Time   3-5 minutes

Props   Large box of items that will stimulate the senses, including objects such as tea bags, air freshener, scented candle, chocolate scratch 'n sniff stickers, hand lotion, coffee beans, maple syrup lollipop, small cedar box, an orange peel, rubber raincoat or galoshes, inked stamp

Use this activity to make the point that we must use more than one "sense" to make an accurate assessment when solving problems, conducting investigations, and supervising people.

> *In my ongoing work in a variety of organizations, I find that a consistent deterrent to dealing effectively with behavior and technical problems is an unwillingness to use all senses to analyze a situation and to determine potential solutions. Some of those senses include business sense, historical sense, personal sense, financial sense, sense of time and space, relational sense, others' sense, ethical sense, practical sense, sense of fit, sense of observation, sense of propriety, sense of levity, and sixth sense.*

Instructions
1. Before your session begins, collect your sensory articles and put them in a box.
2. Explain that the box contains items that one person will have an opportunity to identify just by using their senses.
3. Ask for one volunteer and blindfold that person.
4. Remove the items from the box one at a time. Hold an item up to the volunteer with instructions to smell the item to guess what it is. If the guess is correct, affirm it and put that item in one place. If the guess is incorrect, say so, put that item in another place, and hold up the next item.
5. When you've been through each item, give the volunteer another chance to guess the missed items by hearing them one at a time (shake near the ear). Once again, if the guess is incorrect, say so, put that item aside, and hold up the next item.
6. Next time around, place each unidentified item on the table one at a time in front of the volunteer and ask the person to feel the item to determine what it is.
7. For the final step, remove the blindfold.
8. When you're finished, make the point that in our desire to come up with an answer, we often jump to conclusions based on our first

sensory experience. We frequently hear comments like: "I could tell she did it from the expression on her face," or "I heard it was the best way to go." The point is that a situation is not always what it appears to be at first glance. Therefore it is important to use all possible senses before forming conclusions, even if only for confirmation about the decision.

Variation

Use about half of the items on the first volunteer, then ask for a second volunteer and proceed in the same way with the remaining items.

Tips

1. This can and should be a lot of fun.
2. Mix items that are easy to guess by smelling with others that could not possibly be guessed by the nose only.

Notes

_____

_____

_____

_____

_____

_____

_____

_____

_____

_____

Show and Hide

Purpose

Introducing a topic; Getting closure; Physical energizer; Energizing a long, dry presentation

Group Size

10-40

Level of Physical Activity

High

Estimated Time

2-4 minutes

Props

10 large cards with emotions written on them

Participants will enjoy the expressions of others in this activity of showing and hiding emotions. Use it during supervisory, customer service, or communications skills training.

> *One of the most useful skills a person can acquire is the ability to remain objective in verbal and body language when one chooses to. When I've been asked which skills are the most important for a manager to learn, I've said "facilitation skills" for that reason. As a facilitator one learns to remove personal emotional content and to listen and respond to all people and situations objectively.*

Instructions

1. Before the session begins, choose emotions from the following list or decide on your own and write ten of them on large index cards, card stock, or posterboard: disappointment, anger, appreciation, resentment, happiness, concern, disbelief, annoyance, enthusiasm, frustration, stress, and relief.

2. Ask participants to stand.

3. Explain to participants that in their given jobs, they will need to show and hide emotions—depending on the situation. Sometimes it is important for them to let the listener "hear" what they are truly feeling. At other times, it is very important that they appear to be objective, hiding that display of emotion.

4. Ask them for examples of emotions they may feel in their jobs. Now ask them for examples of situations when it is important to show emotions, and those in which it is crucial not to display emotions.

5. Remind participants that besides the words they speak, they use facial expressions and body language that readily display their emotions. Explain that in this activity they will practice showing or hiding facial and body expressions of emotions.

6. Tell them that you will hold up a card and either say "Show _____ (the emotion on the card)" or "Hide _____ (the emotion on the card)". They should

demonstrate the emotion through facial and body expressions, and look around at others' display of emotion.

7. Begin the activity by holding up a sign and saying "Show _____" or "Hide _____."

Variations

1. Have participants suggest the emotions they might use and pull from that list for the activity.
2. Ask for volunteers to lead the activity.
3. Have participants turn toward the center of the room so people will be looking at one another.
4. Play this like Simon Says. Participants show emotions when you call out the name of an emotion, unless you say "hide" before the emotion.

Tips

1. This activity is a lot of fun if the mood is set that way.
2. Encourage people to overdramatize their emotions by modeling one first.

Notes

_____

_____

_____

_____

_____

_____

_____

_____

_____

Spinning an Ideal Yarn

Purpose	Team building; Introducing a topic; Getting closure
Group Size	6-24
Level of Physical Activity	High
Estimated Time	3-6 minutes
Props	Ball of yarn

Participants will take turns adding to the "story" of an ideal organization. Use this at the beginning of a session for people to hear from one another and frame a picture of the possible future; during the session to energize participants; or at the end of the session to gain closure.

> *Many organizations continue to pass the ball without thinking about and designing for ultimate outcomes of decisions and events.*

Instructions

1. Ask everyone to stand in a circle.
2. Tell them the opportunity in this activity is to create a story of an ideal organization (or team).
3. Explain that one person will begin the yarn by telling one thing that would happen in this "ideal organization," for example: "In this organization, everyone understands and is committed to the vision."
4. Explain that the first person will then pass the ball of yarn to the next person to add to the story. This continues until everyone has added to the "yarn."

Variation

Have the story relate to one individual's experience in this ideal organization.

Tips

1. The ball can be passed from person to person in a circlular manner, or passed to the next person who has an idea to form a web.
2. As the story builds, participants get more ideas; don't limit the yarn to one time around unless you have many people.

The Domino Challenge

Purpose   Team building; Introducing a topic; Pure fun

Group Size   6-12

**Level of Physical
Activity**   High

Estimated Time   6-10 minutes

Props   Dominoes (at least 96)

Many conclusions, watch-outs, and suggestions come from this activity in which everyone plays a different role in creating a successful domino effect. This works well with groups that enjoy a challenge and strategizing. Use it before launching a new system or as the introduction to a planning session.

> *When my in-laws, Walt and Goldie, came to visit last year, we rediscovered dominoes. By the third night of their visit, we had some hot and heavy competition going. Dominoes seems like a simple game, but everyone has their own rules—that's where the challenge comes in.*

Instructions

1. Divide participants into three teams: Implementers (two people), Builders (half the group), and Proposers (all the rest).
2. Explain that the task of the group is to successfully complete one run of all dominoes (meaning each falls in order). The Proposers will design the route, the Builders will build the pattern, and the Implementers will get the dominoes going.
3. Explain that the group has five minutes to achieve its goal.
4. Begin the activity.
5. After five minutes, or when the group has successfully achieved its goal, debrief the activity by asking the following question and allowing the group to respond:

"How is this activity like the business task before us?"

Variations

1. Create a competitive event with two or more groups.
2. Give small teams their tasks (design the pathway, set up the dominoes, and start the dominoes falling) and ask them after the event for comparable organizational groups or roles.

Tips

1. Since you've given them only the completion time, the groups will urge each other on to meet the deadline—like groups in organizations.
2. If you allow them to make the analogies at the end, they'll gain more relevant insight.

THE TORTOISE AND THE HARE

Purpose   Introducing a topic; For non-icebreaker types

Group Size   6-30

**Level of Physical
Activity**   Medium

Estimated Time   5-7 minutes

Props   Flip chart paper, one piece per group posted on walls or easels, markers, The Tortoise and the Hare Activity Sheet

      Use this activity as an introduction to decision making or problem solving to help participants recognize when it is necessary to take time in decision making or problem solving to do research, consider options, and get buy-in.

> *We have all witnessed a group go through power and control struggles that cost time, money, and integrity, because they didn't see the value in reaching consensus up front on a crucial issue. You know the familiar saying, "Pay me now, or pay me later."*

Instructions

1. Organize participants into groups of two to five around posted flip chart paper.

2. Ask each group to designate a Scribe for the group.

3. Tell groups to generate every type of decision (or problem, depending on the topic) that currently exists in their departments (or company). Explain that they have one minute to complete the list.

4. After one minute, introduce the tortoise and the hare by showing the picture. Ask a volunteer to tell the fable.

5. Instruct them to take one minute to apply the tortoise and the hare test to each of the decision or problem situations they listed in the following way:

   ■ They should discuss each one and make a group decision about whether it warrants a quick decision or a decision that requires a more time-consuming, methodical approach.

   ■ As they agree on each, they should draw a tortoise or a hare in front of it.

6. When one minute is up, ask each group to list on chart paper the reasons for choosing the tortoise for some; then do the same for the hare group.

7. After about two minutes, ask each group to report its reasons for choosing tortoise or hare. Make sure the following points are covered:

- Decisions and problems need tortoise treatment if they require the involvement of many people for commitment, historical or informative research, or more options.
- Decisions and problems deserve hare treatment if they have small stakes, have a tight time frame, are emergencies, do not warrant additional research, or have limited options.

Variations

1. Develop sheets for people to use at their tables.
2. If time permits, ask each group to share its lists, and allow for dialogue.

Tip

To create interest, make a transparency of the picture and project it before you begin the activity.

Notes

_____

_____

_____

_____

_____

_____

_____

_____

_____

_____

THE TORTOISE AND THE HARE ACTIVITY SHEET

Up, Down, All Around the Town

Purpose Team building; Introducing a topic; Grouping people

Group Size 12-60

Level of Physical Activity Medium

Estimated Time 4-6 minutes

Props Up, Down, All Around the Town Activity Sheet, one card per person, one building per group

In this activity, participants get a brief chance to experience community living in Smalltown. It works best near the beginning of a program to group people, and at any time to introduce a topic on building community, ethics, or service orientation.

Ah, Smalltown, U.S.A.! At one time or another, many of us think about the lifestyle in a small community where people know each other and take pride in community achievements. Some of us have had that experience, and some of us are still there.

Instructions

1. Pass out cards to participants that are in the shape of public community buildings.
2. Ask participants to group themselves from the public building pictures they received.
3. Tell groups they have one minute in their groups to generate a list of all the services their organizations offer to the community.
4. After one minute, invite each group to quickly report its services.

Variations

1. Ask participants to get into groups by making a sound associated with the community organization (e.g., police or fire siren, church bell) and then finding others making a similar sound, hopefully representing the same organization.
2. Give formed groups two minutes to decide on a sound associated with their community organization. Ask them to share their sounds with the total group.

Tips

1. This is a great introduction to a community service session or to introduce ethics or systems.
2. If participants in the group already serve in one of these capacities (e.g., fire service, clergy, etc.), ask them to become a member of a different group.
3. This activity may be light and fun or more solemn. Your demeanor will set the stage.

UP, DOWN, ALL AROUND THE TOWN ACTIVITY SHEET

Courthouse

 Firehall

 Church

School

Police Station

 Hospital

YOUR HEART ON YOUR SLEEVE

Purpose

Introducing a topic; Getting closure; Physical energizer; Pure fun; Energizing a long, dry presentation

Group Size

8-40

Level of Physical Activity

Medium

Estimated Time

4-5 minutes

Props

Your Heart on Your Sleeve Activity Sheet, 8 cards per partner group

Participants will guess each other's emotions by watching for nonverbal cues. This activity can be used effectively to get ideas for a particular goal or problem, as a mental energizer, or as a way for participants to get to know one another better. Some groups are very goal directed; make it specific for them.

Many people in business have learned not to wear their hearts on their sleeves. And I'm sure that's a good thing, but not always. Compassion and empathy come from the heart.

Instructions

1. Make emotion cards for each partner group by writing eight different emotions on eight cards numbered 1 to 8.

2. Organize participants into pairs.

3. Give one participant in each pair a set of odd-numbered cards and the partner a set of the even-numbered cards.

4. Ask participants to stand and face their partners.

5. Explain that many times, whether we intend to or not, we "wear our hearts on our sleeves," meaning that others get an impression from our body language and facial expressions about how we think and feel at the moment. Explain that this is both good and bad. It is good when we want to show that emotion; it is bad when we want to show a particular feeling and don't, or when we don't want to convey a particular feeling and do—in other words, when our thoughts and hearts don't match what we're showing.

6. Tell them that this activity will remind them about "wearing their hearts on their sleeves."

7. Explain the rules:

   - The participants who have the #1 card in each pair will go first. Your job is to show emotion #1 through facial and body expressions without stating it directly.

   - Your partners must now guess emotion #1.

   - Then those holding the #2 emotion cards will display that emotion, while your partners try to name the emotion.

- Continue the activity until you have each guessed the emotions written on each other's cards.
- You will have two minutes for this portion of the activity.

8. Begin the activity.

Variation

Ask participants to think of emotions they feel and demonstrate them.

Tip

Begin by demonstrating a couple of emotions and having participants guess them.

Notes

_____

_____

_____

_____

_____

_____

_____

_____

_____

YOUR HEART ON YOUR SLEEVE
ACTIVITY SHEET

1	2
3	4
5	6
7	8

MEETING STARTERS

Auto Biography

Purpose   Meeting starter; Getting to know you better; Introducing a topic

Group Size   2-150

**Level of Physical
Activity**   Low

Estimated Time   10 minutes

Props   None

Using their first cars as a source of inspiration, participants will get in the mood to think about the benefits of your meeting or program with this activity. This is best used following an explanation of the agenda.

Most people (particularly those of the middle-aged variety) have fond memories of their first cars, and enjoy talking or reminiscing about them. They will smile broadly while describing the car in detail, usually ending with a sentence like, "It was so cool...."

Instructions

1. Ask participants to find a partner and introduce themselves.
2. When everyone has a partner, ask them to take two minutes to describe their very first cars to one another by responding to the following statements:
   - Describe the appearance and other *features* of the car.
   - Describe what the car meant to you and did for you.
3. When five minutes are up, explain to participants that the meeting or training program is about _____ (your topic). But for them to really make their time worthwhile, they need to recognize how this meeting can do something for them.
4. With the same partners, ask the participants to explain to each other what they believe the meeting will do for them in terms of knowing, experiencing, feeling, and participating.
5. After five minutes, ask for volunteers to report.

Variations

1. If the group is small, have each pair report on its discussion at the end.
2. At the end of a meeting or program, have participants return to these topics and first explain how they thought they could benefit, then add specifics to the original responses.

Tip   Start the activity by lavishly describing your own first car.

Building an Agenda

Purpose	Physical energizer; Introducing a topic; Meeting starter
Group Size	6-20
Level of Physical Activity	Medium-High
Estimated Time	3-5 minutes
Props	Agenda items in envelopes, blank sheets of paper or posterboard for building the agenda

This activity is particularly good if you have asked participants to help build the agenda in advance of the session. Use Building an Agenda to get people active and focused in the beginning.

> *Agendas. Everyone has them. Each person's was built in a different way. They help us succeed and they help us stay stuck. The key is in knowing when and how to stick to our agendas. It's hard to admit that someone else's agenda is equal to or better than our own. People don't battle; agendas do.*

Instructions

1. Before the session, write out the agenda on a piece of flip chart paper or other large sheet of paper.
2. Cut the agenda into separate items.
3. Now cut up each item into many pieces and put the pieces from each item into an envelope.
4. When the session begins, explain that you need help from the group to build the agenda.
5. Organize participants into groups of two to four.
6. Give each group an item envelope and ask them to tape the pieces together to create an agenda item.
7. In order, ask groups to come up and insert their items on a blank sheet of paper entitled "Agenda."

Variations

1. Give each participant or group an envelope containing an 8½" × 11" or a 5" × 7" agenda cut into puzzle pieces. Ask them to put together the agenda for themselves.
2. Use this for grouping by giving participants pieces and asking them to find the other people with pieces of their puzzle to sit with.

Tips

1. Explain that the purpose of this activity is to have them active in the beginning of the session, to illustrate that the agenda actually was built by using pieces of information from each of them, or to demonstrate that the information they'll be dealing with in the session will help them piece together their roles or processes.
2. Make agenda items attractive.

CAN IT!

Purpose
Meeting starter; Introducing a topic; Getting closure

Group Size
8-40

Level of Physical Activity
Medium

Estimated Time
3-5 minutes

Props
One basket, candy jar, and plenty of scrap paper per participant table

Having participants write out what's bothering them, then "can it" makes for a good quick way to get negative thoughts out on the table (literally!) at the beginning of a session; people can then make more room for positive thoughts. Use this sparingly—it's best when you feel people will resist what's on the agenda or have so much going on that they will not be able to concentrate.

In the book, 1,001 Logical Laws, Accurate Axioms, Profound Principles, Trusty Truisms, Homey Homilies, Colorful Corollaries, Quotable Quotes, and Rambunctious Ruminations For All Walks of Life,* *there's a section called "The Cynic's Reflection: I'd be a pessimist, but it wouldn't work anyway."*

Instructions

1. Put baskets on each of the participant tables.
2. Tell participants that it is important that they get rid of negative thoughts and keep an open, clear mind for the day in order to get something positive from the session.
3. Explain that the next activity is worth points and prizes (since giving up some of our most prized possessions can be difficult).
4. Explain the agenda or topic for the session.
5. Ask participants to take some scrap paper from the table and write one preconceived or negative thought that they may be having on each piece. It can be any thought that may interfere with their objective analysis of issues during the day.
6. Give participants about two minutes to write down their negative thoughts and perceptions, then instruct them to wad up the trash papers and throw them in the basket on the table one by one. If they miss the basket, they should try again. They should keep track of the number of trash pieces they throw.
7. As they finish, tell them they can take as many pieces of candy from a candy jar as the number of "trash ideas" they threw away.

*Compiled by Peers, John (1979) *1,001 Logical Laws, Accurate Axioms, Profound Principles, Trusty Truisms, Homey Homilies, Colorful Corollaries, Quotable Quotes, and Rambunctious Ruminations For All Walks of Life.* New York: Fawcett Gold Medal, Ballantine Books.

8. Encourage them to write down each negative thought as it comes to them, throw it in the basket, then reward themselves with a piece of candy.

Variations

1. Put one trash can in a single location and ask participants to walk to the can to rid themselves of trash.
2. Use this as an activity to get rid of preconceived ideas or judgments that are not necessarily negative.
3. Use this to get rid of personal distractions that participants are dealing with.

Tip

The type of candy should reflect the seriousness of the negativity. For example, thoughts that aren't very negative would be worth cheap, hard candy, while really hostile thoughts rate Godiva chocolates. (Negativity that is immovable may need watches, cameras, and video recorders!)

Notes

_____

_____

_____

_____

_____

_____

_____

_____

_____

HERE WE ARE

Purpose

Getting to know you better; Team building; Meeting starter; Introducing a topic; For non-icebreaker types

Group Size

10-20

Level of Physical Activity

Medium

Estimated Time

4-8 minutes

Props

Here We Are Activity Sheets

This is a low-risk activity for participants to find out more about one another, to give you, the leader, information about the expectations of participants, and to encourage participants to take responsibility during the session.

If you lead meetings, deliver speeches, or deliver training, you know there's a chance that at least once in your life you'll come across a person who is sorry they are in your session. We seasoned veterans look for the signs early on: fidgeting, exasperated sighs, nonconformance, belligerence, and so on. Since I have experienced the feeling of being locked into a session that has no meaning or relevance for me, I usually approach such attendees early in the session to find out if they had other expectations, ask what we might do to adjust the session, or at least let them know that I understand. (By the way, I usually remind them that leaving is an option—when it is.) But this fall, I was totally fooled. I conducted a session at a conference that I thought went very well: every person voluntarily and actively participated, everyone smiled, and everyone thanked me profusely at the end. That evening, I read the class evaluations and one of them jumped out at me. The participant had responded that he got nothing from the session, although he thought the session itself was great. The next day, this person came up to me and said, "I suppose by now you've read the evaluations and realized which one was mine. I just wanted to make sure you realized that I really appreciated your delivery. The topic just wasn't the one I wanted." I asked him why he stayed. He said he used it as a time to relax, which he desperately needed, and to get to know the other participants. After he left I felt better. He did get something out of it.

Instructions

1. Organize participants into pairs.
2. Explain that this activity will help them discover what their partners would like to get from the session.
3. Pass out Here We Are Activity Sheets. Tell participants they have two minutes each to interview their partners and write down pertinent information.

4. When they finish, ask each person to tell the rest of the group the partner's name and information from items 2, 3, or 4.

Variations

1. Make up your own interview sheets based on the topic and history of the group members.
2. Close the activity by asking each person, "Give one reason why your partner should be a part of the session."
3. For large groups, eliminate step 4.

Tip

You may want to choose which item—2, 3, or 4—participants report, and capture the information on a flip chart.

Notes

_____

_____

_____

_____

_____

_____

_____

_____

_____

_____

HERE WE ARE ACTIVITY SHEET

Name _____

Interviewee name _____

1. Please state your name, company, current position, and length of time in that position.

2. What are your goals for the session?

3. How do you think this session will benefit you and others?

4. What assets do you have that could be helpful in this session?

5. What liabilities do you have that will prevent you from making the most of this session?

6. What will you contribute to this session?

7. How can I help you achieve your goals for this session?

I Spied

Purpose	Meeting starter; Team building; Introducing a topic; Energizing a long, dry presentation
Group Size	10-20
Level of Physical Activity	Low
Estimated Time	2-3 minutes each time
Props	None

Participants will be more focused on the session as they hope to "spy" certain behaviors and activities. This activity works particularly well when a group of people are already focusing on behaviors, such as when a team is working on ground rules for meetings, a group is working on recognition and reward programs, or supervisors are thinking about giving specific and regular positive feedback.

Years ago I made a conscious decision to begin telling people when I appreciated something they did. Some simple examples: when a person at a checkout is pleasant; when a family member makes me laugh; when my husband shows consideration for someone in need; when a coworker shows enthusiasm for a project. No one seems to object, and I tend to look at the positive much more than I used to. I guess everyone wins.

Instructions

1. Explain to participants that during the course of the session they are to notice when people in the group contribute to the success of the session by giving ideas; listening to others; giving feedback; asking relevant questions; complimenting someone; or using any other behavior that contributes to comfort, learning, and enjoyment.

2. Explain that periodically during the session, you will stop and lead them in a session called I Spied, when they will each have the opportunity to name people and behaviors beginning with the phrase "I spied...." For example, a participant might say, "I spied Lisa supporting Chris's idea of developing new systems by asking questions and showing enthusiasm."

3. Begin by saying, "I already spied ..." and complete the thought with any positive behavior you noticed from someone in the session.

Variations

1. Take the emphasis away from persons and focus it on behavior by asking them to say "I spied ..." and completing the thought with a behavior but no name.

2. Organize participants into partners. Periodically ask them to play I Spied with one another.

Tip

Include yourself in the activity each time by talking about things you spied.

It's a Toss Up

Purpose   Meeting starter; Introducing a topic

Group Size   6-15

**Level of Physical
Activity**   High

Estimated Time Ongoing

Props   Koosh™ ball, bean bag ball, or other soft throwing object

Participants enjoy throwing a ball to someone who has a thought or idea. Use this activity when you have a topic or idea-generating session that will generate a host of varying opinions. It is a good way to keep control of discussion and reminds participants to allow others to have their complete say.

We have wonderful friends whose family style allows for one to interrupt during the course of any given conversation whenever one has something to interject. All interruptions are accepted and respected. It took me half an evening to catch on; if you want to say anything, interrupt knowing that the first few words you utter are the most important because the others may never get spoken. My husband is still working on it. At first he never spoke. Now his unique contribution to the group is starting conversations for everyone else to finish.

Instructions   1. Explain to participants that there will be times during the meeting or session when people are called upon to express opinions or generate ideas. The natural tendency during those times is for people not to listen to one another or to cut one another off mentally or verbally because of the allegiance to their own ideas or opinions.

2. Explain that in order to make sure that all ideas or opinions are fully expressed, you will throw the ball out to the group. The person who has the ball will speak. No one else may speak when someone has the ball. When that person is finished, the ball will be thrown to someone else to speak. The ball will be passed around the group until opinions and ideas have been exhausted or until the leader signals for time.

3. Do a practice round using a simple topic such as "Who do you think will win the Super Bowl?" or "What is your favorite color and why?"

Variations   1. Ask participants to always pass the ball back to you after speaking so you can make sure it is getting passed to people with dissenting viewpoints.

2. Ask participants to take the responsibility to pick up the ball and begin tossing when there is a need for listening to ideas or opinions.

Tip   I like to put a ball on each table. The group begins monitoring themselves, tossing the ball when someone begins to speak.

Story Time

Purpose Introducing a topic; Meeting starter; Winding down/relaxation; Energizing a long, dry presentation

Group Size 8-600

Level of Physical Activity Low

Estimated Time 3-5 minutes

Props None

In this activity, people listen to a story and make comments afterward. Use this as an introduction to a topic, as an energizer or thought provoker at any time during a session, or as a way to get people sharing their own thoughts.

Everyone loves to hear a bedtime story—even when it's not bedtime. I find that when I read short stories during the course of my presentations, people are often either touched or amused. I don't think I've ever read or told a short story and not had people come up to me afterward and share a story of their own. They often say, "You know that story you read? Well, I had a similar thing happen …"

Instructions
1. Choose a short story or anecdote that suits your goals.
2. Read the story aloud to participants.
3. After reading, ask participants if they have any thoughts or ideas that complement the story.

Variations
1. Read the story, then ask participants to share thoughts that have come to them while listening with a partner or in small groups.
2. If you're introducing a topic, ask pairs or groups of three to discuss the relevance to the topic, then share with the whole group.

Tips
1. Practice reading the story in advance; cut out unnecessary parts to keep it short.
2. Use inflection when you read.

Notes

_____

_____

_____

_____

_____

_____

Tuning Up

Purpose	Meeting starter; Physical energizer; Team building
Group Size	6-30
Level of Physical Activity	High
Estimated Time	10 minutes
Props	Audio tape of orchestral music (optional)

Get your group "in tune" and "ready to play" with this simple role-playing exercise. It works well as an opener or energizer.

> *One of my favorite parts of a performance by a symphony orchestra is the pre-concert "getting in tune" exercise by the members. There's a certain dramatic effect that occurs when the cacophonous sounds of individual instruments stop abruptly, followed by a pause—and then an eruption of totally harmonious sound spilling out in a glorious burst of passion (unless, of course, the piece is by Stravinsky).*

Instructions

1. Explain to participants that before any great musical performance, performers spend time getting in tune. We've often heard the expression "playing from the same sheet of music." But accomplished musicians know that a polished performance goes beyond that—instruments also need to be in tune.

2. Ask participants to imagine a symphony orchestra with all the different types of instruments represented. Ask them to choose one, and imagine themselves as musicians playing that instrument.

3. Now ask these "musicians" to stand and get their bodies in position to warm up their instruments to begin the piece. Tell them to begin warming up at any time, but to watch for a signal from you to pause, and then to start the piece when you bring your arms down in a conductor's downbeat motion.

4. Allow the musicians one to three minutes to warm up. Then raise both arms in the air as a signal to stop (pretend you have a baton poised in the air) and after about thirty seconds, bring your arms down as if on a downbeat to signal the start of the symphony.

5. Conduct the participant orchestra for about one minute, then signal them to stop playing.

6. Explain that you're now all on the same sheet of music, in tune, and ready for the meeting (or the next segment of the meeting) to begin.

Variations

1. To include movement, have participants move to one side of the room and then make a grand entrance to their seats.
2. Assign each person a particular instrument to play.

Tips

1. Play an audio tape of an orchestra warming up and then beginning to play a piece.
2. Provide a list of orchestral instruments to stimulate participants' ideas.

Notes

_____

_____

_____

_____

_____

_____

_____

_____

_____

_____

What in the World?

Purpose
Mental aerobics; Team building; Pure fun; Energizing a long, dry presentation; Meeting starter

Group Size
5-20

Level of Physical Activity
Low-medium

Estimated Time
2-5 minutes

Props
Current newspaper

This is a Jeopardy-like current affairs activity in which participants will create questions to go with answers about world news. Use it at any time during a session as a mental energizer or as a small group competition activity.

What in the world is going on? I learned the expression in my home, but I know that other parents and teachers also use it.

Instructions
1. On the day of the session, write 8 to 12 questions and answers about current events of the day.
2. Tell participants that you know they keep current with world events either by listening to the radio, watching television, or reading the newspaper.
3. Explain that this activity will give them the chance to show off their knowledge.
4. Tell them you will read the answer to a question about a current event. If they know the question, they should respond by raising their hands.
5. Begin the activity.

Variations
1. Organize participants in partners or small groups to come up with answers.
2. Make the activity competitive.
3. During each break, put a card with the answer face down on group tables. When groups return, give them thirty seconds to write the question for the answer. Ask each table for its question.

Tip
This is fun as group competition.

MENTAL AEROBICS

AIR WAVES

Purpose   Team building; Mental aerobics; Pure fun; Introducing a topic

Group Size   4-20

**Level of Physical
Activity**   Medium

Estimated Time   8-10 minutes

Props   List of radio call letters, one per pair

In this icebreaker, participants will pair up to create meaning behind common radio call letters—meanings that didn't exist prior to this day. Participants will enjoy pairing for this fun activity at any time during a meeting or session.

WII FM—What's in it for me?—is a common question in organizations today. A bit different from John F. Kennedy's message, "Ask not what your country can do for you, but what you can do for your country."

Instructions
1. Organize participants into pairs.
2. Give participants three minutes to share with their partners what their favorite radio stations are and why.
3. Ask the total group if they know what the call letters of their stations are, what they stand for, and how they got them.
4. Pass out call letters to each pair.
5. Explain that for the purpose of this activity, they may pretend not to know the origin of the call letters they received.
6. Tell them that their task is to work with their partners for five minutes to choose some call letters from the sheet and write what they stand for. Give the example of WII FM as What's In It For Me and WETA as White Elephant Trunk Area.
7. After five minutes, ask pairs to exchange with other pairs and read their responses.
8. At a break, write the call letter explanations on a sheet. Post the sheet where everyone can see it. Encourage participants to add to the list.

Variations
1. Ask the whole group to name local radio station call letters. Then proceed with the activity, asking pairs to use call letters from the list the group created.
2. Ask participants to create their own call letters and explain their meaning.
3. Have participants relate call letters to things happening in the organization.

Tips

1. For local radio station call letters, consult your telephone directory Yellow Pages.
2. Play music on a radio, of course, as they work. I think Baroque is best for brainstorming (Wire Baroque Best for Brainstorming And Music—WBBB AM).

Notes

_____

_____

_____

_____

_____

_____

_____

_____

_____

_____

EVOLUTIONARY IDEA

Purpose

Introducing a topic; Getting to know you better; Team building; Mental aerobics; For non-icebreaker types; Energizing a long, dry presentation

Group Size

5-40

Level of Physical Activity

Medium

Estimated Time

3-6 minutes

Props

Evolutionary Idea Activity Sheets, one per participant

Participants will get to expand and comment on each other's ideas in this unique brainstorming activity. This activity can effectively be used to get ideas for a particular goal or problem, as a mental energizer, or as a way for people to get to know one another better. Some groups are very goal directed; make it specific for them.

I have concluded that the word idea *is often thought of as a possessive noun: if one doesn't possess it, it can't be good; if one possesses it, one had better not share it or someone else might take possession of it.*

Instructions

1. Organize participants into groups of five to six.
2. Explain that the goal of this activity is to build on one another's ideas.
3. Give each participant an Evolutionary Idea Activity Sheet.
4. Explain the directions:
   - Each of you should write a goal you think would be good for the company at the top of your activity sheet. You will have thirty seconds to do this.
   - When I call time, pass your sheet to the person on your right. That person will build on the idea for twenty seconds, at which point I will call time.
   - The same process will continue until each idea sheet is back in the hands of its original owner.
   - You will then read your sheet aloud to group members.
5. Begin the activity.

Variation

If you know a company or group is working on a particular theme (such as empowerment of the workforce or network integration), use these as the broad topics for ideas to be built on.

Tips

1. It doesn't matter whether group members work in the same department or workspace or not. They will get good suggestions anyway.
2. Encourage them to put down any ideas, particularly those they are likely to bring up in conversation, such as "If the people in this company were smart, they would…"

Notes

_____

_____

_____

_____

_____

_____

_____

_____

_____

_____

EVOLUTIONARY IDEA ACTIVITY SHEET

Topic: _____

I.
    A.
        1.
        2.
        3.
    B.
        1.
        2.
        3.
    C.
        1.
        2.
        3.

II.
    A.
        1.
        2.
        3.
    B.
        1.
        2.
        3.
    C.
        1.
        2.
        3.

III.
    A.
        1.
        2.
        3.
    B.
        1.
        2.
        3.
    C.
        1.
        2.
        3.

FUNNY FABlES

Purpose
Introducing a topic; Pure fun; Grouping people; Mental aerobics

Group Size
8-20

Level of Physical Activity
Medium

Estimated Time
8-10 minutes

Props
Funny Fables Activity Sheets; copies of fables

This activity allows participants to use humor to describe the realities of life. Use it as an energizer or as an example of thinking beyond the obvious.

When I was a child, my parents gave me a book of Aesop's Fables *which I absolutely cherished. Being a lover of animals had something to do with it, I suppose. As I got older, my appreciation for the fables increased and along with that (thanks to Aesop) I developed a tongue-in-cheek sense of humor. Tongue-in-cheek generally refers to a dry or ironic sense of humor—for example, a short story with a twist at the end.*

Instructions
1. Ask participants to pair up.
2. Distribute Funny Fables Activity Sheets and copies of fables.
3. Read the Funny Fables Activity Sheet aloud.
4. Tell pairs they have five minutes to read two fables and add their tongue-in-cheek moral to it.
5. After five minutes, ask each pair to read their fables aloud and report their tongue-in-cheek morals.

Variations
1. Organize participants into groups of three to four.
2. Use fables without morals and ask pairs to create the morals.
3. Ask participants to act out one fable and then add their tongue-in-cheek moral.

Tip
Choose fables that are familiar to the members of the group. For a great resource, track down a copy of *Aesop's Fables*.

Notes
_____

_____

_____

_____

_____

FUNNY FABLES ACTIVITY SHEET

Have you ever heard the story of the boy who cried, "Wolf!" one too many times? Or how about the story of the country mouse and the city mouse—a great story to make us count our blessings. And if you've ever heard anyone say, "Appearances are deceiving," they're probably referring to the story of *The Wolf in Sheep's Clothing*. All of these are animal fables attributed to Aesop. Fables are tales or legends written to provide important moral lessons in a fun, and often humorous, story format.

First read the brief synopsis of Aesop's famous *The Hare and the Tortoise* fable below, then review both the real moral and the tongue-in-cheek morals we've provided. Now take a look at the fable your session leader has given you. It's your turn to find the real moral and come up with your own tongue-in-cheek morals.

The Hare and the Tortoise

The tortoise, as most of you know, is a slow-moving, placid creature who doesn't go anywhere in a hurry. The hare, on the other hand, is a quick-moving, spirited animal that moves quickly from place to place. One fine day in the meadow, the hare challenged the tortoise to a race. Being an agreeable sort, the tortoise accepted the challenge. They determined a starting line and a finish line, then began the race. The tortoise slowly took off heading around the meadow, directly toward the finish line, while the hare started quickly bouncing off ahead of him. The hare got far enough ahead that the tortoise couldn't see him anymore, so he decided to take a shortcut through the woods and use the time he saved to take a nap. His intention was to tell the whole meadow how he had taken a nap, yet still beat the tortoise to the finish. He didn't want to raise suspicion by winning by too much, however, so he settled down for his nap just shy of the finish line. The hare meant to wake up when the tortoise came by, jumping ahead of him to the finish. Unfortunately, the hare woke from his nap just in time to see the tortoise cross the finish line. In Aesop's words, "Plodding wins the race."

The morals of the story:

- Consistent and careful hard work results in getting a project done right.
- Cheaters never prosper.
- It's not good to become overly confident or too sure of your success.

Tongue-in-cheek morals:

- Never race a tortoise.
- Never race anyone smarter than you.
- If you think you're going to win, at least have some money riding on it.
- If you do decide to race someone, get someone to watch the course to make sure your opponent doesn't cheat.
- Cheating is okay, as long as you do it right and don't let your guard down—or take a nap.

News Edit

Purpose	Mental aerobics; Pure fun
Group Size	6-12
Level of Physical Activity	Medium
Estimated Time	3-5 minutes
Props	News Edit Activity Sheet transparency; one newspaper article per participant

Everybody loves to tamper with somebody else's writing, so give participants this chance. Use this activity as a mental energizer for participants who enjoy a verbal challenge.

> *Newspapers help define who we are. For instance, there are* New York Times *people,* Washington Times *people,* Wall Street Journal *people,* Washington Post *people, community newspaper people, etc. There are many reasons for choosing a newspaper besides the layout, editorials, contributing writers, classifieds, sports, and specific information. Some people choose newspapers by cost, some for prestige, some for political slant, and others for just plain ease of delivery. Whichever the reason, newspapers for some people are as essential as morning coffee (well, almost).*

Instructions

1. Make a transparency of the News Edit Activity Sheet.
2. Give each participant a newspaper article, or ask them to furnish their own.
3. Explain that News Edit is a mental energizer to get them thinking differently, much as they have to do on the job.
4. Show the News Edit transparency. Point out that the article has been subjected to a News Edit—the crossing out of words to create a new and very different story. Read it aloud.
5. Instruct participants to read their articles silently. Explain that when they understand the article, they should apply a News Edit, and—have fun.
6. After participants are finished, ask them to tell the rest of the group what the original article was about, and then read the News Edit.

Variations

1. Give each person a copy of the same article. Ask them to apply News Edit to it. Then hear the different results from each person.
2. Ask participants to make their articles relevant to the organization through the edit.

Tips

1. Choose newspaper articles that will be fun for participants to work with.
2. One could use this activity before introducing an organizational change.

NEWS EDIT ACTIVITY SHEET

News Edit #1

NEW YORK, March 31—The daffodils here in Bryant Park had just started to sprout when the city was hit with a messy storm of snow and sleet. Springtime was put off just a little bit long. Winter would not pass. At least not yet.

And on the runways, it seemed that retro fashions would forever refuse to give way to modern silhouettes.*

News Edit #2

NEW YORK, March 31—The daffodils here in ~~Bryant Park had just started to sprout when the city was hit with~~ a messy storm ~~of snow and sleet. Springtime was put off just a little bit long. Winter would not pass. At least not yet.~~

~~And~~ on the runways~~, it seemed that retro fashions would forever~~ refuse to give way to modern silhouettes.

Final Story

NEW YORK, March 31—The daffodils here in a messy storm on the runways refuse to give way to modern silhouettes.

*From "A Real Flare For the '70s" by Robin D. Givhan in *The Washington Post,* April 1, 1996.

OXYMORONS

Purpose   Mental aerobics; Pure fun; Introducing a topic

Group Size   6-20

**Level of Physical
Activity**   Low

Estimated Time   2-3 minutes

Props   Flip chart; markers

Participants will brainstorm a list of oxymorons in this activity. Use this for humor and to get the group mentally energized and re-freshed.

> *Subtle red. That's the label on a deep, matte-finish, alluring lipstick. Oxymoron? Not when you compare it to a flaming red, glossy, "in your face until I wear off which may be never" lipstick.*

Instructions   1. Write the word oxymoron on a flip chart.
2. Explain that an oxymoron is a two-word phrase with each word having an opposite meaning from the other. Provide examples such as *pretty ugly* or *military intelligence*.
3. Ask participants to name oxymorons and write them on the chart.

Variations   1. Ask participants to create their own oxymorons which relate to the topic or their business.
2. Organize participants into groups of three to four and ask them to list oxymorons with definitions to share with the total group.

Tip   Leave the list up so participants can add to it throughout the session.

Pavlov

Purpose

Mental aerobics; Introducing a topic; Team building; Physical energizer; Pure fun; Getting closure

Group Size

10-40

Level of Physical Activity

Medium

Estimated Time

5-6 minutes

Props

Bell; candy or food for prizes; questions or statements

I'm not sure participants will noticeably salivate, but they will enjoy responding to questions that are reinforced with prizes. Use this activity at any time in a program to reinforce the learning of information or understanding of concepts.

Remember Psychology 101: Pavlov's experiments on reinforcement techniques with animals? A progression of his formula follows:
1. Sight and smell of food = dog salivating
2. Sight and smell of food + bell = dog salivating
3. Bell = dog salivating

Instructions

1. Organize participants into groups of five to eight and arrange groups in lines facing a bell on a table about 20 feet away.
2. Instruct each group to designate a single runner (or as Pavlov would say, a subject).
3. Explain to the groups that you will be asking them a series of questions and their responses will allow them to compete for points which will be used to obtain food prizes at the end.
4. Explain the rules of the game:
   - The groups will discuss each question or statement I read and come up with a group response.
   - When a group has a response, your runner should run to the bell and ring it to designate your readiness to answer, then return to the group.
   - The first runner to ring the bell gets to speak first with a response. If correct, that group gets one point.
   - If the response is incorrect or needs further elaboration, the second runner to ring the bell gives a response.
   - This continues until the full correct response is given. Whichever group provides the correct response gets a point.
5. After ten to twenty questions or statements, ask groups to tally their points.

6. Award food prizes to the winning group, and prizes to everyone else—for salivating, of course.

Variations

1. Have each team submit an equal number of questions to use.
2. Give each member of a team a piece of candy each time they get a point.

Tips

1. Use a fun bell such as a cow bell.
2. Include some humorous questions, perhaps about session participants.

Notes

_____

_____

_____

_____

_____

_____

_____

_____

_____

Phobia Mania

Purpose   Mental aerobics; Introducing a topic; Pure fun

Group Size   10-40

Level of Physical Activity   Low

Estimated Time   5-7 minutes

Props   Flip chart paper; markers
     This is an activity in which participants confront and name their true fears—those never named before—in a humorous way. It is best used as a mental and emotional energizer anytime during a program or as an introduction to the fear of a topic such as organizational change.

> *I recently came upon a humorous book that listed phobias with proper definitions for each. Reading through the entries, I realized that there were many missing from that listing that I have either encountered myself or watched other people exhibit. Take, for example, the fear of brushing your teeth early in the evening lest you decide to snack afterwards and have to brush them again. Or how about the fear of having your dentist discover that you haven't been flossing because your gums bleed when they're cleaned? If you think these fears aren't real, tell me why people wait until five minutes before bedtime to brush their teeth. And (now tell the truth) do your flossing patterns directly coincide with your dental appointments?*

Instructions
1. Organize participants into groups of three to five.
2. Explain that there are currently many named phobias, but there must be a few that have yet to be discovered.
3. Give examples of phobias and ask for a show of hands for each phobia participants have heard of.
4. Explain that they will now have three minutes with their groups to create and list names for phobias never before named. Provide an example such as *grasspest phobia: the fear of walking barefoot on grass and being stung by a bee hidden in the long blades.*
5. Instruct groups to write their phobias and definitions on flip chart paper.
6. When the three minutes are up, ask each group to report its phobias and definitions.

Variations
1. Ask groups to choose one phobia and illustrate it before sharing it with the group.
2. Use work phobias as the topic for participants to work within.

Tips

1. Keep it light; this isn't a therapy session.
2. Don't make fun of real fears that people suffer from.
3. Examples of phobias: acrophobia—fear of heights; claustrophobia—fear of enclosed spaces; arachnephobia—fear of spiders.

Notes

_____

_____

_____

_____

_____

_____

_____

_____

_____

_____

Radio City

Purpose	Team building; Mental aerobics; Introducing a topic; Pure fun
Group Size	8-40
Level of Physical Activity	Low
Estimated Time	5-10 minutes
Props	Radio City Activity Sheets, one per participant and one per group

Participants share favorite radio stations while adapting some call letters of their own in this activity. It's a great creativity activity, a way for people to create shows about the organization, or a team building energizer for that dead time after lunch.

> *NPR, National Public Radio, is one of our favorite stations. Saturday afternoons include "Car Talk" and "Prairie Home Companion"—decent, nonviolent, unoffensive, fun, and, at times, inspirational programming. Radio has a certain nostalgic quality to it; it calls forth remembrances of days by the fire in the kitchen with family and friends listening to "The Shadow" or "Amos and Andy." (Or so they tell me.)*

Instructions

1. Organize participants into groups of four to eight.
2. Ask participants to name nonmusic radio shows that they listen to or are familiar with.
3. Invite participants to reminisce with you about radio shows of the past.
4. Tell them that they will now have five minutes in their groups to design a new radio program that will air on prime time and have a wide audience.
5. Pass out a Radio City Activity Sheet to each participant, plus one for each group to fill in together.
6. Explain that each group should complete one final sheet, but that all group members should fill in their own sheets while coming up with program ideas.
7. After ten minutes, invite groups to share their program ideas with other groups.

Variation

Ask that program ideas relate to the organization.

Tips

1. Have a radio playing softly in the background.
2. Bring in radio memorabilia to display on a table.

RADIO CITY ACTIVITY SHEET

Radio City

Program Name:
Program Type:
Run Time (length):
Air Time (days, time of day):
Show Host(s):

Show Sponsors (advertisers):

Program Description:

Radio City

Program Name:
Program Type:
Run Time (length):
Air Time (days, time of day):
Show Host(s):

Show Sponsors (advertisers):

Program Description:

SAY IT WITH FLOWERS

Purpose   Mental aerobics; Team building; Pure fun

Group Size   6-24

Level of Physical Activity   Low

Estimated Time   2-4 minutes

Props   Paper; pens

Participants will brainstorm the ways flowers appear in popular music, poetry, and movie titles. Use this activity as a mental energizer and as a way to get small groups energized either at the beginning of a session to spark enthusiasm, or later to take a break.

> *One of our most common forms of communication is flowers. Think of all they say: thanks for having us; thanks for your help; Happy Birthday/Mother's Day/Valentine's Day/Hanukkah/Groundhog Day; congratulations on your new job/new baby/raise; best wishes in your new home; we appreciate your friendship/relationship; I'm sorry; I miss you; I love you; and I don't have time for you but these flowers do.*

Instructions
1. Organize participants into groups of four to five.
2. Explain the rules:
   - You will have two minutes to list quotations, phrases, and song, book, play, or movie titles that have the name of a flower in them. For example, the song "I Never Promised You A Rose Garden."
   - You may not use proper names such as Aster Street.
3. At the end of two minutes, hear from each group.

Variation   Make this an individual or pairs competition.

Tip   This works well in the spring when people are planting and thinking about flowers.

STREET SMARTS

Purpose Getting to know you better; Introducing a topic; Mental aerobics; Pure fun; Team building

Group Size 8-40

Level of Physical Activity Medium

Estimated Time 6-8 minutes

Props None

Everyone can identify with this activity in which participants will recall street names—with light competition sprinkled in. Use this activity for people to get to know one another better, as an introduction to a recall or brainstorming activity, or to energize the group after lunch.

My husband has an Uncle Clyde who lives in San Antonio on the corner of Rawhide and Buckboard Streets. We never forget his address.

Instructions

1. Organize participants into groups of three to six.
2. Suggest to participants that there are many street names that are repeated in different towns and countries, and many other street names that appear to be original.
3. Explain the rules of the game to participants:
    - Individuals will have one minute to write down a list of the names of all the streets you have lived on or that exist in your present town.
    - The group will then have one minute to create a group list, using each street name only once.
    - Groups will then have one minute to add other street names, but you must be able to say where every name on the list is located.
    - The winning group will be the one with the greatest number of street names that other groups have not named.
4. Begin the activity by telling participants to individually write street names as quickly as they can.
5. After one minute, tell them to get with their groups and spend one minute consolidating their individual lists into one team list.
6. After one minute, tell the groups that they now have one minute to generate more street names for their lists.
7. After one minute, ask each group to read its list.

8. Explain that as each group reads its list, the other groups should say "Street Smarts" when a name also appears on its list. All groups should then cross that common name off their lists.

9. After each group has read its list, ask groups to count the number of street names they have not crossed off their lists and assign each one a point.

10. Now ask each group to read its short list. Explain that the other groups have the right to challenge any name they think isn't real; the group who named that street then has to state where the street appears. If they can, the challenging team loses one point. If they can't, they must subtract two points from their own score.

11. Tally the scores and announce the winning group.

Variation

Make this an individual activity only.

Tip

Don't tell participants that they will be crossing out common names until it's time for them to do it.

Notes

_____

_____

_____

_____

_____

_____

_____

_____

_____

_____

The Lettermen

Purpose

Physical energizer; Mental aerobics; Team building; Introducing a topic; Getting closure

Group Size

24-100

Level of Physical Activity

High

Estimated Time

2-4 minutes

Props

One 8½" × 11" letter of the alphabet for each participant; envelopes

In this activity participants will compete by arranging themselves to form words with the letter cards they're given. This activity is purely for energizing—getting people up and moving about. It is especially challenging for those who like to work with words.

> *When I was in seventh grade I lost a regional spelling bee by spelling correctly at first—and then changing and misspelling— the word "rheumatic." In the weeks following, I replayed that scenario in my mind over and over again until I was over it. Or so I thought. In the eighth grade my son, Ron, after spelling many very difficult words, misspelled a simple word in a NY State Spelling Bee Contest. It all came back.*

Instructions

1. Before the session, place the same alphabet letters in envelopes for groups, with each envelope containing one letter for each group member and at least four vowels.
2. Organize participants into groups of twelve to sixteen.
3. Give each group an envelope full of letters, one letter per participant.
4. Move groups to an open space for standing and moving about.
5. Ask groups to distribute one letter from their envelope to each member of the group.
6. Explain that groups will be competing against one another. Give instructions:
   - I will name a category.
   - Your group will line up to form a word that is in that category.
   - It is not necessary to use all letters (and people) each time.
   - The group that lines up with a legitimate word first wins.
7. Give a practice round asking them to form the name of a person.
8. Give them the following categories, one at a time:
   - Form the name of a flower.
   - Form the name of a game.
   - Form the name of a song.

- Form the name of a candy bar.
- Form a word that uses the greatest number of letters your group has.

9. After each round, name the winning group.

Variations

1. If your group has fewer than 20 participants, do it as a total group.
2. Use topic or business related categories.

Tip

This can be used periodically during a session.

Notes

_____

_____

_____

_____

_____

_____

_____

_____

_____

_____

WORDplexing

Purpose Mental aerobics; Pure fun; For non-icebreaker types

Group Size 8-40

Level of Physical Activity Medium

Estimated Time 3-8 minutes

Props Wordplexing Activity Sheets, one per participant

Participants will create new words to aptly describe those previously undefined moments in life. Use this activity to mentally energize an audience, preferably ones who enjoy thinking games.

> *They say that the first step to conquering a fear is to name it; I wonder if that's true for frustrations as well. So ... if I have this right, for me to conquer the unbelievable anger, frustration, and annoyance I feel from receiving weekly (or more) mealtime telemarketing calls for a woman and her husband who never lived here but who have remained on mailing lists for three years now despite our numerous attempts to install changes, I must give it a name. Okay. It's worth a try ... How about "malphonedigestion?"*

Instructions

1. Explain to participants that there are just not enough words in the dictionary to adequately explain all situations or describe some feelings and observations.

2. Tell them that this activity will give them the chance to create those words. For example, one name for the phone calls that occur right at mealtime might be "dinneruptions."

3. Suggest that there are different ways to create appropriate words: one may use syllables that have meaning such as "uncoolable" (used by teenagers referring to the futility of attempting to bring their parents up to worldly speed); combining words such as snooze and snugly to form "snoogly" (the blanket one curls up in to fall asleep on the couch); or using sounds or feelings such as "shooshed" (describing how someone passed you during a road race).

4. Ask participants to pair up.

5. Give each pair a list and two minutes to make words to accompany the given definitions.

6. After two minutes, read each definition and have each set of partners give its words for that definition.

*Hall, Rich & Friends (1984) *Sniglets*. New York: MacMillan Publishing Company, Inc.

Variations

1. If you have more time, ask them to write a definition and pass it to another group to create the word. Make sure each set of partners has a different definition. Share the words.

2. Vote on which word is best for each definition.

Tips

1. The fun of this activity is in the sharing of words, more than in the creating of wordplexes.

2. You might want to give them examples from *Sniglets** or other variations on the theme.

Notes

_____

_____

_____

_____

_____

_____

_____

_____

_____

_____

WORDPLEXING ACTIVITY SHEET

Create words for the following definitions:

- The moment right before a storm or conflict bursts _____

- The feeling in your teeth when you bite into a cold Popsicle™ _____

- What happens to everyone in a room when a puppy or a new baby is brought into the room _

- The moment when you first wake up, but are not yet oriented to your surroundings _____

- The look someone has after they have been crying hard _____

- The feeling that you've forgotten something but have no idea what it is _____

- The feeling that you're too tired to get up off the couch and go to bed _____

- When you're so bored you want something to eat, but you're not really hungry _____

- When you're hungry, but can't decide what you want to eat _____

- Those "important" people who drive on the shoulder of the road when traffic is backed up ___

- The moment of decision when a traffic light ahead of you turns yellow and you have to judge whether you can make it through or should stop suddenly _____

- The sales phone calls you receive right when you sit down to dinner with the family _____

- What happens when a fire engine or ambulance drives through the neighborhood and everybody rushes out to see where it's going _____

- That slow-motion feeling you get when you realize the car behind you may not be able to stop in time _____

- The excited anticipation of people on the night before a big event when they will get gifts, such as Christmas, graduation, or a birthday _____

OUTDOOR ACTIVITIES

Ball Bobble

Purpose

Physical energizer; Team building; Outdoor activity; Introducing a topic; Pure fun

Group Size

12-24

Level of Physical Activity

High

Estimated Time

3-6 minutes

Props

3 beach balls

Participants will toss a ball around the group until each person has a chance to catch and throw—the trick is, they have to toss it in the same order each time. Use this as a challenge with any group that would welcome energizing.

Learning to juggle is a rite of passage. I remember well when both of my boys decided it was time (not at the same time, thank goodness). Naturally, they chose items that would give them the greatest challenge; it's part of the rite. Balls and bean bags just don't do it. It's the conquering of the oranges, water balloons, and, finally, the eggs that truly ushers in the next stage of maturity.

Instructions

1. Ask participants to stand and move apart so there's space between them.
2. Explain the rules:
   - The object of the activity is for the group to establish a forward and reverse pattern while throwing one ball around; then repeat the same pattern with two other balls.
   - The first person will pass the ball; wait until the fifth person in the pattern has caught it and pass a second ball; wait until the fifth person in the pattern has caught it and pass a third ball.
   - If you are the last person to get the first ball, you reverse the pattern by throwing the ball back to the person who threw it to you. You do the same with the other two balls.
   - Play continues until all balls are back in the possession of the first person who started the pattern.
3. Begin a practice round with just one ball.

Variation

Use a Koosh™ ball, bean bag, or other object instead of a beach ball.

Tips

1. If the group gets good, add a fourth ball.
2. Some groups can only be successful with one ball. If they're having difficulty during the practice round, just use one ball.
3. Naturally, some people will drop the ball. Encourage them to pick it up and keep it moving. If they can't, begin again.
4. Part of the fun is the bobbling of balls as they pass, going forward and in reverse.

Beach Party

Purpose	Physical energizer; Pure fun; Outdoor activity; Team building
Group Size	8-20
Level of Physical Activity	High
Estimated Time	3-5 minutes
Props	3 beach balls; Beach Party Activity Sheets, one card per participant

This is recess for adults. Use it with any group as an energizer (or when you'd rather be outdoors than teaching a session).

Have you ever witnessed school children out on the playground at recess time? The sounds are delightful: laughing, directions being called out, cheering for individuals and teams, arguing over rules, sing-song rhymes and clapping hands for jumping rope, name calling, hushed conversations, bats and balls colliding, ball bouncing, and the skipping of hopscotch. Adults need more recess.

Instructions

1. Take participants outside and ask them to form a circle.
2. Give out number cards randomly so that sequential numbers are not in a row.
3. Explain the rules:
   - The object of this activity is to keep the balls within the circle and in the air.
   - Beginning with one beach ball, a person with a #1 card will go to the middle of the circle, hit the ball into the air, and yell "#1."
   - A #2 must then run into the circle and hit the ball into the air while yelling "#2."
   - #3 follows #2, #4 follows #3, and so on.
   - After the first four people have hit the ball, #1 will start a second ball by hitting it in the air and yelling "#1."
   - The game will continue until there are three balls all going at the same time with each being hit in consecutive order by their numbers.
   - Participants must listen for the number prior to theirs so they can be prepared to get that ball.
   - If the ball hits the ground, the person who was supposed to hit it should pick it up, hit it into the air, and call his or her number.
   - Continue through one round for each ball. The last person should hit the ball out of the circle.

4. Begin the activity and continue playing until all three balls have been hit once by all group members.

Variations

1. Just use one ball and have the person in the middle call the number of a person who will then hit it.

2. Do it indoors if there is ample safe space.

Tip

Encourage people to hit the ball high into the air to give time for the next person to get in and under it.

Notes

_____

_____

_____

_____

_____

_____

_____

_____

_____

_____

BEACH PARTY ACTIVITY SHEET

1	2	3	4
5	6	7	8
9	10	11	12
13	14	15	16
17	18	19	20

CHEERS!

Purpose
Getting closure; Physical energizer; Team building; Outdoor activity; Pure fun

Group Size
10-50

Level of Physical Activity
High

Estimated Time
3-5 minutes

Props
None

Participants will love creating cheers—especially when it relates to their own project or group. Use Cheers! as a closure activity to give positive uplift at the end of a session or as a team building exercise to gain a sense of community. All groups enjoy this one.

Cheerleading prepares one for life. Think about the extensions: coaching little league baseball; selling a product; coaching a birth; training your dog; supporting friends in tough times; encouraging your idle automobile on a freezing day as it turns over and over and over ...

Instructions
1. Organize participants into pairs.
2. Explain that they will have an opportunity to cheer for _____. (You name the category: perhaps a goal, a skill, a group, or a project?)
3. Give them aloud the beginning of the cheer—"Rah, rah, sis, boom, bah ..."
4. Explain that they now have one minute to create the second line.
5. After one minute, ask pairs to take turns standing up and delivering their cheers.

Variations
1. This could also be an individual or a small group activity.
2. Don't give participants the first line.

Tips
1. Make up your own cheer and give it as an example.
2. Provide a set of pom-poms for pairs to use when presenting their cheers.

Notes
_____
_____
_____
_____
_____

Fast Forwarding

Purpose

Physical energizer; Pure fun; Outdoor activity

Group Size

48-104

Level of Physical Activity

High

Estimated Time

4-10 minutes

Props

Four different-colored Koosh™ balls, beach balls, Frisbees™, or balloons; Fast Forwarding Activity Sheets, one per web site leader and one for the leader of the activity

This activity gets people up, moving, and cooperating as they pass balls around in a pattern. Use this activity indoors or outdoors, but it is best outdoors where participants can spread out, hence increasing the chance for error.

I can understand why moving is high on the list of personal stressors. In very overt and many more subtle ways, as we live in an area we define and create the physical and interactive networks and webs that support our consumer, health, and lifestyle choices.

Instructions

1. Using the diagram in the Fast Forwarding Activity Sheet, organize participants into web-like formations in an open space with participants standing about three feet from one another. Designate web site leaders A1, B1, C1, and D1.

2. Give each web-site leader a ball and a Fast Forwarding Activity Sheet so they understand directions for throwing the ball.

3. Explain the practice round:
   - During the first round a ball will travel the entire A to D square formation.
   - To begin this, web leader A1 will throw the ball to A2; A2 will then throw to A3, and so on, until the ball has gone completely around the A-square formation and is returned to A1.
   - A1 will then throw the ball to B1 who will complete a similar process in the B square and then throw to C1.
   - C1 will complete the process in C square and throw to D1.
   - When the process is completed in the D square, D1 will throw the ball to A1 signaling the completion of the round.

4. After the practice round, explain the rules:
   - The goal is for four balls to begin at each web site simultaneously, travel the complete square formation of all four web sites, and return to the original web-site leaders—all arriving at the same time.

■ To accomplish this, each web-site leader will throw a ball at the same time to #2 in their squares.

5. Repeat as many times as necessary until throws are synchronized and balls arrive back at web sites at the same time.

Variations

1. For inside activity, have participants pass rather than throw the ball.
2. Make it competitive; first web site to get the ball back wins.

Tip

If outdoors, beach balls or Frisbees™ work well. Inside, Koosh™ balls or balloons are better.

Notes

_____

_____

_____

_____

_____

_____

_____

_____

_____

FAST FORWARDING
ACTIVITY SHEET

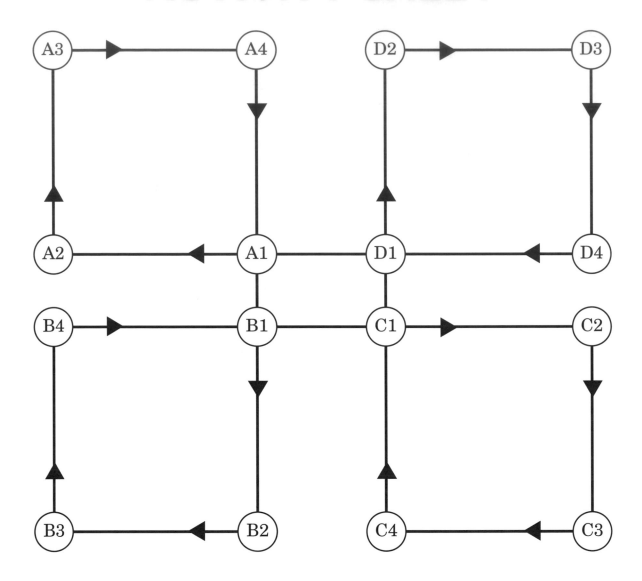

Each circle represents a participant. Fill in the lines between circles with equal numbers of participants to form four perfect squares. The four center people each get a ball. Begin with a practice round by having the ball passed around each small square.

The goal of placing people in this formation is for all four balls to cycle through all four squares and return to web-site leaders at the same time.

Web-site leaders will first throw the balls to the #2 participants in their squares (A1 to A2, B1 to B2, C1 to C2, D1 to D2). After the balls have traveled the squares and are returned to the web-site leaders, leaders will throw the balls to the next designated web-site leader (A1 to B1, B1 to C1, C1 to D1, D1 to A1).

IN SHAPE

Purpose

Team building; Physical energizer; Outdoor activity; Pure fun; Especially for big groups

Group Size

24-200

Level of Physical Activity

High

Estimated Time

5-10 minutes

Props

In Shape Activity Sheet, one copy for the leader; numbered cards, one per group

Groups will work together to form shapes in this high-energy activity. Use this as an energizer when you have adequate space with a group who appreciates a challenge and movement.

Shapes: at different ages we're naming them, using them, defining them, creating them, admiring them, working at them, recalling them, struggling to keep them, reminiscing about them ...

Instructions

1. Organize participants into groups of twelve to twenty.
2. Ask each group to name a leader and give each leader one large card with a number on it.
3. Explain that they will now be engaged in group competition. You will call out the name of a shape and each group should take on that shape.
4. Tell them to practice by forming a circle. Then ask them to form a square.
5. Explain that you will call shapes in rapid succession. As soon as one group has formed the shape, they should hold up their number. You will call out the number of that group and then call out the next shape.
6. Explain that the object of the activity is for groups to score points by completing the shape first.
7. Begin the activity.

Variations

1. Allow each group to complete the shape before moving on.
2. If it's a well-educated group, use shapes like rhomboid or parallelogram.

Tips

1. If you have a large group, make sure you're using a microphone or megaphone so that you can be heard over the din.
2. The more room there is, the freer groups feel about running around.
3. To decide how many shapes to call, sense the interest of the group.

IN SHAPE ACTIVITY SHEET

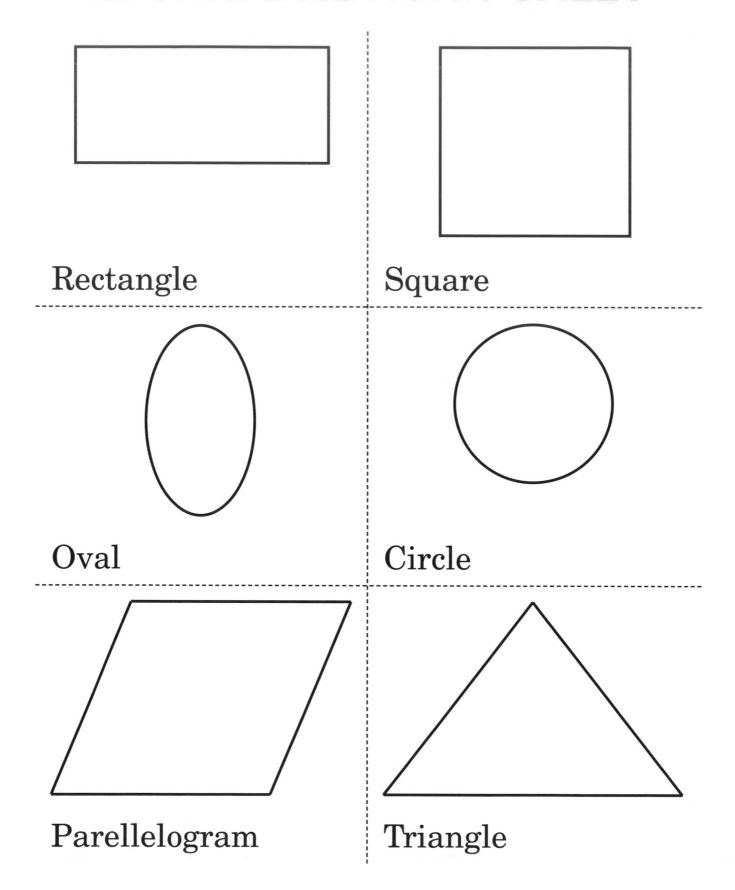

Rectangle

Square

Oval

Circle

Parellelogram

Triangle

The Waves

Purpose
Outdoor activity; Physical energizer; Team building; Energizing a long, dry presentation; Especially for big groups; Pure fun

Group Size
15-100

Level of Physical Activity
High

Estimated Time
3-5 minutes

Props
None

Many people have experienced the wave—that uplifted arm movement that moves through stadium crowds like a wave crashing on water—so this appeals to all audiences. It is a great energizer, outdoors or indoors, and may become as elaborate as you dare to make it.

Many years ago we were fans of the University of Vermont Catamount Hockey Team. I mean diehard fans—a status that involved standing in line outside at 4:30 a.m. in –20° temperatures for a 9:00 or 10:00 a.m. opening at the box office to purchase tickets for a nighttime game. At the time, the team had just started playing Division One hockey, and was a very exciting team to watch. During the warm-up, prior to the National Anthem (which I never heard all the way through), there was a power surge that coursed through the crowd. For me, the wave of emotion lasted into the wee hours of the morning, while I tossed and turned, replaying passes and goals, and reliving the crowd-swelling feeling of victory or total devastation.

Instructions

1. Organize participants standing in a semi-circle with everyone facing in and you standing at one end.
2. Demonstrate the typical wave by throwing your arms up and asking the person next to you to follow, and so on, all the way down the line, with the last person bringing arms down, at which point each person in turn brings their arms down until it is back to you.
3. Explain that there is more than one type of wave.
4. Ask them to follow with the same wave pattern each time you lead.
5. Lead them by taking one step to the right while throwing your arms over your head and to the right.
6. When that wave comes back to you, take two fast steps forward while throwing your arms forward.
7. When that wave comes back to you, spin around on one foot 180°and stand facing in the opposite direction.
8. Continue the activity with any other version of the wave you can think of. The rest is up to you. Have fun!

Variations

1. Ask a participant to be the leader or have participants take turns leading.
2. If participants are dressed appropriately, perform waves from a sitting or lying position.

Tip

Have great fun with this: laugh with the mistakes, increase the speed, and perform outrageous moves.

Notes

_____

_____

_____

_____

_____

_____

_____

_____

_____

YARD STICKS

Purpose	Outdoor activity; Physical energizer; Team building; Especially for big groups; Pure fun
Group Size	20-200
Level of Physical Activity	High
Estimated Time	5-10 minutes
Props	Prizes

Yard Sticks energizes and builds skills of collaboration and cooperation as participants measure a distance using only themselves, without tools or measuring devices. Use this activity to energize any group who likes a challenge.

Do you "measure up" to the standards set by your coworkers or boss? How about your family and friends? Do you "measure up" to your own standards? Sometimes we spend an enormous amount of time and energy trying to measure up to a standard (a length) that no one has meted out.

Instructions

1. Mark off a distance of about 30 to 40 feet (but make sure it is an uneven number, like 29.5 feet) by making a long line on either end of the activity space.
2. Organize participants into groups of six to twenty.
3. Explain the rules of the game:
   - The object is to make an educated guess as to the exact length of the distance.
   - The groups may use whatever means, short of actually using a ruler, tape, or yardstick, to measure the distance.
   - You'll have five minutes to come up with an answer.
4. Tell them that the winner is the team that comes up with the most accurate guess by the time five minutes is up.
5. Begin the activity.
6. When five minutes are up, ask groups for their educated guesses.
7. Award a prize to the team that comes the closest.

Variation

If you have a large group, for example 100 to 200 people, use larger groups and increase the length of the line to be measured.

Tips

1. Encourage people to be creative in the ways they may get the answer.

2. Some ways that groups measure the distance include: lying down end to end and adding heights; walking the length off; measuring by arms' lengths, etc.
3. Each group has its own line.

Notes

_____

_____

_____

_____

_____

_____

_____

_____

_____

_____

Physical Energizers

Advanced Placement

Purpose Physical energizer; Team building; Pure fun; Outdoor activity

Group Size 30-60

Level of Physical Activity High

Estimated Time 2-4 minutes

Props None

Participants will physically arrange themselves as the parts of a whole object in this activity. This is a great way for participants to interact while getting energized. Use it many times during a long session.

> *I am convinced that the test of true consensus often happens—or not—around mealtime. At any time in our family, when we are trying to decide what to do for a quick, easy dinner together, someone will invariably say, "Well, why don't we just send out for a pizza?" Just, you say? Glenn likes pepperoni, mushrooms, and green peppers—no black olives please; Ron likes sausage, onions, and extra cheese; Kim likes the works without mushrooms; Todd likes white pizza with veggies; and I like unsalted pizza. So, after about thirty minutes of trying to agree on pizza toppings, we vote unanimously to order KFC individual dinners.*

Instructions

1. Organize participants into groups of ten to twenty people.
2. Explain that the name of the activity is Advanced Placement.
3. Give these instructions:
   - I will name an object.
   - It will be the job of the groups to simulate the insides of that object and recreate the placement of parts.
   - To do that, each person will choose to be one part and get in the position of that part. For example, if I said "pizza," people would distribute themselves evenly in a circle or a rectangle as cheese, pepperoni, green pepper, sausage, broccoli, etc.
4. To begin, give a practice round. Tell participants to become an oak tree.
5. When groups are in place, ask them to call out their parts one at a time.
6. For the first round, tell groups to become a watch.
7. Choose one of the following whenever the group needs to be energized:
   - computer

- human body
- motorcycle
- purse
- chicken

Variation

Use the human body each time and tell them that each time they have to become a different part.

Tips

1. Make sure there is plenty of space for people to spread out for this one. It increases the fun factor.
2. When I give the first example, I take the time to ask participants what they would be on the pizza.

Notes

_____

_____

_____

_____

_____

_____

_____

_____

_____

_____

BICYCLE BUILT FOR TWO

Purpose Physical energizer; Team building; Pure fun

Group Size 2-200

Level of Physical Activity High

Estimated Time 5 minutes

Props Music (optional)

Partners in sync! Getting energized! That's what this activity is about. Use it with any group or twosomes to get an energizing quick fix.

> *Picture this: Ocean City, N.J., 8:00 a.m., August 1. It's a sunny morning and you're bicycling on the boardwalk with your favorite person. Aaah.*

Instructions

1. Organize participants into pairs.
2. Ask pairs to place their chairs one behind the other and sit down.
3. Explain that they will replicate riding on a bicycle built for two.
4. Set the stage by asking participants to close their eyes and imagine the sun warming them; cool ocean breezes blowing gently against them; and the smells of the surf wafting across their nostrils.
5. Tell them to begin peddling; the front person should set and vary the pace, while the back person keeps in sync.
6. Explain that they'll have one minute to bike, then ten seconds to rest, then another minute to bike and another ten seconds to rest.
7. Begin the activity.
8. When the activity is over, ask partners to comment on the ease or difficulty of keeping in sync.

Variations

1. Use bicycles built for three or four.
2. Offer the activity a couple of times and then have everyone change partners.

Tips

1. This activity should be fun; encourage participants to quicken the pace, climb and go down hills, etc.
2. Play music with varying tempos.

Notes

_____

DYNAMIC DUOS

Purpose   Grouping people; Physical energizer; Team building; Pure fun

Group Size   10-40

**Level of Physical
Activity**   High

Estimated Time   8-10 minutes

Props   Dynamic Duos Activity Sheets, one card per participant
                       This activity is great to get people into pairs and on their feet as they act out the roles of their dynamic duo. Be prepared to discover hidden talents! Use this one at any time during a session; your audience will love you for it.

                       We know and love them all—Burns and Allen, Steve and Edie, Ben and Jerry, Abbott and Costello. Dynamic duos. Terrific twosomes. Powerful pairs.

Instructions   1. Organize participants into pairs.
                       2. Give each pair a card with the names of a dynamic duo on it.
                       3. Explain to the participants that since nobody else in the room knows who their dynamic duo is, they'll have to play the part. Each pair will have two minutes to plan a thirty-second routine to perform for the group, who will then try to guess the names of each dynamic duo.
                       4. Give the signal for the pairs to begin planning and practicing.
                       5. After two minutes, ask each dynamic duo to perform its routine, pair by pair.
                       6. Encourage the other participants to guess the duo.

Variations   1. Encourage participants to use props.
                       2. Allow the groups to come up with their own dynamic duos.

Tips   1. Use as much or as little time as you have for this depending on your objective.
                       2. For the fun of it, give prizes for courage.

Notes   _____

                       _____

                       _____

                       _____

DYNAMIC DUOS
ACTIVITY SHEET

Bonnie & Clyde	Bonnie & Clyde
Romeo & Juliet	Romeo & Juliet
Tarzan & Jane	Tarzan & Jane
David & Goliath	David & Goliath
Santa & Rudolph	Santa & Rudolph
Fred Astaire & Ginger Rogers	Fred Astaire & Ginger Rogers
Jack & Jill (of nursery rhyme fame)	Jack & Jill (of nursery rhyme fame)
Lucille Ball & Ricky Ricardo	Lucille Ball & Ricky Ricardo
Charlie Brown & Lucy	Charlie Brown & Lucy
Cinderella & Prince Charming	Cinderella & Prince Charming
Dorothy & the Scarecrow	Dorothy & the Scarecrow
Mary & Joseph	Mary & Joseph
Samson & Delilah	Samson & Delilah
The Lone Ranger & Tonto	The Lone Ranger & Tonto
Darth Vader & Luke Skywalker	Darth Vader & Luke Skywalker
Peter Pan & Tinkerbell	Peter Pan & Tinkerbell
Road Runner & Wiley E. Coyote	Road Runner & Wiley E. Coyote
The Tortoise & the Hare	The Tortoise & the Hare
Red Riding Hood & the Big Bad Wolf	Red Riding Hood & the Big Bad Wolf

HEALTH Club

Purpose   Physical energizer; Winding down/relaxation; Pure fun

Group Size   10-100

Level of Physical Activity   High

Estimated Time   5-10 minutes

Props   Whistle

This is a great miming activity. Participants will perform a routine they may perform at a health club—without equipment. Use this with any group to relax and reduce stress. It also serves as an energizer—just as going to a health club does.

I had a most embarrassing experience in a health club. Here's the set-up: I was a relatively new member in a club that limited access for men and women—women could use the club on Mondays, Wednesdays, and Fridays, men could attend on Tuesdays, Thursdays, and Saturday mornings, and both could participate on Saturday afternoons and Sundays. Prior to this experience, I had only attended during the week. My story takes place one Saturday afternoon when I went to the club. After using the machines, I changed into my bathing suit and started out to the pool area. Right before the pool area was a rest room, so I stopped in before going to the pool as I had each time in the past. Imagine my surprise when I emerged from a booth and faced a full-length mirror with the image of a man standing, well, in his birthday suit. Mustering up my composure, I looked directly into his eyes and said, "Oh, I'm sorry. I thought this was a women's rest room." His reply was just as composed: "No, on weekends, this is only for men. But I can understand your confusion. It's not well marked." I walked out quickly, my head in the air, pleased at how well I had handled the situation. That is, until I walked into the sauna and faced the same person alone again and, finding it awkward, said, "It's nice to see you again."

Instructions

1. Ask five or six participants who have attended a health club to act as trainers, choosing one activity to mime with the group.

2. Ask participants to stand in a place with some room to stretch and move a bit.

3. Explain to participants that the best time to go to health clubs is during the day because they're not crowded. Suggest that you brought the health club to them since they couldn't attend.

4. Introduce the trainers. Explain that they will lead them through some routines.

5. Ask participants to imagine equipment, leotards, and mirrors!
6. Tell each trainer to lead the group through about 30 seconds of an activity.

Variations

1. You lead the activity.
2. Do one activity at a time during the course of a longer session.

Tip

Examples of routines might include: rowing machine, treadmill, weights, nautilus machines, and mild aerobics.

Notes

_____

_____

_____

_____

_____

_____

_____

_____

_____

_____

Line Language

Purpose	Physical energizer; Team building; Pure fun; Energizing a long, dry presentation
Group Size	24-60
Level of Physical Activity	High
Estimated Time	6-8 minutes
Props	None

This activity is a combination of body language, sign language, charades, and mime in which participants will create their own language other than words. This is a great culminating or closing activity. It also works as an energizer midway through a session.

> *"Read my lips." An expression we hear today, meaning "I'm serious about this and you're not listening to (or are intentionally ignoring) my words and actions."*

Instructions

1. Organize participants into groups of six to twelve, standing in line.
2. Explain to participants that they will have the opportunity to send a short message to the other groups. To do this they will choose a group language, but not a verbal one. Remind them about mime, charades, sign language, songs, and any other method you can think of.
3. Tell them they have one minute in their groups to think of a phrase or a short sentence message they want to send to the other groups.
4. Tell them they have three minutes to first decide how they will show the other groups their message, and then take time to practice sending it. Explain that they don't have to remain in line.
5. When time is up, ask each group to show its stuff while the other groups guess.

Variations

1. For a shortened version, ask groups to come up with a closing statement and repeat the statement in a line with each person saying one word.
2. Ask groups to create a culminating statement by writing words on pieces of paper and hanging them on a string with clips. They can then hold it up for the audience to read.

Tip

This activity may be lengthened quite effectively.

Notes _____

Off the Wall

Purpose　　　　　Team building; Physical energizer; Introducing a topic

Group Size　　　　16-100

Level of Physical Activity　　High

Estimated Time　　10-12 minutes

Props　　　　　　Tape; rubber, tennis, or ping-pong balls (one per group); wall space

You'll need a big room and lots of wall space for this activity, since participants will actually get into groups and take turns hitting the ball off a wall in an activity that, like racquetball, discourages ball hogging. Use this activity when you want participants to think about teamwork, when you want to get participants up and moving about for physical stimulation, or when you're introducing the need for systems and organization within a group.

> *Whether in sports or business, the term "ball hog" adequately describes the behavior of some individuals much of the time and many individuals some of the time. Ball hogs aren't any fun, especially since handing the ball (or task) over to a team member can sometimes make the difference in scoring points.*

Instructions

1. Designate locations for groups on the floor with tape or some other marker. The teams will be facing a blank wall approximately ten feet away with no obstructions in between. Groups will be hitting a ball off the wall.
2. Organize participants into teams of ten to twenty.
3. Ask the teams to stand in the prearranged locations around the room.
4. Explain that this activity will assess their abilities to work together toward a team goal.
5. Give each group a tennis, rubber, or ping-pong ball.
6. Explain the game. The object of the game is to bounce the ball against the wall until each person on the team has successfully hit the ball. The team that completes the task first wins. The following rules apply:
   - Each person on the team must hit the ball two times.
   - A person may not hit the ball two times in a row.
   - There may be no more than one bounce between a hit and the wall and one bounce between the wall and a hit.
   - If the rules are broken, play is resumed by another player and the player who broke the rules must do the two hits again.

7. Give teams three minutes to plan their strategies.
8. After three minutes, ask teams to get ready, get set, and go!
9. When one team has finished, stop play for all groups.

Variation

Use large balloons or beach balls.

Tip

If there are people who are unable to play, ask them to be the judges, making sure rules are followed.

Notes

_____

_____

_____

_____

_____

_____

_____

_____

_____

_____

SNAP SHOT

Purpose   Team building; Physical energizer; Outdoor activity

Group Size   20-40

Level of Physical Activity   High

Estimated Time   3-8 minutes

Props   Sample pictures such as a Norman Rockwell picture, George Washington crossing the Delaware River, the Marines raising the flag at Iwo Jima; Polaroid camera (optional)

Use this midway through or at the end of a session to energize the group. It works well right after lunch.

An event truly becomes an event when it is captured on film or in a painting. How many daily events would we change if we thought the scene would be displayed for years to come?

Instructions

1. Organize participants into groups of five to ten.
2. Show them the famous action pictures.
3. Explain that their job is to physically depict what might someday be a famous painting.
4. Explain the rules:
   - Each group has two minutes to decide on and practice a famous event, scene, or incident from history that they would like to depict.
   - Everyone in the group must be in the scene.
   - After two minutes, each group will physically demonstrate its scene while one person from the group names the scene.
5. Remind them that the scenes show action but are still—as if they were snapshots or paintings.
6. Begin the activity.

Variations

1. Give them pictures of famous paintings which they have to depict.
2. Ask them to depict scenes from happenings in the organization.

Tips

1. If time permits, allow them to do more than one.
2. Take pictures of the groups and put them up on the wall. If you only have one team, have the picture enlarged and framed for the group to display at work.
3. Encourage groups to think creatively and choose a scene they would truly enjoy doing.

SWIMMING LESSONS

Purpose   Physical energizer; Pure fun; Outdoor activity; Especially for big groups

Group Size   4-400

Level of Physical Activity   High

Estimated Time   5-8 minutes

Props   None

Enjoy Swimming Lessons anytime participants need a physical break or you need a humor break. Since some people feel funny about acting out their swimming strokes on dry ground, this works best with people who are willing to engage in a rather unsophisticated activity.

According to many fitness experts, swimming is one of the best forms of exercise. Unfortunately though, many of us are not near enough to pools or other bodies of water to engage in this activity. Why let the lack of water restrict us?

Instructions

1. Ask participants to stand and move far enough apart from one another so their fingers don't touch when they stretch their arms straight out to the sides.
2. Review and model (or ask a participant to model) the technique of several swimming strokes, one at a time—breaststroke, backstroke, freestyle (crawl), butterfly, and dog paddle.
3. After each modeling, encourage participants to perform the stroke.
4. On the last turn, ask participants to choose their own stroke.

Variations

1. Ask participants to swim around the room.
2. Use diving formations instead.

Tips

1. If you have flippers, a nose plug, or a bathing cap, wear them—just for fun.
2. You might want to play music while participants are swimming. (How about Handel's *Water Music* or *Splish, Splash*?)

Notes

_____

_____

_____

_____

The Shape You're In

Purpose

Getting to know you; Getting to know you better; Physical energizer; Team building; Outdoor activity; Pure fun; Introducing a topic; Meeting starter

Group Size

12-24

Level of Physical Activity

High

Estimated Time

3-5 minutes

Props

The Shape You're In Activity Sheets, one card per participant

The Shape You're In is an engaging way to get people quickly involved in working together to create new shapes from the geometric pieces they are given. Use it with groups that appreciate a quick challenge.

Remember all those theorems we learned in high school geometry class? Useful, huh? Why, just the other day I was mentioning to a colleague that Theorem #68 was my favorite; he came right back in support of Theorem #16 truly having the most clout ... Just kidding, of course.

Instructions

1. Pass out one shape card to each participant.
2. Explain to participants that The Shape You're In will allow them to find out which contributions others make to the organization; it will also force them to think of the significant value they contribute each day.
3. Explain to participants that the shape each person has in hand is a complete shape by itself. However, those shapes in combination with other pieces could make a different shape. Give the example of two triangles put together to make a square.
4. Tell them that each participant's job is to find at least three other individuals whose shapes can be combined with their shape to make a different shape.
5. Instruct them to put the parts together on a flat surface. After they put their pieces together, they should explain one by one at least one "piece" of value that they bring to the organization.

Variations

1. Give all the same pieces, such as all triangles, and allow them to make up their own shapes.
2. Choose a geometric design for groups to make.
3. Make shapes at least two feet in diameter and encourage them to construct their shapes on the floor.

4. Group participants and ask them to physically make solid, three-dimensional figures.

Tips

1. If you laminate the pieces, you'll be able to use them more than once.
2. Put the company logo, slogan, or other symbol on each piece.
3. Post a chart or picture of various geometric shapes.

Notes

_____

_____

_____

_____

_____

_____

_____

_____

_____

_____

THE SHAPE YOU'RE IN ACTIVITY SHEET

WEAK DAYS

Purpose
Physical energizer; Getting to know you; Energizing a long, dry presentation; Pure fun

Group Size
20-60

Level of Physical Activity
High

Estimated Time
4-10 minutes

Props
Signs for days of the week; Weak Days Activity Sheet
   This activity capitalizes on people's love of talking about their weeks—their favorite days and their worst days. Use this activity at the beginning of a session as a way for people to quickly connect with many people, and as an energizer at any other time.

   Payday Candy Bar. Sunday paper. T.G.I.F. Daily connotations.

Instructions
1. Put a day sign on each of seven tables in the room (or on the wall if no tables are available).
2. Explain to participants that this is a chance for them to let others know how they feel about the days of the week.
3. Give the following instructions:
   - You will be standing.
   - I will ask a question.
   - You should each move to the table that answers the question for you.
   - When you get to your table, you should share with one another why you chose that day of the week.
   - When I say "Weak Days," you should listen for the next question and move to that table.
4. Begin the activity, asking the questions in the order provided on the Weak Days Activity Sheet.

Variation
Use the same questions, but don't ask people to move. Let them answer with raised hands.

Tip
Keep this activity moving quickly. Don't wait for everyone to finish talking at the tables.

Notes
_____
_____
_____

WEAK DAYS ACTIVITY SHEET
(FOR LEADER)

Questions:

1. On which day are you most likely to read the paper?

2. On which day of the week are you most likely to order a pizza?

3. On which day of the week are you the busiest?

4. Which day of the week do you like the least?

5. Which day of the week do you like the best?

6. On which day are you most likely to eat dinner out?

7. On which day are you most likely to eat lunch out?

8. On which day of the week do you feel most relaxed?

9. On which day of the week are you likely to call family members?

10. On which day of the week are you most creative?

PURE FUN

Clean Machine

Purpose   Pure fun; Team building

Group Size   6-60

**Level of Physical
Activity**   Medium

Estimated Time   10 minutes

Props   One bar of soap and one plastic knife per person
                      In this activity, participants help to create a machine by each
                      carving a bar of soap. It's a fun (and clean!) way for participants to
                      strengthen team building skills by achieving a common purpose. It is
                      also works as an energizer, particularly right after lunch or before an
                      afternoon break.

> *Many creative thoughts are born in the morning shower. Unfortunately, we're often alone in this activity, so we don't get to share those ideas at the moment of inception; as a result, they are often lost. This is a chance to share creative ideas about building a machine—ideas that could have been washed down the drain had they originated under a showerhead. (By the way, did you know that "machinery" can either refer to an assemblage of machines, such as the machinery of a factory, or the parts of a machine, as in the machinery of a watch?)*

Instructions
1. Organize participants into groups of two to eight and give each person a bar of soap and a plastic knife.
2. Explain to the groups that they will have two minutes to decide on a machine or machines their group could sculpt from their bars of soap in three minutes. According to *Merriam Webster's Collegiate Dictionary,* the definition of a machine is "an assemblage of parts that transmit forces, motion, and energy." They may choose to make one machine with each soap bar contributing a part to that machine, such as a lawnmower, or they may choose to make more than one machine, with each machine contributing to a common theme, for example, farm machinery or machines one might find in a kitchen. (Admonish them to keep it clean.)
3. Begin the brainstorming.
4. After two minutes, explain that they will now have three minutes to sculpt their machines. Give the signal to begin.
5. At the end of three minutes, ask each group to show and explain its machine(s).

Variations
1. Make this an individual activity.

2. Ask participants to make machines they use frequently and have them explain the benefits to their lives.

Tips

1. Allow participants to wash hands after activity.
2. Soap is sometimes crumbly. To avoid a mess, give participants paper plates or trays, or put plastic tablecloths on the tables.
3. Use soft soaps that are easy to sculpt.

Notes

_____

_____

_____

_____

_____

_____

_____

_____

_____

_____

CRAZY CAPTIONS

Purpose

Mental aerobics; Team building; Pure fun; For non-icebreaker types; Energizing a long, dry presentation

Group Size

8-24

Level of Physical Activity

Medium

Estimated Time

2-4 minutes

Props

Crazy Captions Activity Sheets, one per participant

Participants will work together to create captions for a series of given pictures. Use this to encourage people to work together in pairs at any point in the session that calls for an energizer.

The word caption comes from a French word meaning "to take." To take what—license?

Instructions

1. Organize participants into pairs.
2. Give each participant a Crazy Captions Sheet.
3. Tell pairs they have one minute to write a caption under each picture.
4. After one minute, or so, ask pairs to share their captions.

Variations

1. Make it an individual activity, and pass them out as people are entering the session. Share them later.
2. Have groups come up with captions.
3. Choose your own pictures for captions.

Tip

This activity is purely for fun.

Notes

_____

_____

_____

_____

_____

CRAZY CAPTIONS
ACTIVITY SHEET

_____
_____
_____

_____
_____
_____

_____
_____
_____

_____
_____
_____

_____
_____
_____

_____
_____
_____

HOT AIR EXPRESS

Purpose   Team building; Physical energizer; Pure fun

Group Size   16-100

**Level of Physical
Activity**   High

Estimated Time   5-8 minutes

Props   Balloons, one color per group—one per person plus extras
                     This is a fun, high-energy, competitive activity for building team and achievement. Use it with groups to energize, to use as an example of problem solving, and for a sense of fun.

> *Every time I have mailed a package via Federal Express or Airborne Express it has arrived at the correct location at the correct time. All three times I have used the postal service's express mail (you would think I would learn), the packages arrived a day late. I have concurred that the service is predictably unreliable. What are the chances that on the three occasions I had a package to mail, there were exceptional circumstances that prevented guaranteed arrival???*

Instructions
1. Mark locations in the room for groups to begin and to move balloons to. This could be corners, boxes or circles made with tape, or one solid line.
2. Organize participants into groups of eight to fifteen.
3. Give each person one balloon to blow up and tie off.
4. Explain the activity:
   - The object is for groups to get their balloons to the designated area before other groups. The first group to get all of their balloons into that area is the winning group.
   - Groups must put their hands behind them and clasp them; they may not use their hands to move balloons.
   - Groups will have one minute to decide how to move balloons.
   - Once the activity begins, the strategy may change, but participants must, at all times, keep their hands clasped behind their backs.
5. Give groups one minute to strategize.
6. At the end of one minute, make sure they're positioned, then give the signal to begin.
7. Allow all groups to complete the task before ending the activity.
8. Announce groups in the order they completed the task.

Variation

To stress the strategizing/problem solving aspect of the activity, allow groups more time for strategizing and, at the end of the activity, discuss different strategies groups used and the effectiveness of each.

Tip

People who are unable to participate because of the physical activity may be designated cheerleaders, guides, coaches, referees, or observers who will report observations at the end of the activity.

Notes

_____

_____

_____

_____

_____

_____

_____

_____

_____

OINK, OINK, OINK!

Purpose — Physical energizer; Pure fun

Group Size — 9-18

Level of Physical Activity — High

Estimated Time — 3-5 minutes

Props — Oink, Oink, Oink! Activity Sheet for leader

The story of *The Three Little Pigs* is at the center of this activity that has participants acting out the process of building their houses. Use this as an energizer or just for fun with groups that enjoy being playful. I suspect that types that are impressed with their own importance would not enjoy this one, although I can't say that for sure since I haven't tried it on them.

Laughing is like breathing—it brings life.

Instructions

1. Organize participants standing in a circle.
2. Quickly review a synopsis of *The Three Little Pigs*.
3. Repeat that the first pig built his house from straw and demonstrate a motion that represents straw (such as hands in the air waving). Next explain that the second pig built his house from twigs and show a motion that calls to mind twigs (such as sticking arms out from sides in different directions).

   Finally, repeat that the third pig built his house out of bricks and demonstrate a motion that represents bricks (body with arms to side, feet together, and rigid stance).
4. Ask participants to imitate the motion as you do each: straw, twigs, and bricks.
5. Explain the rules:
   - One person will be chosen to be "it" and take a position in the center of the circle.
   - With eyes closed, that person will turn around in circles until disoriented, and then stop, point at one person, and say, "Three Little Pigs."
   - The person who is pointed to is the second little pig and must make the motion for twigs while saying "Oink."
   - The person to the left of the second pig is the first little pig and must make the motion for straw while saying "oink."
   - The person to the right of the second little pig is the third little pig and must make the motion of bricks while saying "Oink."
   - All three "pigs" should make these motions simultaneously.

- The participant who makes the motion last becomes "it" and play begins again.

Variations

1. Use any analogy that has three sequential movements.
2. Ask someone in the group to review the story.

Tips

1. Keep this moving fast. Stop the activity as the group appears to be losing interest (or just before, if you're psychic).
2. Play with the topic, telling groups that you are not in any way insinuating …
3. This activity can actually be used for the group to make analogies about activity in an organization.

Notes

_____

_____

_____

_____

_____

_____

_____

_____

_____

_____

OINK, OINK, OINK! ACTIVITY SHEET (FOR LEADER)

First read the following synopsis of *The Three Little Pigs,* then demonstrate the motions listed below.

Synopsis:

This is a basic rendition of *The Three Little Pigs.* There were three pigs who were being pursued by a big, bad wolf. Each of the pigs built a house out of different materials. The first little pig built his house out of straw, but the wolf easily blew it down with a huff and a puff. So the first pig ran to his brother's house which was made out of twigs. Again, the wolf easily blew the house down. The two little pigs ran to their brother's house which was made of bricks. Finally, the pigs had found a building material the wolf couldn't blow down!

Motions:

Straw: To indicate building a house of straw, participants should wave their hands back and forth like straw blowing in the wind.

Twigs: To indicate building a house of twigs, participants should stick arms out from sides in different directions.

Bricks: To indicate building a house of bricks, participants should stand in a rigid stance with arms to side and feet together.

Rubbery Band

Purpose

Physical energizer; Pure fun; Team building

Group Size

10-20

Level of Physical Activity

High

Estimated Time

8-10 minutes

Props

Assortment of large rubber bands, several per person

In this activity, participants will create beautiful(?) music from rubber bands. It's fun for any group, but particularly for those with a sense of humor and ingenuity. Use it midway through a session to energize the group, engage their spirit of fun and wit, and get the creative juices flowing.

> *At the Westminster at Lake Ridge retirement community, about twelve residents participate weekly in a "kitchen band." They ingeniously attach, detach, stretch, join, rivet, and connect various kitchen tools and utensils to make "music" (at least that's what they call it) from many different, ordinary utensils and tools. And they practice arduously prior to each "concert."*

Instructions

1. Organize participants into pairs.
2. Give each pair a pile of assorted rubber bands. Explain that they may use as many or as few of them as they want.
3. Tell them that their task is to spend three minutes in their pairs practicing to perform a thirty-second piece on their rubber bands for the rest of the group. The rubber bands may be placed anywhere they would like to play them, and they may use anything they choose to play them with.

Variations

1. Use this activity with groups of four to ten people.
2. You could call this activity a "stretching exercise."
3. Give each participant just one large rubber band.

Tips

1. Lead the group in clapping after each performance.
2. Demonstrate the playing of rubber bands. (Better practice first!)

Story Telling

Purpose

Physical energizer; Team building; Pure fun; Getting closure

Group Size

10-300

Level of Physical Activity

High

Estimated Time

4-5 minutes

Props

Story for the leader to read

Everybody will get to play a role in the telling of a simple story as they repeat a line or noise and add motions that represent their characters. Use this activity to spark enthusiasm and energize participants. It works best with intimate small groups or large groups that enjoy a smile.

> *When I turned 50, my family threw a wonderful surprise party. Most of what they said and did was, quite naturally, related to age. My sister Fran, who is a wonderful storyteller, led us through an icebreaker using the story of Noah's Ark (because Noah lived to be 900!). When I walked in, they had me sit on a rocker with a shawl around my shoulders and a cane by my side. We were all given specific lines and movements for real or imagined characters in the story; someone was Noah, my husband and I were lovebirds, etc. In years to come, one of my fondest memories of my 82-year-old mother (who played God) will be to envision her jumping from her chair, throwing her hands in the air and exclaiming "Awesome" whenever God was mentioned.*

Instructions

1. Prior to the session, choose a story that has a wide variety of characters. (If it relates to your topic, that's even better.) Assign phrases or noises to each of the character roles.

2. Explain to participants that you will read them an interactive story in which they will all have major roles to play.

3. Depending on the number of people in your session, assign each individual, group, or portion of the room a role to play. Explain that whenever their character is mentioned, they should call out their assigned phrase or noise. For example, if your story is Snow White, you could have the group assigned to the witch cackle or say "Mirror, mirror, on the wall" every time the witch is mentioned.

4. Read the story. Have the group participate.

Variation

Pass out copies of a short story with lines highlighted for the group to repeat.

Tip

Everyone gets very involved in this one. Usually they'll ask to do it again.

Who's the Dummy?

Purpose   Getting to know you better; Pure fun; Team building

Group Size   6-12

**Level of Physical
Activity**   High

Estimated Time   3-8 minutes

Props   None

In this activity, participants will get to take on ventriloquist roles of master and dummy as they answer personal questions for their partners. Groups that already know one another are best for this one.

Kermit, Howdy Doody, Kukla and Ollie, Willie the Worm (anyone remember that one?): Everybody loves a dummy.

Instructions

1. Pair up participants.
2. Tell them they will have an opportunity to perform a ventriloquism routine while revealing personal information about their partners to the group.
3. Ask them to decide first who will be master and who will be dummy.
4. Explain the rules:
   - One at a time, each set of partners will come to the front of the room and position themselves to take the roles of master and dummy.
   - Other people in the room may ask two questions of the dummy. Examples of questions are "What was your most embarrassing moment in high school?" and "What is the craziest thing you've ever done?"
   - Since everyone knows that dummies can't talk, the master will answer for the dummy while the dummy's lips move.
   - The master may call a brief conference with the dummy to get help in answering the question. However, that is the master's call, not the dummy's.
5. Begin the activity.

Variation

Tell them there will be prizes for the best ventriloquist pair. After all acts are completed, have the group vote on the best Master and Dummy pair and award prizes.

Tips

1. Model the activity with one participant, letting the group ask questions of you.
2. Position partners with dummy sitting and master seated or standing sideways to the right or left of the dummy with one arm extended behind the dummy's back (as if to be working the dummy's lips).

Self-Disclosure

Bear It and Grin!

Purpose	Self-disclosure; Getting to know you better; Introducing a topic
Group Size	5-40
Level of Physical Activity	Low
Estimated Time	3-6 minutes
Props	Gummy bears, napkins, bowls

Participants feel good about sharing experiences that turned out well. Bear It and Grin! is particularly useful as a leveling activity—with diverse groups of mixed status, ages, etc. Use it when you feel that a basic level of comfort has been reached to help participants reflect on their own experiences, or to gain insight from and about others.

Gotta love those teddy bears. Is it their looks, their movements, or the stories passed down about them? I once read a story in Reader's Digest *about a man caught by a bear who had his head gnawed for an hour. Since then I've been wondering how a bear hug can give the connotation of a warm, fuzzy, desirable experience??*

Instructions

1. Organize participants into groups of four to six, seated around tables.
2. Put a bowl of gummy bears in the middle of each table and give each participant a napkin.
3. Tell participants that Bear It and Grin! is an activity that allows them to share personal stories and be rewarded for it!
4. Instruct participants to think of events that have occurred at work that caused them discomfort—events that were not pleasurable for them at the time, but ones in which the outcomes were worthwhile.
5. Ask participants to take thirty seconds each to share a story about a time they had to bear it in order to get the grin.
6. Explain that as participants finish a quick story, they should reward themselves by taking a handful of gummy bears.

Variations

1. Make the rewards bear stickers instead, which they can attach to their name tags or themselves after sharing their stories.
2. Make this a partnering, rather than a small group, activity.

Tips

1. Offer other treats or different kinds of candy as well—with and without sugar.
2. Expect stories about such things as feedback that proved to be worthwhile, mistrust that was unfounded, a change in career ladder that was beneficial, etc.

BOY, WAS MY FACE RED!

Purpose	Getting to know you better; Introducing a topic; Self-disclosure
Group Size	6-12
Level of Physical Activity	Medium
Estimated Time	3-5 minutes
Props	None

In this icebreaker, participants will share embarrassing moments and equal footing. It works best either as a leveler used with people who are uncomfortable with one another because of differences in professional level, or as a bonding experience with people from the same profession—for example, salespeople, professional speakers, real estate agents.

There I was in the middle of a very heated debate. I was the facilitator. The group was at the pinnacle of disagreement. Tension was thickening. An ideal time to break; they decided against it. Well, at least we could review ground rules. I made the suggestion while slowly backing up to open the external door hoping to let out some hot air and bring fresh air (and perspectives) in. I leaned back hard on the door and pushed. Instantly an alarm sounded. When I turned around, I discovered why. A sign on the door read: Do Not Open This Door—Emergency Only. In a matter of minutes, hotel personnel, police, and firefighters were all over the room. Was my face red!!

P.S. It worked.

Instructions

1. Set the stage by telling a story of your own about a time that you were red-faced.
2. Explain that participants will have an opportunity to do the same.
3. Give participants one minute to think of an embarrassing situation.
4. Instruct them to tell their stories to the rest of the group.
5. Explain that the last sentence of each story should be, "Boy, was my face red!"
6. When the first person comes to the close of the story, lead the group in repeating with that person, "Boy, was my face red!"

Variation

With a larger group, ask participants to share stories in small groups or pairs.

Tips

1. When you tell your own story, dramatize as much as needed to truly make this a humorous activity.
2. Some people will say they have no embarrassing stories; often, as they listen to others a story will come to mind. If not, don't force it.

MEMORY LANE

Purpose	Self-disclosure; Getting to know you better; Pure fun
Group Size	10-200
Level of Physical Activity	High
Estimated Time	5-10 minutes
Props	None

In this activity participants will learn something of the history of other participants as they use the singing of songs to replay the experience. Use this with any group that wouldn't mind having some fun and don't mind feeling a bit silly if they can't sing.

> *Music has played a major role in the recording of history. Differences in cultures and differences in ages are often signaled by differences in musical preferences. If one does not exist, I suspect that somewhere in the near future someone will design a personality inventory based on tonal preferences. Now wouldn't that be interesting?*

Instructions

1. Explain to participants that music has been a recorder of history throughout the ages.
2. Ask participants to think of a song that reminds them of a piece of their own history—that has strong memories for them.
3. Give an example of a song that has meaning for you by explaining the significance and then singing a few bars. Encourage participants to join in.
4. Beginning with one participant, ask each to first explain the significance of the song, then sing a few bars while others who know the song join in.

Variations

1. Have participants hum the tune and have the others guess what the song is.
2. Ask participants to tell the name of the song and some of the words, rather than singing.

Tips

1. Discourage comments about the quality of singing.
2. People who sing off-key generally bring humor into the experience, so encourage any singing.

Notes

_____

_____

Pillow Talk

Purpose	Self-disclosure; Getting to know you better
Group Size	6-15
Level of Physical Activity	Low
Estimated Time	Varies
Props	Decorative pillow

    The pillow in this exercise symbolizes safety and security, thus encouraging your participants to talk comfortably about difficult or personal issues. Use this anytime you think it would be best to up the security ante.

> *Children often carry a pillow with them on trips or even just to the grocery store. The "why" is simple: Pillows provide safety. Disclosing information about oneself is difficult for some people. To provide an element of safety, we can reach back to a childhood favorite—the pillow.*

Instructions

1. Have participants sit in a circle, either in chairs or on the floor.
2. Introduce the activity as "pillow talk" and show the pillow. Explain that they will pass the pillow from person to person, each sharing something about themselves when they hold the pillow.
3. Give the pillow to the first person and instruct that person to begin.
4. When everyone has had a turn, take the pillow back and ask if anyone has thought of something they would like to add. Pass the pillow to anyone who wants to talk again.

Variations

1. Ask participants to share something they wouldn't usually share without a pillow.
2. Explain to participants that the pillow is available anytime during the session when they have something they would like to share.

Tip

Set a mood that matches the occasion. If this is a counseling session or training session around a theme that warrants self-disclosure and analysis, set a serious tone of comfort and safety, symbolized by the pillow. If this is a general training program or meeting, use the pillow to create a light, fun mood.

Notes

_____

_____

Pin 'em Down

Purpose

Self-disclosure; Getting to know you better; Team building

Group Size

5-40

Level of Physical Activity

Low

Estimated Time

5-10 minutes

Props

Clothespins of any size (five per participant)

This activity provides an opportunity for participants to give some history about themselves, without just being asked to "tell about themselves." Use it at the beginning of a session or after lunch for participants to get to know one another better.

One chore that my sister and I were expected to do as teenagers was hanging out the laundry on washday. Sometimes we did it together, but many times we took turns. Whenever my sister hung clothes alone, the clothespins became her playmates. She talked to them, laughed with them, and admonished them. We would watch with amusement from the kitchen window. Consequently, I learned that clothespins can bring out many sides of a person ...

Instructions

1. Organize participants into groups of five to eight.
2. Explain that they will now have an opportunity to get to know members of their group better by "pinning them down."
3. Encourage the group to take turns in the following activity and explain the rules.
   - One person in each group is chosen to act as the "Self."
   - One member of the group should ask the "Self" one question about his or her life. Examples of questions are: "Who was the person who contributed the most to who you are today and how did they do that?" or "Tell us which job you have liked best and why it was the best for you?"
   - The "Self" will answer the question.
   - If the questioner believes the "Self" has responded with a truly self-disclosing response, he will reward the "Self" with a clothespin that he will attach to the "Self's" clothing. (Self-disclosing responses are those in which a person reveals a piece of information that other participants in the group didn't know before, and that are more than one- or two-word answers.)
   - The activity continues until each person is wearing at least one clothespin.
4. Begin the activity.

Variation

Have participants randomly wander around the room asking one another open questions and rewarding self-disclosing responses with clothespins.

Tips

1. Let participants turn in clothespins for prizes.
2. Encourage participants to choose their questions thoughtfully so as not to embarrass or annoy the "Self."
3. I use tiny, colorful clothespins found in an office supply store.
4. If groups have more than five participants, limit the activity to one questioner and one question per participant.
5. For groups of five to eight participants, do the activity as one group.

Notes

_____

_____

_____

_____

_____

_____

_____

_____

_____

_____

PROJECTION

Purpose   Getting to know you; Getting to know you better; Self-disclosure

Group Size   10-1,000

**Level of Physical
Activity**   Medium

Estimated Time   5-10 minutes

Props   None

This is an interesting way for people to share things about themselves, without feeling overly self-conscious. Use this activity with groups that understand the subtlety of projection—any time, any place, any way.

The American Heritage Dictionary, Second College Edition *defines projection as the "process of projecting a filmed image onto a screen or other viewing surface" and "the naive or unconscious attributions of one's own feelings, attitudes, or desires to others."*

Instructions

1. Organize participants into groups of three.
2. Explain (or ask a participant to explain) the meaning of projection.
3. Tell participants that they will have an opportunity to share an interesting or humorous experience by projecting it on another person.
4. Explain the rules of the activity:
   - For each Projection round, each triad of participants will assign roles as the Projector, the Projection, and the Questioner.
   - The Projectors will think of a very pleasant experience they have had, but when describing those experiences, they will speak as if they happened to the Projection.
   - After the Projectors describe the experiences, the Projections take ownership in the experiences and create the responses and feelings they would have.
   - The Questioners may then ask questions of the Projections, such as "How did you feel?" or "What did you do next?"
   - The Projections will answer the questions.
   - When all questions have been answered, the three players change roles and repeat the process.
   - The activity stops when all three participants have had a chance to be Projector.

Variations

1. Use this same activity for people to express opinions about hot topics, etc.
2. Use duos, leaving out the role of the Questioner, and calling the activity You Statements.

Tips

1. Model this with two participants before beginning.
2. This can be either a humorous or a serious activity. Set the stage at the beginning according to your purpose.
3. Some humor arises when the Projections can't imagine the experiences happening to them, and therefore can't describe them, or change the story considerably when responding to the Questioners. (An example is a Projector who was a person in obviously very fit condition and who talked about competing in a bike race. When the Questioner asked the Projection how he felt, he said he was exhausted for a month—and completely left out any description of an incredible "high." They all laughed.)

Notes

_____

_____

_____

_____

_____

_____

_____

_____

_____

_____

THINGS THAT ARE ...

Purpose	Getting to know you better; Team building; Self-disclosure
Group Size	6-26
Level of Physical Activity	Medium
Estimated Time	2-4 minutes
Props	Things That Are ... Activity Sheet for leader

This is a quick, interesting way for participants to learn things about one another. Use it periodically during a session, rather than just once. All audiences enjoy it.

> *"You're kidding. Do you really enjoy that?" Someone asked me that question when I described leading games for large groups at conferences. The person's next statement was, "I would die. Four people in front of me is more than I can handle."*
>
> *My son, Todd, uses the expression "whatever floats your boat."*

Instructions

1. Explain to participants that in life there are things that "just are ..." In the same situation, each of us has different experiences and reactions. For one person, caring for an ailing relative may be a positive experience; for another, it is just plain difficult. For one, making sales calls may be stimulating; for another, it's totally draining.

2. Tell them that in this activity they will be finding out about "Things That Are ..." for each of them.

3. Explain that you will give the category, and they should each respond with their own answers. For instance, if you say "things that are hard," they will each finish the sentence by choosing something that is hard for each of them.

4. Begin the activity with the first "Things that are ..."

5. Ask participants to share their answers with the total group.

Variations

1. Have participants complete responses on a flip chart while working in small groups.

2. Ask participants to form responses that are related to work. For instance, you might say, "Things that are solid in this organization are...."

Tip

Choose either the personal or work-related, humorous or serious, based on your objective and on the audience.

Notes

_____

_____

_____

_____

_____

_____

_____

_____

_____

THINGS THAT ARE ... ACTIVITY SHEET (FOR LEADER)

What do you think of when you think of things that are ...

Blue

Fast

Relative

Fun

Hard

Easy

Solid

Stupid

Exciting

Tall

Sweet

New

Old

Desirable

TEAM BUILDING

Happily Ever After

Purpose
Team building; Getting to know you better; Physical energizer; Introducing a topic; Pure fun

Group Size
10-40

Level of Physical Activity
High

Estimated Time
10-20 minutes

Props
Happily Ever After Activity Sheets, one per group

Groups will think about the morals behind their favorite fairy tales and get a chance to act them out. Use this activity for team building, affiliation, or the understanding of organizational culture and norms. Use this with groups from all levels of the organization.

Much has been said about the effects of fairy tales on children and adults. There have even been rewrites of a few of the favorites. Whatever the effect, fairy tales are an important part of our culture.

Instructions

1. Organize participants into groups of five to eight.
2. Instruct groups to take one minute to list values they think are of importance to the group and then prioritize them.
3. After one minute, pass out one Happily Ever After Activity Sheet to each group and explain the rest of the activity:
   - Groups should identify a fairy tale or short story that they all know about and that they can use to act out one or more of their chosen core values. It does not have to be from the list provided.
   - The groups will then have three minutes to practice and one minute to act out their fairy tales for the other groups. Their versions of the fairy tale should clearly and emphatically emphasize their priority values. (For instance, a group may use "Goldilocks and the Three Bears" to demonstrate the values of generosity and undaunting courage, exaggerating those throughout.)
   - After each group acts out its story, the other groups will guess the values that were being portrayed.
4. Begin the activity and explain that groups now have three minutes to practice their fairy tale production.
5. When people have finished practicing, ask each group to act out its fairy tale for the other groups. Allow for the guessing of values at the conclusion of each performance.

Variations

1. Give each group an already identified core value and ask them to act out a fairy tale emphasizing that core value.

2. Ask participant groups to make up their own fairy tales.

3. Rather than providing the Activity Sheets, ask participants to brainstorm fairy tales.

Tip

People actually have fun with this activity, but take the values seriously. Support that.

Notes

_____

_____

_____

_____

_____

_____

_____

_____

_____

_____

HAPPILY EVER AFTER ACTIVITY SHEET

Examples of fairy tales:

Cinderella

Snow White and the Seven Dwarfs

Peter and the Wolf

Little Red Riding Hood

The Little Match Girl

Hansel and Gretel

Peter Cottontail

The Little Red Hen

Squirrel Nutkin

The Old Woman in the Shoe

Goldilocks and the Three Bears

Rapunzel

The Princess and the Pea

Rip Van Winkle

The Legend of Sleepy Hollow

Paper Dolls

Purpose
Physical energizer; Team building; Pure fun

Group Size
6-20

Level of Physical Activity
High

Estimated Time
5-8 minutes

Props
Plain white paper, such as one tablecloth per group; scissors; wall to post dolls

Making paper dolls is harder than it looks—especially when the dolls have to represent the group. This activity is a great one for building teams, even if they are temporary teams. Use this with groups that are open to being creative and having fun.

> *I remember from my childhood that paper dolls was one of those activities that one could play totally alone; as a matter of fact, they were better played that way. There was no need for another live person when one had make-believe characters and lives to portray; another person just changed or distorted the story. That's not unlike the feelings we get sometimes about working in groups or teams: Some groups function quite effectively while others have distorted stories.*

Instructions

1. Organize participants into groups of two to four.
2. Explain that this activity is a chance for them to compete with other teams. They'll compete by cutting out paper dolls. Show them an example of paper dolls strung together.
3. Explain that their challenge as a team is to cut out a string of paper dolls that most represents the team in three minutes. Explain that the whole group will vote on which string of dolls is the most representative.
4. Begin the activity. After three minutes, ask groups to display their paper dolls on the wall.
5. After each group has displayed and described its paper dolls, take a vote as to which is most representative of the entire group.

Variations

1. Give groups paper dolls and ask them to draw on the figures to make them look like their team.
2. If you are able to allow more time, the quality will rise.

Tips

1. Many small groups won't know how to cut stringing dolls. Give no assistance; that's part of the fun.

2. When voting, if each group votes for its own dolls (which sometimes happens), you pick the most representative, but make light of it or let it go without further judging, exclaiming that they are all winners.

3. Make sure you have plenty of extra paper.

4. Don't give out markers, crayons, or other writing tools, but don't say they can't be used.

Notes

_____

_____

_____

_____

_____

_____

_____

_____

_____

PERSONIFICATION

Purpose   Team building; Introducing a topic; Meeting starter; Getting closure; Pure fun

Group Size   6-25

Level of Physical Activity   High

Estimated Time   3-7 minutes

Props   Flip chart paper, one sheet per group; markers

Participants will get to personify a particular word in this activity, but you can use it for specific purposes. If your purpose is to build a team, let participants personify the name of the work group. If you want people to understand and appreciate one another's departments, let them personify departments (such as Marketing, Human Resources, Production, or Graphics.) If they're from different organizations, let them personify the organizations. Or use it with qualities, characteristics, or qualifications.

> *Years ago, I came across a delightful book called* The Book of Qualities *by J. Ruth Gendler.* Gendler has captured the spirit of qualities by personifying them in a whimsical but captivating manner. An example is inspiration: "Inspiration is disturbing. She does not believe in guarantees or insurance or strict schedules ... Surrender. She knows when you need her better than you do."*

Instructions
1. Organize participants into groups of three to six.
2. Explain to participants that personification is taking an inanimate object or abstraction and giving it a persona. Simple examples include calling a boat a she or a hurricane a she or he. Explain that the group will now be using personification to describe what you have chosen (e.g., their departments).
3. Explain that their group task is to sketch and then write descriptions of their personification.
4. Give each group a sheet of flip chart paper and markers and tell them they have five minutes to personify and sketch.
5. When they are finished, have groups share their sketches and descriptions.

Variation   If the objective is team building, ask people to pick qualities they think are important for team members. Then ask each member to personify one of those.

---

*Gendler, J. Ruth (1984) *The Book of Qualities*. Berkeley, CA: Turquoise Mountain Publications.

Tip

If you use this at the beginning or in the middle of the session, refer back to it when you can.

Notes

_____

_____

_____

_____

_____

_____

_____

_____

_____

Rhymes Revisited

Purpose
Getting to know you better; Team building; Introducing a topic; Pure fun

Group Size
2-24

Level of Physical Activity
Medium

Estimated Time
8-10 minutes

Props
Nursery rhymes
 Rewriting their favorite nursery rhymes will elicit participants' smiles and teamwork. Use this activity as an energizer, or as an introduction to innovation. Use it with thinking audiences.

> *I've often wondered what would have happened to Jack and Jill if they hadn't had such a horrible mishap. Of course I'm referring to the nursery rhyme that says:*
> *Jack and Jill went up the hill*
> *to fetch a pail of water;*
> *Jack fell down and broke his crown*
> *and Jill came tumbling after.*
> *Suppose it said:*
> *Jack and Jill went up the hill*
> *to fetch a pail of water;*
> *The sky was dark, the moon just right,*
> *their purpose didn't matter!*

Instructions
1. Organize participants into groups of two to five.
2. Explain to participants that they will now have an opportunity to innovate together, to come up with a different, and perhaps better, solution.
3. Pass out copies of nursery rhymes.
4. Tell groups that they will have four to six minutes to select one rhyme and change the final stanza in any way they would like.
5. After four to six minutes, ask groups to read their rhymes—first the original, then the revised version.

Variations
1. Rather than passing out nursery rhymes, ask participants to come up with them.
2. For an even greater challenge, have participants rewrite first stanzas.

Tips
1. Give an example of your own creation, or work with the group to create an example.
2. Remember that not everyone knows nursery rhymes. This may be an introduction for some people.

Star Quality

Purpose
Team building; Introducing a topic

Group Size
4-40

Level of Physical Activity
Medium

Estimated Time
10 minutes

Props
Five-pointed stars drawn on large pieces of paper or posterboard (one per small group); tape or flip charts; markers (one per small group)

Is quality a heavenly concept? Groups will readily engage in this activity after there is a clear understanding of team goals (another heavenly concept).

Instructions

1. Organize participants into small groups. Place one of the large stars near each group.
2. Provide a definition of qualities. (According to *Merriam Webster's Collegiate Dictionary, Tenth Edition*, qualities are either inherent features or distinguishing attributes.)
3. Give small groups two minutes to brainstorm the qualities needed for achieving team goals.
4. After two minutes, instruct small groups to choose their top five qualities and write them inside the five points of their star.
5. When points are filled in, instruct groups to agree on other star qualities and list them in the center of the star.
6. Ask each group to share their star qualities with the rest of the group.

Variations

1. If a group has fewer than twelve participants, do the activity together as one group.
2. Provide a list of "star qualities" and ask groups to prioritize them.
3. Use this as a goal-setting activity.

Tip
Encourage groups to use illustrations and color when listing qualities on the stars.

STAR QUALITY
ACTIVITY SHEET

Thanks Giving

Purpose

Team building

Group Size

6-20

Level of Physical Activity

Low

Estimated Time

2 minutes

Props

Thanks Giving Activity Sheets

This activity encourages coworkers to remember past kindnesses with thank you notes. Use this activity with an intact group or team of people when you observe or feel they are working together well.

Thank you—one of the most powerful phrases in the English language. Enough said.

Instructions

1. Explain to the group that the phrase "thankless job" is one that can be applied to many positions or specific tasks. Ask if they have ever felt that way about job tasks. Explain that sometimes one simple phrase coming from the right source can change that descriptor; that phrase is "thank you."
2. Distribute blank thank you notes to team members.
3. Invite them to write a note at any time during the session when they remember a particular time, event, or behavior for which they would like to thank another team member.
4. Before each break, invite participants to put their thank you notes at the appropriate coworkers' places.

Variations

1. Ask people to distribute cards at the end of a session for recipients to take and read at their leisure.
2. Give one note per team member to each participant and encourage them to write at least one thank you note for each individual.

Tips

1. Since these notes are personal between sender and recipient, do not explore them further as a group. The power of this activity is in the result, not the process.
2. If no one writes notes, you begin the process by writing a note yourself.
3. If you think the group will be reluctant to participate, structure the activity by suggesting they complete a certain number of notes, or by suggesting they write them for each person.
4. Saying a "thank you" is not a touchy-feely thing to do. It is civil and courteous, and just happens to make people feel good.

THANKS GIVING
ACTIVITY SHEET

Cut along the solid lines and fold along the dotted lines.

Thank You! *Thank You!*

Thank You! *Thank You!*

Warning Signs

Purpose
Team building; Introducing a topic; Getting closure; Self-disclosure; Getting to know you better; Especially for big groups

Group Size
6-600

Level of Physical Activity
Medium

Estimated Time
3-5 minutes

Props
Warning Signs Activity Sheets, one per participant

A set of warning signs helps stimulate discussion as participants think of workplace analogies for each sign. Use this activity with supervisors, managers, and leaders to help them recognize their own strengths and limitations. It also works well for team building and conflict management because it helps people to recognize their own pressure points as well as those of others. This is a light activity when used with a large group, but can become very self-disclosing when used with a more intimate group.

What pushes your buttons? It's one of the first questions couples should ask of one another. What could be more helpful than knowing up-front exactly which phrases and behaviors to avoid in the interest of keeping peace?

Instructions
1. Give each participant a Warning Signs Activity Sheet.
2. Tell them to take two minutes to write underneath each sign those work situations that correlate to the sign.
3. After two minutes, organize participants into pairs.
4. Ask them to share their signs and work situations with their partners.

Variations
1. Have participants work in groups and list all situations possible under each sign.
2. Have participants make the list a "Watch Out" list for themselves and use it as a closing activity.

Tip
Introduce the activity by giving examples of your own that fit the signs.

WARNING SIGNS ACTIVITY SHEET

DANGER
CONFINED SPACE
ENTER BY
PERMIT ONLY

_____
_____
_____
_____

DANGER
DO NOT
DOUBLEDECK

_____
_____
_____
_____

DANGER
EXPLOSIVES

_____
_____
_____
_____

DANGER
HARD HAT
AREA

_____
_____
_____
_____

DANGER
LASER
OPERATING

_____
_____
_____
_____

DANGER
NO
ADMITTANCE

_____
_____
_____
_____

DANGER
NO PEDESTRIAN
TRAFFIC

_____
_____
_____
_____

DANGER
PINCH POINT

_____
_____
_____
_____

DANGER
DO NOT TRAVEL
WITH
FORKS RAISED

_____
_____
_____
_____

WE'RE ALL IN THE SAME BOAT

Purpose   Team building; Physical energizer; Especially for big groups; Pure fun

Group Size   10-200

**Level of Physical
Activity**   High

Estimated Time   3-5 minutes

Props   None

This energizing activity gets people moving and doing things together. I find the best use for this activity is in the middle or near the end of a program to make a point about working together.

One's boating experience can be related to life cycles: dependence, interdependence, independence, interdependence, and back to dependence. I remember riding in a rowboat as a small child while my father rowed; sharing the middle seat and rowing with my father; taking the rowboat out by myself…. As children, we plead, "Please let me row by myself." As elderly adults we silently scream, "Please let me take my own oars."

Instructions

1. Organize participants into groups of ten to twenty.
2. Ask for six volunteers from the total group who have done some boating, sailing, crewing, or sculling to come up front and decide on six different physical movements that they will take the group through with verbal expressions or repetitions to repeat.
3. Explain that teamwork—understanding specific roles and responsibilities and having everyone do their part with precision—is very evident in boating and sailing competitions.
4. Instruct groups to arrange themselves into boat-like structures.
5. Ask the six volunteers to individually or collectively lead the groups through the activities.

Variations

1. Encourage each group to decide what kind of boating it will be doing and script its own movements.
2. Have the group make the formation of one large boat and do the exercises.

Tip

This activity may be treated as a light energizer or as an integral part of your session—depending on what you want it to be and how you set it up.

Winding Down/Relaxation

ENERGY SOURCES

Purpose

Winding down/relaxation; Introducing a topic

Group Size

6-20

Level of Physical Activity

Low

Estimated Time

2-4 minutes

Props

Soft, soothing music

This activity is a relaxation activity. It works well at any point in a session. Thinking, busy audiences respond best to the concept.

> *There's an equation that goes something like this: X amount of energy out + X amount of energy in = a well-balanced lifestyle. The difficulty is in determining the components of X.*

Instructions

1. Explain that we give and get energy from people and other natural sources on a daily basis, but that those sources differ with each of us. An example of energy drain is SADS, a depression caused by a need for sunlight for some and not enough exercise for others. An example of energy boost for some people is partying with friends, while for others an example is taking time alone to be still and relax.

2. Ask participants to close their eyes and think of three of the greatest sources of energy for them. Explain that sometimes we can get energy from just thinking about those sources. Give examples of your own energy sources.

3. Tell them that you will put on soothing music and that they will get to spend three minutes focusing on those energy sources.

4. Ask participants to get into a position of relaxation: neck relaxed, arms relaxed, legs relaxed, and so on.

5. Turn the music on and explain that they should think of their first source.

6. At the end of the first minute, call for the second source and at the end of the second minute, call for the third source.

Variations

1. Have participants focus on one energy source for three minutes.

2. Three times during the session, break for a one-minute energy charge.

Tips

1. Some participants will come to the realization that they have insufficient energy sources in their lives at the time.

2. Some participants will think this activity is hokey. Tell them to use the time just to relax or to think about other things.

ON YOUR TOES

Purpose   Physical energizer; Winding down/relaxation

Group Size   1-500

Level of Physical Activity   High

Estimated Time   2-4 minutes

Props   None

This is a stretching exercise to help participants relax and get energy. The only groups that don't like this one are those who would rather choose their own ways of stretching.

They say that ballet dancing is one of the most strenuous of all physical activities. And yet, it looks effortless—at least when you watch the true professionals. What beauty, grace, and precision!

Instructions

1. Explain to participants that On Your Toes is a stretching exercise.
2. Ask participants to stand in a comfortable position.
3. Explain the following instructions:
   - Relax your body, feet comfortably apart, shoulders and arms relaxed.
   - Slowly life your arms and reach for the ceiling until you're on your toes.
   - Slowly lower your arms until you're in a relaxed, standing position.
   - Repeat four times.

Variations

1. Repeat the activity after a one-minute rest.
2. After stretching toward the ceiling, instruct them to slowly bring their arms down to their toes.

Tips

1. Modulate your voice so that it is relaxed and soft.
2. Soft music often helps people relax.

STRESS RE-LEAf

Purpose	Getting closure; Meeting starter; Introducing a topic; Winding down/relaxation
Group Size	1-20
Level of Physical Activity	Medium
Estimated Time	4-8 minutes
Props	Brightly colored paper leaves, 3 per participant

In this activity, participants reduce stress by listing their stressors and articulating ways to change. Participants respond best to Stress Re-Leaf at the end of a program that has raised stressful issues for them or as an introduction to a program about stress.

> *Spring and fall both symbolize new beginnings. Spring, obviously, brings new life—and green leaves—to plants and trees. Fall brings with it the energy of cooler weather, with a focus on new work projects and learning activities. For many parts of the U.S., brilliantly colored leaves symbolize these new beginnings.*

Instructions

1. Pass out three leaves to each participant.
2. Remind participants that we all accept stress as a part of our lives and that stress itself is acceptable. However, when stress has a negative affect on our health, work, energy, abilities, or family and social lives, it's time to re-examine its necessity and do what we can to reduce it.
3. Ask participants to identify the three greatest stressors in their lives for which they recognize negative effects. Have them write one stressor on each of their leaves.
4. Whatever the season of the year, explain that we always have the opportunity to turn over a new leaf and make changes in our lives that will reduce the effect of stress on us. For example, fall brings new learning opportunities, winter offers the start of a new year, spring delivers new life and summer is a time for reflection and renewal.
5. Ask participants to think about what it would take to "turn over a new leaf" in an effort to reduce negative stress. Instruct participants to turn their leaves over one at a time and write three ways to reduce the negative aspects of that particular stressor.
6. When participants have finished, explain that they now have options for "re-leaf" and encourage them to look at the leaves each day—first at the stressor side, then the relief side—to help them work on reducing the stress in their lives.

Variations

1. Have them share with partners.
2. Designate one leaf for family, one leaf for work, and one for personal issues.

Tip

Play peaceful, soft music while participants are writing ways to "turn over a new leaf."

Notes

_____

_____

_____

_____

_____

_____

_____

_____

_____

_____

STRESS RE-LEAF ACTIVITY SHEET

The Eye of the Beholder

Purpose

Getting to know you better; Winding down/relaxation; Introducing a topic; Outdoor activity

Group Size

4-20

Level of Physical Activity

Medium

Estimated Time

2-10 minutes

Props

None

   As participants enjoy the beauty outside the window, this quick activity will help reinforce a point about differences in value judgments. Use it with any group when you are in a room with windows.

   "Wit to persuade; and beauty to delight." (Sir John Davies, Orchestra)
   "Beauty is bought by judgment of the eye." (Shakespeare, Love's Labour Lost)
   "A thing of beauty is a joy forever." (John Keats, Endymion)
   Bless those romantics!

Instructions

1. Ask participants to stand and face, or come near, a window.
2. Instruct them to look out and observe things of beauty.
3. Ask participants to share a thing of beauty they have noticed and to explain why they find it beautiful.
4. Ask for participant observations, or make any of the following points:
   - Beauty is not always linked to momentary observation; sometimes it stems from context, memories, and experience.
   - It is important to look for beauty, particularly at times when it is not obvious.
   - Beauty may be temporary or seasonal.

Variations

1. If a window is not available, ask participants to think of things of beauty and describe them.
2. Use this activity several times during a longer session—choosing objects the first time from outside, the second time in the room, and the third time from memory.

Tip

Start the activity yourself by naming a thing of beauty that you took note of that day and describing it.

TUNE-UP

Purpose	Physical energizer; Winding down/relaxation; Getting closure
Group Size	2-40
Level of Physical Activity	High
Estimated Time	6-10 minutes
Props	Relaxing music; index cards, one per participant

Most people attend regularly to vehicle maintenance, but not so regularly to personal maintenance. Use this activity as an energizer midway through a serious session, or as a stress reducer at the end of an intense session.

About eight years ago, I learned a hard life lesson. My Volvo wagon's engine seized up because it didn't have oil in it. Fifteen hundred dollars later, it was back on the road. Since that time my cars have received regular maintenance, and then some. After all, I couldn't live without my car.

Instructions

1. Suggest to participants that vehicles often have it better than we do. They are pampered on a regular basis by people who truly care about them and have an interest in increasing their life span—which is not always true of how we treat one another and ourselves.

2. Ask participants if they get their vehicles tuned up regularly and, if so, what happens to them.

3. Explain that this is an opportunity for participants to treat themselves to a mini tune-up.

4. Ask the group to suggest aloud examples of things they might do to re-energize, recharge their batteries, or change their oil. Some examples might include: do ten deep knee bends, close your eyes and inhale and exhale deeply, or put your feet up and relax your muscles.

5. Give an index card to each participant.

6. Ask participants to write five to ten things they could do to tune themselves up. Tell them to include three things they could do right there in the room in the next five minutes.

7. When they've finished writing their ideas down, put on relaxing music and tell them to tune-up by using one or more of the ideas they wrote on their cards.

8. After five minutes, end the activity and suggest that they take the cards with them as a reminder to attend to regular tune-ups.

Variations

1. Ask participants to share their tune-up suggestions with another participant before engaging in the activity.
2. You lead one relaxing exercise and then allow them five minutes more for their own tuning up.

Tips

1. Give them ownership of the time.
2. Do a tune-up of your own while they do theirs.

Notes

_____

_____

_____

_____

_____

_____

_____

_____

_____

_____

About the Author

Edie West lives in Northern Virginia with her husband Glenn. They have three sons, two daughters-in-law, two grandchildren, and one dog named Jordan.

Edie is the President of Edie West™, a company that delivers consulting and speaking services for corporations, associations, and public sector agencies. They also design and deliver services for conferences and special events. In 1994 Edie West™ began creating, packaging, and marketing products for speakers, teachers, facilitators, and trainers that engage the audience in listening and learning.